7 8 9   BKM BKM   0 9 8 7 6 5

140885-1

Hill books are available at special quantity discounts to use as premiums and sales
ns, or for use in corporate training programs. For more information, please write to
or of Special Sales, Professional Publishing, McGraw-Hill, Two Penn Plaza, New
10121-2298. Or contact your local bookstore.

lication is designed to provide accurate and authoritative information in regard to
ct matter covered. It is sold with the understanding that neither the author nor the
r is engaged in rendering legal, accounting, or other professional service. If legal
other expert assistance is required, the services of a competent professional person
e sought.
Declaration of Principles jointly adopted by a Committee of the American Bar Association
mmittee of Publishers.

of Congress Cataloging-in-Publication Data

ng, David, 1950-
estment performance attribution : a guide to what it is, how to calculate it, and
to use it / by David Spaulding.
.   cm.
ntents: Equity attribution — Fixed income attribution — Global attribution —
netric attribution — Linking across time, arithmetic — Linking across time,
netric—Other attribution concepts—Attribution challenges—Using the information
arching for an attribution system — The future of attribution.
N 0-07-140885-1.
vestment analysis. 2. Portfolio management. 3. Rate of return. I. Title.
4529.S61985 2002
63'2042—dc21
                                                    2002011249

INVESTMENT PERFORMANCE ATTRIBUTION

A Guide to What It Is, How
and How to Use It

DAVID SPAULDING

Boston, Massachusetts   Burr Ridge, Illinois
Dubuque, Iowa   Madison, Wisconsin   New York, Nev
San Francisco, California   St. Louis, Missouri

The McGr

Copyright
America. E
publication
data base

4 5 6

ISBN 0-07

McGraw-
promotio
the Direc
York, NY

This pub
the subj
publishe
advice o
should
—From
and a C

Library

Spauldi
Inv
how

C
Geo
geo
— S
ISB
1. I

HG
332

For
William G. and Ana K. Spaulding
Edward G. and Elizabeth M. Sinkinson

CONTENTS

FOREWORD

For the nearly 35 years that I have been involved in the field of investment management, the subject of performance measurement and evaluation has been a source of constant fascination for me. It is an absolute delight to find that David Spaulding has now put together this comprehensive book on performance attribution to accompany his earlier work, *Measuring Investment Performance*.

Investment performance measurement, while not trivial, is unlikely to be of much value to us beyond its accounting and reporting metrics. However, performance evaluation in the form of attribution analysis is something that can provide us with valuable insight into the processes that generated the returns we are examining. I think the reader will find that Dave has made a wonderful contribution in bringing performance attribution techniques to light in a rigorous yet highly readable fashion. This is no small task, given the inherent complexities that are involved in the arithmetic of attribution.

Reporting standards put in place by the Association for Investment Management and Research (AIMR)® have greatly improved the integrity of the performance numbers themselves and addressed some of the blatant misrepresentations in the past. When I first came into the business in the 1960s, it was not uncommon for someone to represent, for example, that over the last two years they had an average investment return of 20%. When, upon inquiry, one would find that this was "computed" from a return of 100% in year one followed by a return of −60% in year two. We know that the meaningful number here is an average annual return of about −10.6%. Fortunately, these types of misrepresentations are no longer an issue.

To a rather disturbing degree, however, accurately reported performance numbers from investment managers are routinely misunderstood and often misused by clients, consultants, and the media. Even with these accurate representations of performance numbers, we are still plagued with challenges surrounding their interpretation. Human nature seems to drive many to use past performance as a guide to the future. Yet the landscape is littered with the failures of this observational technique. Even for a manager who has the skill to produce value-added performance, there is little reason to assume that this skill will persist into a future that is unlike the past. Worse, past performance may simply be a random accident. Does a random past outcome tell us anything about the future? There are statistical interpretation problems associated with performance data no matter how high the quality of that data or how fairly it is presented. One of my great regrets over the course of my career is that the interpretation of investment performance, even by professionals, rarely incorporated even the most basic statistical tools. The tendency is to apply the past to derive future expectations when the volatility, data points, and time horizon of the past performance makes this a futile exercise with dangerous consequences. One only has to observe what happened during the "bubble" build up in the late 1990s equity markets and the subsequent events to gain an appreciation for the fragilities of past performance as a guide to the future.

While performance attribution does not overcome the statistical challenges associated with placing performance numbers in the proper perspective, it does take us a step further down the evolutionary road to a better understanding of why the performance occurred. It allows us to ask the relevant questions about what portfolio decisions were made and how they impacted the result that we observe. These internal portfolio diagnostics further our insights about the returns, and at least offer us an improved opportunity to then interpret the data in a more meaningful frame of reference. This is particularly true if we are able to compare the *ex post* results of the attribution anlaysis to *ex ante* representations by the manager.

A hallmark of this book by Dave Spaulding is that it provides a robust array of attribution applications for a variety of portfolio objectives. This is accomplished while alerting the reader to the various attribution techniques that may be applied, and providing the necessary cautions regarding interpretation of the results. It would seem that both the students and practitioners in the field of investment management would benefit substantially from reading this book and utilizing it as a reference source in the application of performance attribution methodologies.

Gary P. Brinson
July 2002

"We don't know a millionth of one percent about anything."
—Thomas Alva Edison

My motivation for writing my first book, *Measuring Investment Performance*, was similar to what has motivated me to tackle a book on investment performance attribution: the recognition that there is an absence of collected material on this topic.[1] In the case of attribution, there is clearly a great deal that has been written on it. The publication that I founded and publish, *The Journal of Performance Measurement*®, has itself published numerous articles on this topic.[2] But where was someone to turn to (a) gain a grounding in this topic, and (b) to delve further into it without doing a topic search and scouring the various industry publications? Nowhere, and this was becoming an increasing problem for performance measurement professionals. As interest and demand has grown, we've needed a way to introduce people to this topic.

Like the French author Midhat Gazalé, whose books[3] on mathematics strive to avoid complex notations and language typically found in math books and articles, I've attempted to simplify the material I cover. As he wrote in his book on numbers, *"Ce qui se conçoit bien s'énonce clairement!"* (That which is well conceived is clearly stated.)[4] It is my sincere hope that the reader finds my pre-

---

[1] There's definitely not an absence of material—numerous articles have been written. But there hasn't been a source that consolidated much of the thinking, nor has there been the presence of introductory material.

[2] Many of which I have drawn upon for source material.

[3] *Gnomon: From Pharaohs to Fractals* (Princeton, N.J.: Princeton University Press, 1999) and *Number From Ahmes to Cantor* (Princeton, N.J.: Princeton University Press, 2000).

[4] Gazalé [2000], page xi.

sentations easy to grasp. I recognize that there are some who feel that this treatment does not do the subject justice, as it fails to include the rigorous math that they may prefer.

"There is no royal road to learning."
Euclid

In writing my second book, I thought I'd benefit from my experience with the first in a few ways. First, in how to attack the book. In the interim, I discovered a concept called *mind mapping*.[5] After studying this concept, I came to believe that had I learned of it prior to my first writing effort, my approach would have been quite different—that I would have utilized the *mind mapping* techniques to put the book together. And so I put a mind map together (see figure 1), which became the basis for how this book is laid out. While this notion was supposed to help me breeze through the writing, it didn't. Granted, it helped, but this was still a challenge.

[5]Buzan [1991].

FIGURE 1

A Mind Map for the Book's Design

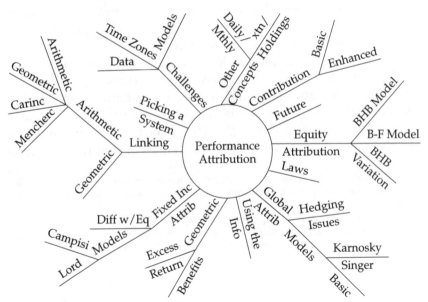

Just like my first book, finding the time to write was a chore. That was the greatest hurdle.

Second, I benefited from my previous writing experience in how I spent my time writing this one. In my first effort, I thought I'd spend time on a regular basis devoted to writing, but I actually crammed much of it into a rather short period towards the end in order to make the deadlines (that had already been revised) established with the publisher. Well I found it even *more* difficult this time to find time to write. This was compounded by my even more hectic consulting and speaking schedule, and by my taking on a second, "part-time" job as the mayor of my home town.[6] Consequently, I've had to *find* time to write. For example, I'm writing these words as I sit in a hotel room in Sydney, Australia.[7]

I used my first book as the basis of a class I teach, titled "Introduction to Performance Measurement." Shortly after I began the class, I added material that I wished I had included in the earlier book (and plan to include in a major revision). Well, I'm now writing this book while I'm putting a class together on performance attribution. Hopefully, this too will yield a better and more complete book.

Actually, since I was able to put the class together, I was able to use much of that work as the basis for what you see before you now!

> *"Big book, big bore."*
> Callimachus

I *really* hope that you don't agree with Callimachus in regards to this book. Granted, a math book can be boring, and that's essentially what this is. A lot of math. A lot of numbers. But I've hopefully included enough humor to keep the book light.[8]

---

[6]I was sworn in to a four-year term as Mayor of North Brunswick, New Jersey, on January 1, 2000. It's not unusual for me to spend 20–30 hours per week in this "part-time" position. You're invited to visit our Web site (www.NorthBrunswickonline.com).

[7]I came to Sydney to teach a two-day introductory class on performance measurement and to speak at an industry conference. I intentionally brought materials along with me, in hopes that I'd be able to spend time writing.

[8]Granted, my humor may be easy to miss. (It usually is.) When I speak publicly, my jokes are sometimes overlooked by the audience, who require me to point them out. While I'm tempted to include some sort of symbol to alert you to the presence of a joke, my dignity (and publisher) won't permit it. If you need help in finding my pearls of humor, let me know, and I'll point them out for you.

"It behooves us to place the foundations of
knowledge on mathematics."
Roger Bacon

As I was completing the draft, I was quite excited by the laudatory comments I got from Steve Campisi, one of the manuscript's early reviewers. He wrote: "This is a great piece of writing. I was commenting to one of my associates about the masterful way you've expressed some highly technical information in a very readable, almost conversational manner. I believe this helps tremendously with the reader's comprehension."[9] I hope that you find my style helpful.

I often tell people that performance attribution has become the "hottest" area of performance measurement today. And I believe that most performance professionals would agree. It's become pretty standard to include one or more sessions on attribution in performance measurement conferences; in fact, many conferences that used to refer to themselves simply as the "Performance Measurement Conference" have added attribution to their name (e.g., "Performance Measurement and Attribution Conference") to give this topic greater emphasis.

I like a line that appears in an early Gary Brinson article on attribution: "Performance attribution, while not new, is still an evolving discipline."[10] The attribution evolution is alive and well, with quite a bit being done.

THE BOOK'S MAKEUP

"The readers and the hearers like my books
But yet some writers cannot them digest
But what care I? for when I make a feast
I would my guests should praise it, not the cooks."
Sir John Harington

There's a saying that goes something like, "To learn a subject well, teach it." This is definitely applicable to some of the material I include here, since before I began to teach it, I hadn't taken the time really to understand it. A corollary to this line might be, "to learn a

---

[9]Campisi [2002].
[10]Brinson [1986], page 40.

subject well, write about it." I had to spend many hours (often, many early-morning hours) researching, testing, etc. I appreciate the assistance and patience that others showed me as I delved deeper into the material to provide you with the best, most accurate, and hopefully most useful text that I could.

With this text, I attempt to address most of the key aspects of attribution. I begin by addressing the issue of contribution. Many folks argue that this formula isn't actually attribution. Well, while the *purists* may feel this way, we've found that most people include it with attribution.[11]

Domestic equity attribution is probably the most developed area, which probably isn't surprising.[12] I include discussions on three common models, contrasting their differences.

Fixed income attribution, on the other hand, has a long way to go. While we've begun to see a lot more attention devoted to it, it's not nearly as well developed. I give you some insights into why this area requires greater attention, and provide you with a basic approach to this analysis. As you'll see, I have relied heavily upon the work of Tim Lord and Steve Campisi to provide you with this information.

Thanks to the early work of Denis Karnosky and Brian Singer, we have a well-regarded model that has a global base of support. Performance measurement software vendors from North America, Europe, and Australia have embraced their approach to this important area. I give you some insights into the approach that they employ.

As we move to shorter *measurement* periods (to improve the accuracy of the results), while continuing to want to maintain relatively long *reporting* periods for the results, we find a growing need for linking attribution effects over time. I demonstrate several different ways to accomplish this important step, from the basic to the mathematically intense.

I also touch upon other aspects of attribution, including some of the challenges and the special requirements of doing software searches for attribution systems.

Since this is the first book devoted solely to investment performance attribution, and since there aren't any well-defined

---

[11]The Spaulding Group [2002]; our preliminary results showed that over 75% feel this way.
[12]As domestic equity gets the greatest attention.

"rules" regarding this field, I've taken the liberty of promulgating some "laws," which I hope will become widely accepted and adhered to.[13] As you'll see, the notion of formal attribution standards is still under consideration. In the meantime, I feel that we need some agreed-upon "dos and "don'ts." Hopefully, these laws will begin to serve this purpose.

CREDITS

"There is nothing more difficult to take in hand,
more perilous to conduct,
or more uncertain in its success,
than to take the lead in the introduction of a
new order of things."
Niccoló Machivaelli

Attribution would not be where it is today without the analysis and design work of several people. Among these are Gary Brinson and his various coauthors (including Gilbert Beebower, Nimrod Fachler, L. Randolph Hood), Denis Karnosky and Brian Singer, Tim Lord, David Cariño, and Jose Menchero. I offer my thanks for their work, as I've liberally borrowed from it.

I've also benefitted from help from Carl Bacon, who I call the "crusader for geometric attribution," who helped me a great deal to uncover the finer points of this alternative method of deriving attribution effects. Steve Campisi, who teaches an attribution class with me, provided me with much of the basis for the chapter on fixed income attribution. Both of these gentlemen spent many hours assisting me with this project. Jose Menchero, too, went out of his way to provide me with additional material.

Kevin Terhaar of Brinson Partners provided me with some sample materials that helped me greatly in not only learning more about the Karnosky/Singer model, but also in demonstrating how the answers aren't always obvious when it comes to attribution analysis.

I appreciate the folks who reviewed the early manuscript for this book. They include Carl Bacon, Jose Menchero, Brian Singer,

---

[13]So far, the discussions I've had with various performance measurement professionals, including members of the Performance Measurement Forum, suggest that there's general agreement with what I propose.

and Steve Campisi. Although I only sent Damien Laker one chapter to review, he pointed out some inconsistences and misinterpretations, which was quite helpful. While I appreciate the effort of my reviewers to uncover discrepancies or errors, I'm confident that a few slipped by (as I learned with my first book). So, if you see any, they're my fault.

When I wrote my first book, the Internet wasn't nearly as advanced as it is today. If, in the course of your reading, you discover something that looks wrong, please e-mail me (DSpaulding@SpauldingGrp.com) and if you're right, I'll post it on my company's Web site (www.SpauldingGrp.com) until a future revision is able to incorporate it. I'll also ensure that the next edition includes corrections, and possibly enhancements, as a result of your comments.

Another change is the inclusion of several end-of-chapter exercises to allow you to try out some of the formulas yourself. The answers are in the back of the book.

If you visit our Web site, you'll also discover the solutions in Excel format, as well as other details from the book in Excel, which I hope will enhance the material even more and contribute to your learning experience.[14]

KNOWING WHEN TO STOP

The reality is that a book on attribution can go on and on—there's so much that can be said and included.[15] New material becomes available almost daily. However, this book isn't intended to cover everything. I want it to provide a solid overview of the major areas of attribution, as well as to delve into some of the more controversial topics. Hopefully, I've succeeded.

With any writing project, there has to be a time when the author says, "enough, already." I'm in Zurich having just finished a

---

[14]We had considered issuing a CD/ROM with this material, but there are a few problems with this approach. First, the CD/ROMs often have problems, and replacing them can be a chore. Second, the flexibility of putting the same information on our Web site is so much greater, in that it allows us to enhance it beyond what we would include on the CD. And third, it allows us to correct any errors that might have made their way through on a disk.

[15]For example, as I was trying to wrap things up, Damien Laker reminded me of an article he and Owen Davies had written (Daves [2001]) that addresses multiperiod attribution. It was simply too late in the process to include their insights, although you're encouraged to explore this material.

talk at a performance and attribution conference, taking advantage of some free time to put the finishing touches on this book. I'm ready to say "enough!"

As always, I appreciate hearing from readers. One of the greatest compliments is to hear from you, by phone, e-mail, writing, or in person. So, whether your comments are positive or not, please let me know your thoughts. Also, please pass along any suggestions as to how to improve the material.

I thank my editing supervisor, Sally Glover, who was phenomenal in cleaning up the manuscript. She did an amazing job and I am indebted to her.

A thank you to Stephen Isaacs of McGraw-Hill for his support and encouragement.

A special thanks to Gary Brinson for providing the foreword. Without Gary's early work, attribution would not be anywhere near where it is today.

I also want to take this opportunity to thank my wife, Betty, who always provides me with inspiration and support to try new things. She also encouraged me to take additional, uninterrupted blocks of time to devote to this project, even though it meant time away from her.

An Overview of Attribution

"Performance Attribution
while not new,
is still an evolving discipline."[1]

I recall my reaction when I read this statement by Gary Brinson and his fellow authors of the 1986 article from the *Financial Analysts Journal*®. Attribution, "while not new." This was in 1986. "Evolving!" Talk about evolving—look at what's been happening over the past five years to the world of attribution.

We're now into the twenty-first century and attribution is *still* an evolving discipline. In fact, I'd suggest it's evolving more now than it ever has, as more and more people try to grapple with it.

The topic is one of those that the more I *learn about it,* the more I *find that I don't know!*

I recall that when I wrote my first book[2] on performance measurement, my main goal was to address rates of return. I felt obligated to include chapters on attribution, risk, and other related

---

[1]Brinson [1986], page 40. In their article, Owen Davies and Damien Laker point out that "at least one paper was written in the early seventies which proposes a framework very similar to the one now recognized as the Brinson method." (Davies [2001], page 13). They refer to "The Measurement of Portfolio Performance for Pension Funds," published by the Working Group of the Society of Investment Analysts (U.K.).
[2]Spaulding [1997].

topics. Although I was somewhat familiar with attribution, my knowledge wasn't nearly as extensive as it is today, five years later.

I called my friend Mike Smith, who at the time worked for Financial Models,[3] to gain some greater insight into the world of attribution. Mike was very helpful and provided me with one of the formulas that appears in my earlier book.[4] Since then, I've spent time with additional models and have discovered many of the challenges and issues relating to this subject.

This chapter will introduce the concept of attribution, including the first two "laws" for investment attribution.

A DEFINITION

A book like this needs some definitions, and one definition that's required is of the subject itself: attribution. What *is* attribution? To put it simply, it's the *act of attributing an event to its underlying cause(s)*.

Don't you just love it when someone uses a part of a word to define it? I think I can do a bit better: attribution is the *act of determining the contributors or causes of a result or effect*.

Is that better? I hope so.

Tim Lord, in his Dietz Award-winning article[5] stated that "the purpose of performance attribution is to measure total return performance and to explain that performance in terms of investment strategy and changes in market conditions. Attribution models are designed to identify the relevant factors that impact performance, and to assess the contribution of each factor to the final result."

I first learned about attribution when I was in graduate school in the 1970s. I was studying operations research, and we would talk about conducting *attribution analysis* to determine what caused something to happen.

---

[3]We don't speak about who Mike works for today, as he has crossed over to the *dark side* and works for a competitor of ours. We're still friends, and I appreciate his help with my first book.

[4]Spaulding [1997], page 66.

[5]Lord [1997]. *The Journal of Performance Measurement* honors its best article of the year with the "Dietz Award," for an outstanding contribution to performance measurement writing. The award is named for Peter Dietz, an individual who some regard as the "father of investment performance measurement."

Somehow, the subject made its way over to performance measurement. It's the same idea. We want to know what *caused* something to happen. In this case, we want to know what caused our return to be what it is.

A manager has a return of 8% for the year 2000. How did he get it? What caused it? Why did the manager get the return she got?[6]

What *could* have caused our excess return? Hopefully it has something to do with the manager's *conscious decisions*. That is, with something the manager *meant* to do. But, in reality, a whole lot of the return might have to do with things the manager *didn't* do, right? Like, the effects of the market at large. The economy. The overall movement of industries relative to actions of the Federal Reserve or other bodies. Even some unintended consequences of the manager's actions. As a result of changes in interest rates, currency movements, etc. Are we going to take into consideration all of these other things, too? Well, no. That would be a whole lot more complicated, and would probably generate a lot of *noise* in our analysis such that in the end, we'd gain little benefit.

But how, then, do we take into account the *things* that the manager couldn't control? We're going to presume that all those things the manager couldn't control are grouped into the benchmark the manager is investing against. Make sense? Perhaps we're taking some liberties here, but it's not a bad approach, and it simplifies things quite a bit.

INSIGHTS

A few years ago, I attended a weekend marketing seminar that was run by a marketing guru named Jay Abraham. During the event, he would introduce and discuss a concept. After he was done, he'd ask 15–20 people to share their *insights* about what they heard, where an insight is meant to refer to some profound thought or idea that may have gone off in a person's head when he heard what Jay offered; perhaps it was a way she could employ the technique in her business, for example. Once Jay was done with this first

---

[6]As I did in my first book, I'll interchange both masculine and feminine pronouns throughout this text.

round, he'd then go around again and ask for insights on the insights (i.e., new thoughts that came to mind when we heard what others had discovered).

Insight is a perfect word for what we discover with attribution. It points out information that we may not otherwise have been aware of, allowing us to gain greater depth and knowledge about our performance and management of the portfolio.

THE PERFORMANCE EVALUATION

Attribution is an analytical technique that allows us to evaluate the performance of the portfolio relative to the benchmark.

A proper attribution tells us where value was added or subtracted as a result of the manager's decisions. Once completed, the portfolio manager can review the results and see what worked and what didn't. Also, in communicating to her clients, the manager can use the results to emphasize her skill or explain why certain decisions didn't work as expected.

I love metaphors and analogies, as they help clarify meanings. One I like to use when it comes to attribution is the situation in which a man is trying to get a date. He's read various books and articles on how to attract women and is ready to put his new strategy to the test. So, he buys just the right car, shops for the latest clothes, buys the perfect cologne, and is armed with just the right "opening line." He approaches a woman, and what happens? He is successful—she says "yes"—he has a date!

Later on, in an attempt to evaluate how each of his actions contributed to his success (and being a good attribution analyst), he asks the young lady what attracted her to him.

"Was it my fancy car?"
Her reply: "Oh, you guys and your cars. To me, a car is simply a mode of transportation."
"Okay, was it my new clothes?"
Her response: "Well, to be honest, your clothes look like something out of the '70s."
"Well, then was it my expensive cologne?"
She responds: "To be honest, it smelled like you used the whole bottle."
"I guess it must have been my opening line, then, right?"
"'Haven't I seen you some place before' isn't exactly a unique phrase, no" is her response.

"Okay, so then why did you agree to go out with me?"
And now he hears the answer: "Well, I hadn't had a date in several weeks and decided this morning to go out with the next man who asked."

Well, perhaps our analysis didn't yield the kind of results he expected, but at least we know what to *attribute* his success to!

Hopefully, when it comes to investment attribution, we'll find that our *intended* actions contributed more to our success than our *unintended* actions or other factors.

FINDING OUT WHERE THE EXCESS RETURN CAME FROM

In attribution, our primary focus is to find the source of the portfolio's "excess return." The excess return is essentially the difference between what the portfolio did (the portfolio's rate of return, or R_P) and how the benchmark performed (the benchmark's return, or R_B).[7]

Figure 1–1 graphically shows what we're doing.[8] As you can see, we have the portfolio and benchmark's returns shown as

[7]I will use the terms "benchmark" and "index" interchangeably throughout the book.
[8]This is based on a chart that Jose Menchero occasionally uses in his presentations. I think it's a good way to depict what attribution is doing.

F I G U R E   1–1

What We're Missing

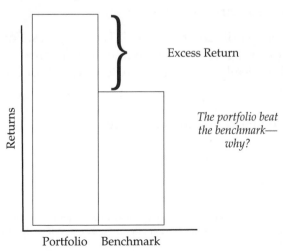

Portfolio   Benchmark

columns, side by side. The difference (in this case, a positive one for the portfolio) is what we're attempting to analyze.

What we're saying is "the amount of the portfolio that's equal to the benchmark came from the benchmark." We want to know where the difference came from. Perhaps this is a simple explanation, but that's essentially what we're trying to do.

WHAT *IS* THE EXCESS RETURN?[9]

Mathematically, excess return can be shown in one of two ways.

If we're talking about it *arithmetically*, it's simply the difference between the portfolio return and the benchmark return:

$$ER_A = R_p - R_B$$

where

ER_A = arithmetic excess return
R_P = portfolio return
R_B = benchmark return

There's also a different approach to arriving at excess return, and that's from a *geometric* perspective:

$$ER_G = \frac{1 + R_p}{1 + R_B} - 1$$

where

ER_G = geometric excess return

Will you get different answers? Typically, yes. For example, if the portfolio has a return of 10% while the benchmark had a return of 8%, arithmetically we'd have an excess return of 2%:

$$ER_A = 10\% - 8\% = 2\%$$

But geometrically, our excess return is 1.85%:

$$ER_G = \frac{1.10}{1.08} - 1 = 1.85\%$$

---

[9]Excess return is one of those performance measurement terms with multiple meanings. You'll occasionally see it defined as Portfolio Return minus Risk-Free Return. Clearly, that's not what we mean here.

There are reasons why we might favor one approach over the other. It appears that Europeans prefer *geometric*, while Americans and Australians seem to prefer *arithmetic*, but this is subject to change as we learn more about each method.

For most of this book, we will refer to excess return from the *arithmetic* perspective (also called "additive"). In chapter 6, we address geometric attribution and go into a little more detail about the benefits of this approach. In chapter 8, we discuss how linking of attribution effects is simplified with the geometric approach.

We know what excess return is mathematically. What does it mean in words? It's essentially what the manager brought to us—the return we can attribute to the manager's actions.

When we speak of attribution, we normally use the term in reference to *active* managers rather than *passive* managers.[10] There is probably an opportunity to develop attribution analysis for passive managers, but this hasn't yet been addressed (see chapter 13). For most of our discussion, we speak in terms of *active* managers.

Because we're talking about active managers, excess return is sometimes referred to as "active return," as it's the portion of the return we attribute to the actions of the active manager. We'll generally use the term "excess return" throughout this book.

WHAT ARE WE ATTEMPTING TO MEASURE?

In performance attribution, we want to know what *caused* the excess return.

Since we're speaking about attribution relative to an *active* manager, it would seem appropriate that we look at those *active decisions* of the manager and see how they contributed to the excess return. Granted, there may have been some portion of the excess return that came from something that we *didn't* mean to do. And, there's room for analysis of this, too. But to begin, we'll focus on analyzing the effects of our intended actions.

---

[10]By "passive" manager, we mean a manager who is attempting to replicate an index or benchmark. The portfolio is being managed in a way that will yield an equivalent (or close to equivalent) return to the benchmark, by structuring it in an almost identical fashion. This is different from an *active* manager who uses various techniques (stock-picking skills, asset allocation strategies, mathematical models, etc.) in an attempt to *beat* the benchmark. The fees paid to a passive or index manager are typically much less than those paid to an active manager, because the passive manager is essentially matching a benchmark.

We've already begun to use a term that's important to the field of attribution: "effects." That's what we're measuring: the *effects* of our actions.

Let's say you're walking down the street and you see two fellows: one is standing and the other is sprawled out on the ground. You may be inclined to ask, "Why is this person lying on the ground?" You may hear, "This other fellow hit me." Thus, you can conclude that the effect "the person is lying on the ground" is the result of the intended action of the other person who *hit* him. Thus, the action of *hitting* had the *effect* or *result* of the man being on the ground. In other words, we can *attribute* the person being on the ground to the *action* of the other man's striking him.

In a broader sense, we have an "effect" of beating[11] (or being beaten by) the benchmark. We want to dissect this difference to arrive at the cause or causes.

THE USE OF MODELS

To measure or analyze the effects of our actions, we need something called a "model." A *model* is a mathematical expression that we will use to analyze the performance results and identify their causes.

The development of a suitable model can be quite a challenge. There are numerous competing models available, and we discuss several within this text.

Some firms use *off-the-shelf* models, models that may have been developed by practitioners or software vendors. Often, they're introduced in publications such as the *Financial Analyst Journal* or *The Journal of Performance Measurement.* There was a time when the math that underlies the models was kept secret. While this is still true today, in most cases, attribution software developers reveal the details of their models.

Some money managers are not satisfied with the models offered by software vendors, so they develop their own, customized models. When this is done, it's not unusual to find that the manager keeps the details secret, as she's invested time and energy into the model's development and may feel she has some competitive advantage to maintain.

[11]This apparent pun (my referring to *beating* a benchmark just after I gave an example of someone being struck) is totally unintended and coincidental.

PICKING THE RIGHT MODEL FOR YOU!

Throughout this book, I'll occasionally introduce attribution "laws." Just as in the fields of mathematics and physics, as well as other disciplines, we find "laws," it's appropriate and important that this area of performance measurement have laws, too, so you'll see a few here. Hopefully, you won't take exception to them but will embrace them because you agree that they make sense and are appropriate for the industry.

Let's start with our first law, which reads as follows:

> ## First Law of Performance Attribution
>
> *The attribution model should represent the active investment decisions of the portfolio manager.*

This means that if we're trying to figure out what caused the excess return, we should be looking at what the manager did—the manager's intended actions. It makes sense that the model fits with the portfolio manager's style of investing.

This doesn't mean that the result (the excess return) may not have arisen from something the manager *didn't* intend to do—and there's room to look at this stuff too. But, at least to begin with, our model should evaluate the causes of the excess return from the perspective of the manager's intended actions.

We like to look at attribution as a "tool set." Since these tool sets come in different styles, you want to make sure you're

First Law of Performance Attribution
The attribution model should represent the active decisions of the portfolio manager.

using the appropriate one. Even though plumbers and carpenters both use tools, often similar ones, their tool sets are generally quite different. Imagine if we mixed the tools up and gave the carpenter the tools belonging to the plumber—how would he be able to work? Granted, he has a box full of tools, but what good is a pipe wrench to someone working with wood? Likewise, what good will simple pliers do for a plumber? Tools are important—having the right ones is critical.

The attribution effects we obtain from the results of our analysis should be attributed to those who are responsible for making the decisions. If an analyst is the one who makes recommendations on stocks, we can determine how good these recommendations were. If a portfolio strategist or economist is the one who dictates asset allocation, then we can grade the effectiveness of these decisions. If a currency analyst recommends when to over or underweight country allocations, we can show where the bets worked and where they didn't.

WHAT *CAN* AN ACTIVE MANAGER DO?

Let's begin from the perspective of an equity manager. (We discuss in greater detail attribution for a fixed income manager in chapter 4.)

Assuming for a moment that the manager has defined a specific benchmark against which she wants to be measured,[12] the manager has a few choices. If it's a domestic benchmark, the manager can:

- make different allocation decisions across industry sectors.
- pick different securities than are in the benchmark.

These are the *classic* effects we generally want to look at. Let's take the first case: making different allocation decisions across industry sectors.

Let's say the benchmark has its securities allocated as shown in Table 1–1.

If the manager is looking for ways to beat the benchmark, she can begin by adjusting the weights. For example, if she feels that banks are going to do very well this quarter, she might overweight this sector relative to the benchmark: instead of having 13% of the portfolio in banks, perhaps she'll allocate 15% of the assets to banks. If she's *bearish* on technology (i.e., she doesn't look favorably upon this sector), she might reduce the allocation (or underweight it) by allocating only 6% of the assets (versus 10% in the benchmark). And so on.

Wouldn't we want to know the *effect* of these decisions? Of course we would. And this is one of the *effects* we'll measure. This effect can go by various names, including *sector selection, industry selection, allocation,* and *timing.*

---

[12]This really isn't such a tremendous assumption since if we *don't* have a benchmark, there's no point in talking about attribution.

T A B L E   1–1

Benchmark's Industry Breakdown

	Benchmark
Basic Mat'ls	11%
Industrials	9%
Transportation	7%
Utilities	13%
Merchandise	5%
Pharmaceuticals	8%
Banks	13%
Technology	10%
Telecommunications	10%
Building materials	14%
Portfolio	100%

What else can a manager do? As noted above, she can pick different securities than what are in the benchmark. She can also pick the same securities but buy more or less of them than are in the benchmark. For example, if the benchmark owns HAL Computer, but the manager prefers to invest in Bell Computer, this would be a security selection difference. By picking different securities, the manager is hoping that *her* choices outperform those in the benchmark.

This *effect* is the result of stock-picking skills: the manager's ability to pick securities that will (hopefully) outperform the benchmark. This effect is called *issue* or *stock selection*.

If we're talking about a global portfolio, then the manager can also attempt to outperform the benchmark by allocating securities across countries differently than the benchmark does. The mere allocation of securities from one country to another won't cause the difference in return. Rather, it's the *effect* of the currency differences that will cause the difference.

For example, if we choose to overweight our dollar-denominated portfolio's portion of assets in the United Kingdom, then the fluctuation of the Pound Sterling (£) to the dollar ($) will have an impact on the portfolio's overall return. Further discussion of the effect of these decisions is discussed in chapter 5.

QUESTIONS WE HOPE TO ANSWER

When we perform attribution analysis on a domestic equity portfolio, we want to find out, from an effect perspective:

- *Sector Selection:* Was the portfolio manager successful at overweighting the sectors that outperformed the benchmark and underweighting the sectors that didn't?
- *Stock Selection:* Did the manager successfully select stocks within each sector to help the manager outperform the market?

THE SECOND LAW

Now that we've identified some of the particulars of attribution, it's time to introduce our second law:

> **Second Law of Performance Attribution**
> *The sum of the attribution effects must equal the excess return.*

Second Law of Performance Attribution

The sum of the attribution effects musts equal the excess return.

Mathematically, this law equates to:

$$\sum_{i=1}^{n} AE_i = R_P - R_B$$

where

AE = attribution effect
R_P = portfolio return
R_B = benchmark return
i = the individual effect
n = the number of effects in the model

We need to account for 100% of the excess return. Consequently, when we've calculated all of the effects (AE, or attribution effects), their sum must equal our excess return.

Some models, as you'll see in chapters 3 and 4, use an "other" or "interaction" effect to make the math work out. While I'm not terribly fond of such models, I'm choosing to delay my comments on this until later. People generally like to see things add up;

they're suspicious when they don't. Suffice it to say, the model, whether it uses such a term or not, must account for the entire excess return. Otherwise, we are forced to ask "what caused the difference?" and won't have an answer.

PICKING THE RIGHT MODEL

As defined in the First Law of Performance Attribution, our model is supposed to represent our style of investing. What about a "bottom-up" manager?[13] Is a model that has a *sector selection* effect appropriate?

At first blush, many folks would say "no," and this is actually in keeping with the first attribution law, isn't it? If the manager didn't make any *sector allocation* decisions, what's the point in measuring her on this? Consequently, I think there's a fair argument to be made that such a model should *not* be used for bottom-up managers.

Now that I've said this, let me have the pleasure of contradicting myself. I think there *are* benefits to looking at the *unintended consequences*. For example, even though we may not have *intended* to overweight one sector and underweight another, the *effect* of these actions may have still had an impact on our return, right? And so, wouldn't it be of some value to look at this, too?

For example, if a manager, in picking stocks, ends up with a lot more invested in banks and technology than the benchmark, we can expect to see an effect as a result of this. While we might want to look solely at the effect of the stock selection, it doesn't hurt to look also at the impact of the unintended effect of the weight differences. This additional information should prove useful.

We might also want to look at our portfolio-benchmark relationship from other perspectives. Again, some may have been the result of our actions but unintended, but the benefit of this analysis can be of value.

---

[13]By "bottom-up," we mean a manager that begins by picking securities. How he does this isn't terribly important for this discussion. But we can conclude that the allocation across sectors may not have been an *intended* decision but rather an *unintended consequence* of the securities the manager picked. Is it of value to measure the effect of sector allocation decisions when there weren't any? That's the question we're facing here.

SUMMARY

The concept of "attribution" isn't limited to investment performance. Rather, it's a concept that we, in the performance measurement arena, have borrowed from others, as it is a great tool for providing *insights* into what's going on with the portfolio—specifically, where the return came from.

Attribution has become the *hottest* area of performance measurement. While we've seen many articles written, presenting various models and linking techniques, we haven't had a single reference to present the basics plus some of the more extensive details.

We also haven't seen "standards" for attribution, and as you see in chapter 13, we're beginning to see some interest in them. However, to have some "dos" and "don'ts" will help. And that's what our "laws" are intended to provide. So far, you've learned of two of them. The third is introduced in chapter 7.

CHAPTER 2

Contribution

What is contribution?

   Contribution is a process to assess how individual securities or sectors (or any subportfolio element) contributed to a portfolio's return.

   When many people think about attribution, at least for the first time, they think about "contribution." Contribution is a fairly straightforward way to determine how various subportfolio elements _contributed_ to the portfolio's overall return. It's that simple.

   There is a different view, however, that says that since contribution doesn't compare the portfolio relative to the benchmark, and doesn't focus on the sources of the portfolio's excess return, then it really isn't attribution.

   Who is right?

   If we define the term attribution as strictly being a measure of the sources of the excess return, then clearly contribution can't be considered a form of attribution. However, since contribution _does_ help us ascertain the sources of (or perhaps, more correctly, the contributors to) the portfolio return, then I would say that it has value and should be brought in as a type of attribution. We may want to use the term "absolute attribution" in referring to contribution.

   Also, as we see later, for bottom-up managers, this is perhaps the best way to measure attribution.

In this chapter, we discuss what contribution is and how it can be used to provide insights into how the various components of a portfolio contribute to the overall return. Two formulas will be presented to demonstrate how contribution is derived.

CALCULATING CONTRIBUTION—THE BASIC FORMULA

The basic formula to derive contribution is very simple:

$$\text{Contribution} = \text{Weight} \times \text{Return}$$

Actually, since the weight[1] has to be expressed in the form of a ratio (relative to the portfolio's overall weight), the formula is more accurately depicted as:

$$Contribution = \left(\frac{(Wt_i)}{\sum_{i=1}^{n}(Wt_i)} \right) \times R_i$$

where

Wt = weight
R = return
i = individual component
n = number of components

We have the individual ratio of the individual security's starting weight (or, more accurately, beginning market value) divided by the sum of all the securities' starting weights (market values), which is equal to the portfolio's starting market value.

$$Contribution = \left(\frac{(BMV_i)}{\sum_{i=1}^{n}(BMV_i)} \right) \times R_i$$

where

BMV = beginning market value

[1]"Weight" refers to the amount of the portfolio that each component represents. It's usually derived by taking the individual component's (be they securities, sectors, or some other segment of the portfolio) market value, and divide it by the portfolio's total market value. This percentage is the weight.

In our discussion, we'll generally refer to the multiplier as "weight."

Basic Contribution Formula
$Contribution = \left(\dfrac{(BMV_i)}{\sum\limits_{i=1}^{n}(BMV_i)}\right) \times R_i$

As far as a formula is concerned, we can't get a whole lot simpler than this, can we? And, we can use this formula at any subportfolio level.

By *subportfolio*, we mean any grouping below the portfolio. Typically, we will calculate contribution for industry sectors and securities. But we could break a portfolio up by market capitalization, country, P/E (price/earnings) ratios, or, for fixed income, by maturity, duration, ratings, or any other group that we can then sum to account for 100% of the portfolio.

Table 2–1 shows the securities that make up a portfolio whose overall return for the period was 1.06%. As you can see, we list the 10 securities, along with their respective rates of return and weights. By simply multiplying each security's return by its weight, we calculate the contribution.

For example, if we take Security A, we have the following:

$$Contribution_A = \left(\frac{Wt_A}{\sum\limits_{i=1}^{n}Wt_i}\right) \times R_A = \left(\frac{11}{100}\right) \times 0.015$$

$$= 0.11 \times 0.015 = 0.17\%$$

T A B L E   2–1

Individual Security Contributions

Security	ROR	Weight	Contribution
A	1.50%	11.00	0.17%
B	1.80%	12.00	0.22%
C	2.00%	1.20	0.02%
D	0.50%	1.50	0.01%
E	0.70%	22.00	0.15%
F	−1.10%	1.30	−0.01%
G	−0.30%	11.00	−0.03%
H	1.00%	20.00	0.20%
I	0.20%	7.00	0.01%
J	2.50%	13.00	0.33%
Overall	1.06%	100	1.06%

USING THE INFORMATION

The reason I favor including contribution with the broad category of attribution is that it provides us with insights into the sources of the portfolio's overall return. Let's take this portfolio as an example.

We know that the portfolio had a return of 1.06% for the period. But where did it come from? We can see that security A gave us 17 basis points,[2] B provided 22 basis points, and so on.

Comparing one security to another, we see that our biggest contributor for the period was security J, which provided us with 33 basis points, or close to one-third of our overall portfolio return (0.33/1.06=0.31=31%). Our next biggest contributor was B, with a return of 22 basis points.

On the negative side, we see that F cost us one basis point and G cost us three basis points.

When a portfolio manager is reviewing her results, she will often want to see how each security compared and how each helped her achieve the overall result. Contribution is an effective way of doing just that.

It also has value for the client who might want to know what securities were *winners* and which were *losers*.

CONTRIBUTION RULE #1

A basic rule with contribution is that the sum of the contribution effects must equal the portfolio's overall return. That is, we must account for 100% of the portfolio's return.

$$R_P = \sum_{i=1}^{n} (Wt_i \times R_i)$$

where

R   = return
Wt = weight

---

[2]Where a basis point is 1/100 of a percentage point (1 basis point = 0.01%).

If we sum the individual security contributions in Table 2–1, we'll find that they add up to the portfolio's overall return of 1.06%.

$$\sum_{i=1}^{n} (Contributions_i) = 0.17 + 0.22 + \cdots + 0.33 = 1.06\%$$

This rule assures us that we are able to identify *all* of the contributors to the portfolio's return. If the sum of the individual com-

> **Contribution Rule 1**
> *The sum of the contribution effects must equal the portfolio's overall return.*

ponents of our group doesn't equal our portfolio return (other than for rounding errors, of course), then we have a problem. Perhaps we failed to account for all of the members of the group, or some of our numbers are wrong.

One question that might come to mind is "which weight do we use in the formula?" The answer is the beginning-period weight.[3] If we're measuring the contributions for a month, then we will use the beginning-of-month weights for each security (or sector). If for a week, then the beginning-of-week weight, and so on.

This "weight" is, in reality, the market value of the security or sector di-vided by the portfolio's market value. As noted earlier, the weight is calcu-

> **Contribution Rule 2**
> *Use the beginning market value; the end-ing market value includes the return's effect.*

lated by taking the component's beginning market value and di-viding by the sum of all the beginning market values. This ratio is what we use, as shown earlier.

ANOTHER EXAMPLE—SECTOR-LEVEL CONTRIBUTIONS

Let's try an example with industry sectors.

Table 2–2 has the sector returns and weights for a different portfolio. In this case, the portfolio's overall return is 0.29%. We use

---

[3]The ending market value reflects the period's return. Therefore, if we were to use this market value, we'd be including the effect of the return twice.

T A B L E   2–2

Sector Contributions

Sector	ROR	Wt	Contribution
Basic Mat'ls	0.25%	10	0.03%
Industrials	0.50%	11	0.06%
Trans	1.00%	8	0.08%
Utilities	−0.80%	12	−0.10%
Merch	2.00%	7	0.14%
Pharm	−0.30%	6	−0.02%
Banks	0.80%	15	0.12%
Technology	0.60%	9	0.05%
Telecom	−0.20%	13	−0.03%
Bldg Mat'ls	−0.50%	9	−0.05%
Overall	0.29%	100	

the same formula as above to derive the individual sector's contributions (weight times return).

To calculate the contribution for the building materials sector, it's simply:

$$Contribution_{BldgMat'ls} = \left(\frac{Wt_{BldgMat'ls}}{\sum\limits_{i=1}^{n} (Wt_i)} \right) \times R_{BldgMat'ls}$$

$$= -0.50\% \times 9\% = -0.05\%$$

We take the building materials sector's weight (beginning market value), divide it by the sum of all the sectors' market values (i.e., the market value of the portfolio at the beginning of the period), and multiply it by the building materials' return.

Again, we can sum the individual sector contributions to arrive at the portfolio's return:

$$\sum\limits_{i=1}^{n} (Contributions_i) = 0.03 + 0.06 + \cdots + (-.05) = 0.29\%$$

WHAT ABOUT CASH?

You might wonder where the cash component is. For our examples, we're assuming that the portfolio is fully invested. But if there is a cash component, then we'd treat it just like our other components of the group: we'd take the cash's beginning-of-period weight, and

> **Contribution Rule 3**
> *Include cash as a component of your contribution analysis.*

multiply it by the cash return for the period, to derive the cash component contribution.[4]

IMPROVING THE ACCURACY

The basic formula for contribution assumes that the manager is exercising a buy-and-hold approach to investing. That is, that there's no trading activity during the period. But, what if this doesn't happen? How do we account for that?

Contribution is considered an estimate of where returns come from; the need to be precise down to the closest basis point is generally not a concern. But we still want our results to be reasonably close. Here's an approach that is used in other areas of performance measurement to bring improvement to the accuracy of the contribution results.

In this method, we will change the weights that we use from the *beginning-of-period market values (weights)* to the *beginning-of-period market values (weights) plus weighted cash flows*. This is an approach that's used, for example, to improve the portfolio weights in a composite.[5] We can use this same concept to improve the contribution of subportfolio groups.

To derive the *weighted cash flows*, we need to introduce the Day-Weighting Factor. This formula comes in two varieties, depending on whether we're assuming that our cash flows occur at the start or end of the day.

First, let's start with the *end-of-day* approach. The formula for the weighting factor is:

$$W_i = \frac{CD - D_i}{CD}$$

---

[4]The portfolio's return is the result of the effect of the securities held as well as cash. If we didn't include the cash, then we'd overstate the contribution of the individual securities (or sectors, or whatever other component we were analyzing). If we only wanted to look at the contribution of the invested portion of the portfolio, then the return we'd use would be net of the cash.

[5]See Spaulding [1997], pages 121–123.

where

    W = weighting factor

    CD = number of calendar days in the period

    D = day of the flow

    i = for each cash flow (individual cash flow indicator)

Weighting Factor Formulas

Start-of-day cash flows:

$$W_i = \frac{CD - D_i}{CD}$$

End-of-day cash flows:

$$W_i = \frac{CD - D_i + 1}{CD}$$

Because we may have more than one cash flow in the period, we need to subscript our weighting factor term (W). The formula takes into consideration the number of calendar days in the period and the day that the particular flow occurred.

For example, if we have a 31-day month and had a flow on the third day of the month, our result would be:

$$W_i = \frac{CD - D_i}{CD} = \frac{31 - 3}{31} = \frac{28}{31} = 90.32\%$$

We can interpret this result to mean that the flow was available for 90.32% of the month and was present for 28 of the 31 days.

If we presume that flows occur at the beginning of the day, then we make a slight adjustment to our formula by adding 1 to the numerator:

$$W_i = \frac{CD - D_i + 1}{CD}$$

By doing this, we add a day back. And, as you'll see, we get a slightly different result for our cash flow on the third:

$$W_i = \frac{CD - D_i + 1}{CD} = \frac{31 - 3 + 1}{31} = \frac{29}{31} = 93.55\%$$

In this case, we're saying the money was available for 29, not 28 days.[6]

At the subportfolio level, cash flows are *buys* and *sells*. That is, we will look at the securities or sectors (or whatever our group-

---

[6]Or, of course, in the case of an outflow, that the money was *not* available for 29 rather than 28 days; that the money left at the beginning of the third day of the month.

ings) and determine what transactions took place. Purchases are treated as inflows, since money had to come into that security to make the purchase; sales transactions are treated as outflows, since the proceeds of the transaction *left* the security. We should also include income (dividends and interest). However, you might be surprised to learn that income is treated as an outflow, since the money can't be kept or stored at the security or sector level; we presume that the money has *left* the security.[7]

The contribution formula is enhanced to account for these weighted flows:

$$Contribution_{Enh} = \left(\frac{(Wt_i + WC_i)}{\sum_{i=1}^{n} (Wt_i + WC_i)} \right) \times R_i$$

where

Wt = weight
WC = weighted cash flow
R = return

> **Enhanced Contribution Formula**
> $$Contribution_{Enh} = \left(\frac{(Wt_i + WC_i)}{\sum_{i=1}^{n} (Wt_i + WC_i)} \right) \times R_i$$

The weighting ratio is enhanced by adding the individual security's weighted cash flows to its beginning weight (or market value). It is then divided by the sum of all the individual securitys' weights and weighted cash flows that make up the portfolio. This slight adjustment to the weight yields a more accurate result.

An alternative way to express the enhanced formula is as follows:

$$Contribution_{Enh} = \left(Wt + \sum_{i=1}^{n} C_i \times W_i \right) xR$$

where

Wt = weight of the sector or security
C = Cash flows
W = weighting factors for each individual flow
R = portfolio or sector's return

[7]It is beyond the scope of this book to discuss this in detail. However, if you recognize that portfolio accounting systems are generally unable to have "buckets"for the cash that "belongs to" a sector or security, then the only way we can account for income is by moving it *out of* the security or sector. It then becomes part of our cash grouping, wihch we discussed earlier.

T A B L E   2–3

Taking into Account the Cash Flows

Security	ROR	BMV	Cash Flow	Cash	Cash Flow	Wtd Flow	Contrib
A	1.50%	$11,000					0.16%
B	1.80%	12,000	3,000	3	0.94	2,806.45	0.26%
C	2.00%	1,200					0.02%
D	0.50%	1,500					0.01%
E	0.70%	22,000	(4,000)	17	0.48	(1,935.48)	0.14%
F	−1.10%	1,300					−0.01%
G	−0.30%	11,000					−0.03%
H	1.00%	20,000	2,000	12	0.65	1,290.32	0.21%
I	0.20%	7,000					0.01%
J	2.50%	13,000	(2,000)	8	0.77	(1,548.39)	0.28%
Overall		$100,000				$612.90	

This formula takes into consideration the possibility of a sector or security having more than one flow in the period.

We now return to our first portfolio, and this time take into consideration the purchases and sales that transpired during the period to see if we arrive at any different results.

Table 2–3 depicts the portfolio, with a few additional columns.[8]

Two of our securities (B and H) had purchases during the month, while two (E and J) had sales.

We'll walk through the calculation of a couple of securities to demonstrate how the weighting is done. Let's take Security E. A sale of $4000 worth of the stock took place on the 17th of the month. We'll assume a 31-day month with start-of-day flows. To begin with, our weight for the flow:

$$W_i = \frac{CD - D_i + 1}{CD} = \frac{31 - 17 + 1}{31} = \frac{15}{31} = 0.4838 = 48\%$$

---

[8] In this table, we use the actual beginning market value of each security and the dollar amount of each cash flow. The effect is the same as our earlier example.

Thus the sale caused this $4000 to be absent from the portfolio for 48% of the month.[9] We now multiply this weighting factor times the cash flow amount to derive the weighted flow:

$$WC = W \times C = 0.48 \times (-4000) = -1935.48$$

Even though $4000 of securities were sold during the month, since the transaction occurred on the 17th of the month, the money is gone for 48% of the month. Its overall effect on the weight for security E is a reduction of $1935.48.

We now take the enhanced calculation for contribution (which accounts for the flow weights):

$$Contribution_E = \frac{(Wt_E + WC_E)}{\sum\limits_{i=1}^{n} (Wt_i + WC_i)} \times R_E$$

$$= \frac{(22{,}000 + (-1935.48))}{(100{,}000 + 612.90)} \times 0.007$$

$$= 0.1994 \times 0.007 = 0.14\%$$

If we compare this contribution amount with the result we achieved earlier (without taking into account the cash flow), we see that the security E's overall contribution dropped by one basis point (15 versus 14).

If we turn our attention to security B, we see that a purchase was made quite early in the month: an additional $3000 of the stock was bought on the third.

Walking through the same steps as above, we first derive the weighting factor:

$$W_i = \frac{CD - D_i + 1}{CD} = \frac{31 - 3 + 1}{31} = \frac{29}{31} = .9355 = 94\%$$

Thus, the additional money was available for almost the entire month: 94% of the month.

We can now calculate the weighted flow amount:

$$WC = W \times C = 0.94 \times 3000 = 2806.45$$

[9]A word about precision: I've shown the percent without the decimal for simplicity (48% versus 48.38%), but my math actually takes into account these decimals.

You can see that we have the benefit of almost the entire $3000 in our weight. This means that the amount security B has on its contribution has been increased by most of this early-period flow.

Security B's enhanced contribution amount can be calculated:

$$Contribution_B = \frac{(Wt_B + WC_B)}{\sum_{i=1}^{n}(Wt_i + WC_i)} \times R_B$$

$$= \frac{(12,000 + 2806.45)}{(100,000 + 612.90)} \times 0.0108$$

$$= 0.1472 \times 0.0108 = 0.26\%$$

B's contribution to the portfolio return is determined to be 26 basis points using this enhanced formula, as opposed to only 22 basis points, which we came up with earlier. This 4-basis-point improvement in accuracy can be viewed as significant, especially since the portfolio's return was only 1.06%, or 106 basis points.

Table 2–4 summarizes the differences between the "basic" formula and this enhanced version.

You can see how we can obtain some differences. And, if the cash flow amount relative to the starting value is even more significant and occurs early in the period, you will see even greater differences. The benefits of these extra steps can be worth the effort.

TABLE 2–4

Comparing the Contribution

Security	Basic	Enhanced
A	0.17%	0.16%
B	0.22%	0.26%
C	0.02%	0.02%
D	0.01%	0.01%
E	0.15%	0.14%
F	−0.01%	−0.01%
G	−0.03%	−0.03%
H	0.20%	0.21%
I	0.01%	0.01%
J	0.33%	0.28%

ADVANTAGES OF CONTRIBUTION

Contribution is an effective and easy way to determine how the securities, sectors, etc. contribute to a portfolio's overall return. The math is simple, the formula and terminology is easy to understand and explain, and it's often what portfolio managers and clients mean when they say "attribution."

The shortcoming of volatility can be overcome to some degree by enhancing the formula and taking into account the cash flows that occur using the enhanced contribution formula.

Calculating contribution is an effective and valuable analytical tool that should be part of the portfolio's statistics.

T A B L E   2–E–1

Portfolio Data

Security	ROR	BMV
A	2.50%	$13,000
B	−1.50%	9,000
C	3.00%	12,000
D	0.44%	7,000
E	−2.00%	12,000
F	1.63%	11,000
G	0.55%	8,000
H	0.90%	9,000
I	0.30%	8,000
J	−1.03%	11,000
Portfolio	0.56%	$100,000

EXERCISES

1. The portfolio in Table 2–E–1 shows an overall return of 0.56% for the month.

   Calculate the contribution of each of the securities to the portfolio's overall return.

2. Using the above table, what happens to the contributions when we take into account the following cash flows?

   Security B   Sale of $5000 on the seventh of the month

   Security J   Purchase of $5000 on the second of the month

   Note: Assume a 31-day month and that flows occur at the *beginning* of day.

Equity Attribution

Use B-F model (p42 ff) [handwritten note]

In chapter 1, we address some of the key contributors to the portfolio's return that we look at in equity attribution. In this chapter, we discuss and contrast some of the models that are commonly used to perform this analysis.

At the conclusion of the chapter, you should have a good grasp of what to look for in comparing models and how to evaluate the relevance of one model versus another.

WHERE THE RETURN COMES FROM

Figure 3–1 shows one view of where a portfolio's return comes from. At the highest level, we have income and appreciation.

OUR BASIC EXAMPLE

As mentioned earlier, there are various ways to do attribution. We use mathematical models to accomplish this, and there are several available. We now introduce you to three such approaches to conduct attribution analysis of an equity portfolio. These three models, while having some similarities, have some striking differences, as well.

In each case, we'll use the portfolio in Table 3–1 to demonstrate how the model is used.

F I G U R E   3–1

Contributors to an Equity Portfolio's Return

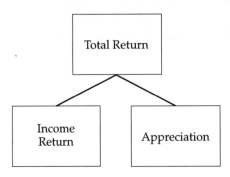

Let's begin by deriving the portfolio's excess return:

$$ER_A = R_P - R_B = 0.29\% - 0.19\% = 0.10\%$$

Using the arithmetic approach (as we present in chapter 1), our excess return is 10 basis points. And, to comply with our second law of attribution, the sum of our attribution effects should equal this amount.

T A B L E   3–1

Basic Equity Portfolio Example

	ROR		Weight	
	Portfolio	**Benchmark**	**Portfolio**	**Benchmark**
Basic Materials	0.25%	0.15%	10%	11%
Industrials	0.50%	0.51%	11%	9%
Consumer Cyclicals	1.00%	1.01%	8%	7%
Utilities	−0.80%	−0.75%	12%	13%
Energy	2.00%	1.95%	7%	5%
Financial	−0.30%	−0.31%	6%	8%
Healthcare	0.80%	0.79%	15%	13%
Technology	0.60%	0.70%	9%	10%
Telecom	−0.20%	−0.21%	13%	10%
Consumer Non-Cyc.	−0.50%	−0.52%	9%	14%
Portfolio	0.29%	0.19%	100%	100%

THE BHB MODEL

We now begin by presenting one of the most commonly used and earliest developed models, which we'll call the BHB model or approach. The "BHB" stands for Brinson, Hood, and Beebower, the authors of this model.[1] *Brinson [1986]*

First, I want to say a word about terminology. In the *Financial Analyst Journal* article in which this method is presented, the authors use the terms "passive" and "actual" to represent what we typically call "benchmark" and "portfolio" or "active." To avoid confusion, I'm going to take some liberties: I'm going to present the model using the same terminology as we use with the other models. You're invited to read the original BHB article—in fact, you're encouraged to do so. But this slight liberty does not detract from the value of the model; it merely keeps us consistent in this text and (hopefully) avoids confusion.

The framework for the model is a grid that depicts the stock selection (in the columns) and sector selection (or "timing," as the authors refer to it) in the rows (see Figure 3–2).

Quadrants are numbered from one to four.[2] Quadrant I, the lower right-hand corner, is the intersection of the benchmark's securities (stock selection) and its sector asset allocation, or timing. When we intersect these values, we come up with the benchmark's return.

FIGURE 3-2

BHB Grid of Attribution Components

	Selection	
	Portfolio	Benchmark
Timing — Portfolio	(IV) Actual Portfolio Return	(II) Policy and Timing Return
Timing — Benchmark	(III) Policy and Security Selection Return	(I) Policy Return (Passive Portfolio Benchmark)

[1]See Brinson [1986].
[2]Brinson, et al prefer Roman numerals, thus we have them from I to IV.

In the diagonal from Quadrant I, we find Quadrant IV (upper left), which is the intersection of the portfolio's stock selection with its asset allocation. This yields the portfolio's return.

The remaining two quadrants (II and III; upper right and lower left) blend the stock selection of one portfolio (benchmark or actual) with the other's asset allocation.

The actual math that is needed to calculate the components[3] of these four quadrants is as follows:[4]

$$IV = \sum W_P \times R_P \qquad II = \sum W_P \times R_B$$
$$III = \sum W_B \times R_P \qquad I = \sum W_B \times R_B$$

where

W = weight
R = return
B = benchmark (passive)
P = portfolio (active or actual)

It's probably not surprising that the lower right corner, Quadrant I, is the sum of the individual benchmark component weights, times their respective benchmark component returns, resulting in the overall benchmark return. Likewise, the upper left (IV) multiplies portfolio component weights by their respective component returns, yielding the portfolio's overall return.

Now that we have the quadrant formulas, we're prepared to derive the actual attribution effects. The BHB model has three effects: timing (or asset allocation), stock selection, and "other," which is the missing piece to satisfy the Second Law of Performance Attribution.[5]

The math works as follows:

Timing (Asset Allocation) Effect

This is simply Quadrant II minus Quadrant I, or

$$\sum W_P \times R_B - \sum W_B \times R_B$$

---

[3]At this stage of our discussion, I'm using the term "component" to represent the subportfolio grouping that we eventually use to calculate the attribution. While this may be sector or security data (or, in reality, some other logical subportfolio group), it's easier at this stage simply to use the term "component." Later, we are more specific and use more precise terminology.

[4]You will note that many of my expressions are simplified; that is, when I show the Riemann sum, I don't show the *from* (e.g., "i = 1") or *to* values (e.g., "n"), nor have I subscripted the elements within the formula. It's my hope that you'll realize that this is what's going on, since I've shown the Riemann sum symbol ($\sum$). I apologize if this is confusing, but I don't feel it necessary to be overly detailed in this regard.

[5]Chapter 10 addresses the use of "other" or "interaction" effects in attribution models.

which algebraically can be reduced to:

$$\Sigma \, R_B \times (W_P - W_B)$$

Here we have the sum of the individual component benchmark returns times the difference between the component's respective two weights (portfolio weight minus benchmark weight).

Stock Selection Effect

To arrive at this effect, we subtract Quadrant I from Quadrant III, which yields:

$$\Sigma \, W_B \times R_P - W_B \times R_B$$

which algebraically can be simplified to:

$$\Sigma \, W_B \times (R_P - R_B)$$

Thus, we are multiplying each of the benchmark's component weights by the difference in returns (portfolio minus benchmark).

"Other" Effect

If you add the timing effect with stock selection effect, you'll see that we haven't equaled the excess return. Therefore, we need to account for the difference, which the model's authors label "other." It's Quadrant IV minus III minus II, plus I, or:

$$\Sigma \, (R_P \times (W_P - W_B) - R_B \times (W_P - W_B))$$

When we add these three effects together, we have the excess return:

Timing (Market Selection)	$II - I$
Stock Selection	$III - I$
Other	$IV - III - II + I$
Total	$IV - I$

LOOKING AT THE SIGNS

I think it's worth considering what the signs will be of the results of our model, even before we use it with actual data. For example, let's look at timing or asset allocation:

$$\Sigma \, R_B \times (W_P - W_B)$$

Let's start with the case where the benchmark return is *positive* and we've *overweighted* the sector (that is, the weight in the portfolio is greater than the weight in the benchmark). What will the sign be?

Since the return is positive and the difference in weights (portfolio minus benchmark) is positive, then our result has to be positive, too, since a positive number multiplied by a positive number yields a positive number. Thus, a manager who overweighted a sector that has a positive return (i.e., a return greater than zero) will be rewarded with a positive effect for asset allocation; the model will say that the resulting excess return received some benefit from this action. The model says she was wise to overweight a sector that had a positive return. Make sense?

How about the case where we have a *positive* return but *underweighted* the portfolio relative to the benchmark? Here, we have a positive return as before, but this time a negative number from our weights (since the portfolio weight is less than the benchmark weight). In this case, our effect will be negative (i.e., the model says we were unwise to underweight a sector that had a positive return). It would say that the better thing to have done would have been to overweight. Thus the manager is penalized for her poor decision.

What if we had a *negative* return and *overweighted* the portfolio? What now? The return is negative and the weights will be positive (as before, if the portfolio weight is greater than the benchmark, the difference will be positive), so our effect is once again negative; we're penalized for overweighting a sector that had a negative (or below zero) return; i.e., we're told that we goofed by putting more of the money in a sector than the benchmark would have had, because the return was negative.

Finally, we have the case where we *underweight* an underperforming sector—one with a negative return. Here, we have a negative number (from the return) times a negative number (because we underweighted the portfolio) which algebraically yields a positive number (because a negative times a negative is a positive). The model rewards us because we underweighted a sector when it was underperforming; something the model feels was a good move on our part; to put less of the client's money in a sector when it didn't yield a positive return.

Do these results make sense? Most people will say "yes."

Figure 3–3 summarizes how the signs will work out, depending on the return of the sector in the benchmark and whether or not

F I G U R E   3–3

Signs for Our Allocation Effect

the manager overweighted or underweighted the sector in her portfolio.

Let's turn our attention to the signs for the stock selection effect.

$$\sum W_B \times (R_P - R_B)$$

where

W_B = benchmark's weight
R_B = benchmark's return
R_P = portfolio's return

Here, the math is much simpler to figure out.

If the portfolio (R_P) outperformed the benchmark (R_B), then this factor in our equation will be positive. A positive times a positive (since we would expect our weight to be positive[6]) will yield a positive. If we underperformed, we'd have a negative times a positive, which gives us a negative. To put it simply, when we outperform the benchmark in a sector, our result is positive; when we underperform, the effect is negative.

Applying the Model to Our Portfolio

We're now ready to use this model to analyze our basic portfolio (from Table 3–1). Let's begin by calculating the quadrant values for each industry. Table 3–2 shows this.

[6]We briefly touch upon this subject in chapter 13.

T A B L E 3-2

Applying the BHB Model to Our Sample Portfolio, Step 1—Calculating the Quadrant Values

	ROR		Weight		Quadrants			
	Portfolio	Index	Portfolio	Index	I	II	III	IV
Basic Materials	0.25%	0.15%	10%	11%	0.017%	0.015%	0.028%	0.025%
Industrials	0.50%	0.51%	11%	9%	0.046%	0.056%	0.045%	0.055%
Consumer Cyclicals	1.00%	1.01%	8%	7%	0.071%	0.081%	0.070%	0.080%
Utilities	−0.80%	−0.75%	12%	13%	−0.098%	−0.090%	−0.104%	−0.096%
Energy	2.00%	1.95%	7%	5%	0.098%	0.137%	0.100%	0.140%
Financial	−0.30%	−0.31%	6%	8%	−0.025%	−0.019%	−0.024%	−0.018%
Healthcare	0.80%	0.79%	15%	13%	0.103%	0.119%	0.104%	0.120%
Technology	0.60%	0.70%	9%	10%	0.070%	0.063%	0.060%	0.054%
Telecom	−0.20%	−0.21%	13%	10%	−0.021%	−0.027%	−0.020%	−0.026%
Consumer Non-Cyc.	−0.50%	−0.52%	9%	14%	−0.073%	−0.047%	−0.070%	−0.045%
Portfolio	0.29%	0.19%	100%	100%	0.187%	0.287%	0.189%	0.289%

We now quickly walk through a couple examples. Quadrant I is derived by multiplying the individual benchmark returns with their respective weights. For example, our basic materials' benchmark return is 0.15% with a weight of 11%.

$$QuadrantI_{BasicMat'ls} = 0.11 \times 0.15 = 0.017\%$$

Quadrant IV uses the return and weight for the portfolio. For basic materials, we get:

$$QuadrantIV_{BasicMat'ls} = 0.10 \times 0.25 = 0.025\%$$

Now that we have the quadrant values, we can derive the attribution effects using our formulas from above, which I restate for you:

> Timing: *Quadrant II − Quadrant I*
> Stock Selection: *Quadrant III − Quadrant I*
> Other: *Quadrants IV − III − II + I*

Table 3–3 repeats the quadrant values and shows the effects we derive by applying our model.

Table 3–4 shows the portfolio's returns, weights, and attribution effects, as calculated using the BHB model. Let's see if the effects make intuitive sense, given what we know about the model.

The basic materials sector found us underweighting the benchmark (10% versus 11%), while the returns in both the portfolio and benchmark were positive. Given what we know about timing, we'd expect to be penalized, since we *underweighted* a *positively performing* sector. And, what do we find? Timing shows a −0.002%.[7] And what about the effect from stock selection? Since we outperformed the benchmark (0.25% versus 0.15%), we'd expect a positive result, and that's exactly what we find: +0.011% or roughly one basis point contributing to the portfolio's overall return.

How about industrials? Since we overweighted this sector (11% versus 9%) and the benchmark had a positive return (0.51%), we should get some credit for superior asset allocation,

---

[7]Normally, we'd probably only show the number to two basis points. We intentionally expanded the numbers to three places to show that there really was a negative effect; had we only shown two, the effect is so small (−0.002%) that we'd encounter rounding and a result of 0.00%, which would have suggested no effect at all, which would have been wrong.

TABLE 3-3

BHB Model Step 2—Calculating the Effects

| | Quadrants | | | | Effects | | | |
	I	II	III	IV	Timing	Stk Sel	Other	Total
Basic Materials	0.017%	0.015%	0.028%	0.025%	−0.002%	0.011%	−0.001%	0.009%
Industrials	0.046%	0.056%	0.045%	0.055%	0.010%	−0.001%	0.000%	0.009%
Consumer Cyclicals	0.071%	0.081%	0.070%	0.080%	0.010%	−0.001%	0.000%	0.009%
Utilities	−0.098%	−0.090%	−0.104%	−0.096%	0.008%	−0.007%	0.001%	0.001%
Energy	0.098%	0.137%	0.100%	0.140%	0.039%	0.003%	0.001%	0.043%
Financial	−0.025%	−0.019%	−0.024%	−0.018%	0.006%	0.001%	0.000%	0.007%
Healthcare	0.103%	0.119%	0.104%	0.120%	0.016%	0.001%	0.000%	0.017%
Technology	0.070%	0.063%	0.060%	0.054%	−0.007%	−0.010%	0.001%	−0.016%
Telecom	−0.021%	−0.027%	−0.020%	−0.026%	−0.006%	0.001%	0.000%	−0.005%
Consumer Non-Cyc.	−0.073%	−0.047%	−0.070%	−0.045%	0.026%	0.003%	−0.001%	0.028%
Portfolio	0.187%	0.287%	0.189%	0.289%	0.100%	0.001%	0.000%	0.102%

38

TABLE 3-4

BHB Model Returns, Weights, and Effects

| | ROR | | Weight | | Effects | | | |
	Portfolio	Index	Portfolio	Index	Timing	Stk Sel	Other	Total
Basic Materials	0.25%	0.15%	10%	11%	−0.002%	0.011%	−0.001%	0.009%
Industrials	0.50%	0.51%	11%	9%	0.010%	−0.001%	0.000%	0.009%
Consumer Cyc.	1.00%	1.01%	8%	7%	0.010%	−0.001%	0.000%	0.009%
Utilities	−0.80%	−0.75%	12%	13%	0.008%	−0.007%	0.001%	0.001%
Energy	2.00%	1.95%	7%	5%	0.039%	0.003%	0.001%	0.043%
Financial	−0.30%	−0.31%	6%	8%	0.006%	0.001%	0.000%	0.007%
Healthcare	0.80%	0.79%	15%	13%	0.016%	0.001%	0.000%	0.017%
Technology	0.60%	0.70%	9%	10%	−0.007%	−0.010%	0.001%	−0.016%
Telecom	−0.20%	−0.21%	13%	10%	−0.006%	0.001%	0.000%	−0.005%
Consumer Non-Cyc.	−0.50%	−0.52%	9%	14%	0.026%	0.003%	−0.001%	0.028%
Portfolio	0.29%	0.19%	100%	100%	0.100%	0.001%	0.000%	0.102%

39

and that's what we find: one basis point (0.01%) contribution
from timing.

This time, we underperformed the benchmark (0.50% versus
0.51%) so our effect from stock selection hurts our performance
(−0.001%).

Let's drop down to utilities. Here, we have a negatively performing sector that we chose to underweight (12% versus 13% in
the benchmark). We'd expect a reward from timing, since we
underweighted a sector that had a negative return. This is what
we find: almost a full basis point (0.008%). Since we underperformed the benchmark (−0.80 versus −0.75), we have a stock
selection of −0.007%, virtually wiping out the benefit we got from
asset allocation.

And finally, let's consider telecommunications, where we find
an overweighted portfolio (13% versus 10%) of a sector that had a
negative return, which means we goofed (i.e., putting more money
than the benchmark would have advised into a negatively performing sector), and the model yielded a disappointing −0.007%
for timing. But we redeem ourselves slightly because we outperformed the benchmark (−0.20% versus −0.21%) and pick up a
small fraction of a basis point (0.001%) in stock selection.

You may notice that I don't comment on the "other" effect,
since there's no intuitive way to anticipate what the result will be.
Fortunately, it has no actual effect for our portfolio, but it can.

Given what we understand the model's intention to be for
stock selection and timing, I think we can conclude that the four
sectors' results make sense. Do you agree?

When we sum the effects, we find that we obtained 10 basis
points (0.100%) from timing (meaning good asset allocation decisions), a fraction of a basis point (0.001%) from stock selection (i.e., almost neutral for stock picking), and nothing (0.000%) from
"other." When we add these effects together, we get 10
basis points, which is the actual excess return for this portfolio (0.29%
− 0.19% = 0.10%). So, we've satisfied our second law of attribution.

A VARIATION OF THE BHB MODEL

The next model is based on the Brinson, Hood, Beebower model
but has a slight adjustment that takes away the need for the "other"
effect.

This model's industry selection uses the calculation for timing from BHB:

$$\sum R_B \times (W_P - W_B)$$

Its signs are therefore the same as we see with the original BHB model we discuss above.

The difference in the two models is in the way that stock selection is derived:

$$\sum W_P \times (R_P - R_B)$$

where

W_p = portfolio weight

In the original BHB model, the weight of the *benchmark* is used; with this variation, we use the weight of the *portfolio*. This slight change eliminates the need for an "other" effect; the sum of the selection and allocation effects accounts for the entire excess return.

Table 3–5 shows the calculations using this model.

Table 3–6 compares the effects of these two models with our portfolio. Not surprisingly, the "timing" and "industry selection"

TABLE 3–5

Variation on BHB Model

	ROR		Weight		Market Effect	
	Portfolio	Index	Portfolio	Index	Stk Sel	Ind Sel
Basic Materials	0.25%	0.15%	10%	11%	0.010%	−0.002%
Industrials	0.50%	0.51%	11%	9%	−0.001%	0.010%
Consumer Cyclicals	1.00%	1.01%	8%	7%	−0.001%	0.010%
Utilities	−0.80%	−0.75%	12%	13%	−0.006%	0.008%
Energy	2.00%	1.95%	7%	5%	0.004%	0.039%
Financial	−0.30%	−0.31%	6%	8%	0.001%	0.006%
Healthcare	0.80%	0.79%	15%	13%	0.001%	0.016%
Technology	0.60%	0.70%	9%	10%	−0.009%	−0.007%
Telecom	−0.20%	−0.21%	13%	10%	0.001%	−0.006%
Consumer Non-Cyc.	−0.50%	−0.52%	9%	14%	0.002%	0.026%
Portfolio	0.29%	0.19%	100%	100%	0.002%	0.100%

T A B L E   3–6

Comparing the Attribution Effects of BHB and Its Variation

	BHB Variation			BHB	
	Stk Sel	Ind Sel	Timing	Stk Sel	Other
Basic Materials	0.010%	−0.002%	−0.002%	0.011%	−0.001%
Industrials	−0.001%	0.010%	0.010%	−0.001%	0.000%
Consumer Cyc.	−0.001%	0.010%	0.010%	−0.001%	0.000%
Utilities	−0.006%	0.008%	0.008%	−0.007%	0.001%
Energy	0.004%	0.039%	0.039%	0.003%	0.001%
Financial	0.001%	0.006%	0.006%	0.001%	0.000%
Healthcare	0.001%	0.016%	0.016%	0.001%	0.000%
Technology	−0.009%	−0.007%	−0.007%	−0.010%	0.001%
Telecom	0.001%	−0.006%	−0.006%	0.001%	0.000%
Consumer Non-Cyc.	0.002%	0.026%	0.026%	0.003%	−0.001%
Portfolio	0.002%	0.100%	0.100%	0.001%	0.000%

effects are identical (since they use the exact same formula). The stock selection effect is slightly different.

BRINSON-FACHLER MODEL

Our third model was developed by Gary Brinson and Nimrod Fachler.[8] It uses the same stock selection formula as the BHB variation:

$$\sum W_P \times (R_P - R_B)$$

where

W_p = portfolio weight
R_P = portfolio return
R_B = benchmark return

The difference, and not an insignificant one (as you'll see), rests with the way that industry selection is determined. Instead of the rather simplistic approach used in both the BHB and BHB variation,

$$\sum R_B \times (W_P - W_B)$$

[8]Brinson [1985].

where

W_p = portfolio weight
W_B = benchmark weight
R_B = benchmark return

which uses the benchmark's return, the Brinson-Fachler model multiplies the weight differential by how well the sector performed in the benchmark, with the overall benchmark:

$$\sum (R_{S_B} - R_B) \times (W_P - W_B)$$

where

R_{S_B} = the benchmark's return for the sector
R_B = the benchmark's overall return
W_B = the sector's weight in the benchmark
W_P = the sector's weight in the portfolio

Here, we subtract the overall benchmark return (R_B) from the sector's return in the benchmark (R_{S_B}).

This, perhaps apparently slight, difference can cause *huge* differences in the results.

Let's begin by analyzing what the signs will be (see Figure 3–4). If we overweight a sector with a positive return, what will we have? In the BHB model, we saw that it was positive (because a positive times a positive is a positive). However, having a positive

FIGURE   3–4

Signs of Industry Selection for Brinson-Fachler

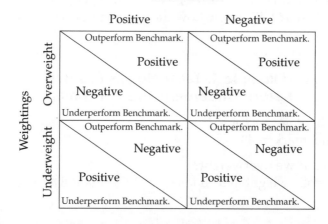

return in the B-F model isn't enough. Here, we have to look at the sector return *relative to* or *in relationship to* the overall return. If the sector was positive but fell short of the overall return (i.e., was less than the overall return), then the difference will be negative and the industry selection effect negative! Why? Because the manager is being *penalized* for investing more in a sector (i.e., overweighting it) that had a return below the overall benchmark, a sector that kept the benchmark return lower than it might otherwise have been. If, however, the sector outperformed the overall benchmark (had a higher return), then the effect will be positive.

If we overweighted a sector that had a negative return, what would the effect be? In the BHB model, it's negative (a negative times a positive is negative). And, it will be negative here, too, but only if we underperformed the overall benchmark. However, if we outperformed the benchmark (that is, even though the sector had a negative return, it was higher than the benchmark), then we'd have a positive effect.

If we underweighted a positively performing sector, the BHB model penalizes us (for underweighting a sector with a positive return). Here, too, we'll be penalized if the sector outperformed the overall benchmark. But, if we underperformed the benchmark, then our underweighting would have been considered wise and the effect positive.

Finally, if we underweighted a negatively performing sector, the BHB model responds positively (a negative number times a negative number). The B-F model will likewise be positive, but only if we underperformed the overall benchmark (had a lower negative number than the benchmark). But, if we outperformed the benchmark (even though the number is negative), we'll get a negative result.

Confused? Let's show how these two models treat the following examples.

Example 1: Technology's Positive Return Underperforms Benchmark

Technology Sector = 2%
Benchmark = 4%

What if we overweight?
Portfolio weight in technology = 10% versus 8% in benchmark.

The BHB model yields an industry selection effect for technology of $+.04\%$, because we overweighted a sector that performed positively (had a return above zero).

$$IndSel_{BHB} = 0.02 \times (0.10 - 0.08) = 0.02 \times 0.02 = 0.04\%$$

The B-F model, however, yields a drastically different result. Here, we see a negative number because we overweighted a sector that didn't help the benchmark; rather, it put a drag on performance.

$$IndSel_{B-F} = (0.02 - 0.04) \times (0.10 - 0.08) = -0.02 \times 0.02 = -0.04\%$$

What if we underweight?
Portfolio weight in technology = 8% versus 10% in benchmark.
The BHB model yields a negative effect because we chose to underweight a sector that had a positive result.

$$IndSel_{BHB} = 0.02 \times (0.08 - 0.10) = 0.02 \times -0.02 = -0.04\%$$

The B-F model, however, gives us a positive number, rewarding us for underweighting a sector that didn't contribute to the benchmark's overall return.

$$IndSel_{B-F} = (0.02 - 0.04) \times (0.08 - 0.10) = -0.02 \times -0.02 = +0.04\%$$

Example 2: Technology's Negative Return Outperforms Benchmark

Technology sector = -2%
Benchmark return = -4%

What if we overweight?
Portfolio weight in technology = 10% versus 8% in benchmark.
The BHB model yields an industry selection effect for technology of $-.04\%$, because we overweighted a sector that had a negative return.

$$IndSel_{BHB} = -0.02 \times (0.10 - 0.08) = -0.02 \times 0.02 = -0.04\%$$

This contrasts quite a bit from the B-F model, which rewards the manager for overweighting a sector that outperformed the benchmark, regardless of the fact that the return was negative.

$$IndSel_{B-F} = (-0.02 - (-0.04)) \times (0.10 - 0.08)$$
$$= 0.02 \times 0.02 = +0.04\%$$

And, if we underweight?

Portfolio weight in technology = 8% versus 10% in benchmark.

The BHB model yields a positive effect because we chose to underweight a sector that had a negative return:

$$IndSel_{BHB} = -0.02 \times (0.08 - 0.10) = -0.02 \times -0.02 = +0.04\%$$

Versus the B-F model, which penalizes us for underweighting a sector that outperformed the benchmark:

$$IndSel_{B-F:} = (-0.02 - (-0.04)) \times (0.08 - 0.10)$$
$$= +0.02 \times -0.02 = -0.04\%$$

What does this mean? I think quite a bit.

We have two models that can give drastically different results. Not only do the numbers change, but they switch from positive to negative—from giving us positive marks for asset allocation to penalizing us for doing a poor job!

The implications can be huge, can't they? Especially if the way we reward our managers or analysts is tied to their asset allocation decisions. It could possibly mean the difference between handing someone a "pink slip" or a bonus check![9]

The BHB model bases its asset allocation component of the model on whether or not the sector's return is above or below zero. There's no reference whatsoever to the sector's effect on the overall benchmark portfolio. I'd say that this model uses logic based on the *absolute* sector return: absolute positive or negative number.

The B-F model doesn't really care if the sector return is positive or negative; rather, it looks at how the sector did in comparison to the benchmark. This model uses logic based on the *relative* sector return: relative to the benchmark.

It's this kind of difference that makes model selection a challenge. How do you wish to measure asset allocation decisions? Would you prefer to reward the overweighting of a sector with a positive number, regardless of how it did relative to the benchmark, or would you only want to reward the overweighting of sectors that contributed to the benchmark return?

I don't think there's a simple answer. While I tend to prefer the B-F approach, the BHB model is widely used and accepted.

---

[9]Perhaps this is a bit of hyperbole, but you hopefully get the point; we can show positive or negative results, based on the same data, simply due to the model we use.

Applying the Model

Let's apply the B-F model to our example portfolio and see what we get. Table 3–7 shows the results of applying the model to this portfolio.

The sum of the effects equals the excess return, showing that there's no need for an "other" effect—we are able to account for the entire excess return from the stock selection and industry selection. The stock selection effects match what we saw in the earlier BHB model, since the B-F model uses the same formula for this effect. The difference, which we discussed at length above, is in the industry selection. Table 3–8 contrasts the industry selection effects we get from the BHB and B-F models.

Because the basic materials' return (0.15%) was positive but below the overall benchmark return (0.19%), and because we underweighted this sector (10% versus 11% in the benchmark), we see a sign flip from negative for the BHB model (which penalized us for underweighting a positively performing sector) to positive for the B-F model (which rewards us for underweighting a sector that underperformed the benchmark). While this is the only case where the signs change, you can see that every sector had a slightly different effect calculated for industry selection.

T A B L E   3–7

Applying the B-F Model to Our Sample Portfolio

	ROR		Weight		Market Effect	
	Portfolio	Index	Portfolio	Index	Stk Sel	Ind Sel
Basic Materials	0.25%	0.15%	10%	11%	0.010%	0.000%
Industrials	0.50%	0.51%	11%	9%	−0.001%	0.006%
Consumer Cyc.	1.00%	1.01%	8%	7%	−0.001%	0.008%
Utilities	−0.80%	−0.75%	12%	13%	−0.006%	0.009%
Energy	2.00%	1.95%	7%	5%	0.004%	0.035%
Financial	−0.30%	−0.31%	6%	8%	0.001%	0.010%
Healthcare	0.80%	0.79%	15%	13%	0.001%	0.012%
Technology	0.60%	0.70%	9%	10%	−0.009%	−0.005%
Telecom	−0.20%	−0.21%	13%	10%	0.001%	−0.012%
Consumer Non-Cyc.	−0.50%	−0.52%	9%	14%	0.002%	0.035%
Portfolio	0.29%	0.19%	100%	100%	0.002%	0.100%

T A B L E   3–8

Contrasting Industry Selection

	BHB	B-F
Basic Materials	−0.002%	0.0004%
Industrials	0.010%	0.006%
Consumer Cyclicals	0.010%	0.008%
Utilities	0.008%	0.009%
Energy	0.039%	0.035%
Financial	0.006%	0.010%
Healthcare	0.016%	0.012%
Technology	−0.007%	−0.005%
Telecommunications	−0.006%	−0.012%
Consumer Non-Cyc.	0.026%	0.035%
Portfolio	0.100%	0.100%

Also note that the portfolio's overall effect for industry selection is the same for each model (10 basis points or 0.10%). The differences lie at the individual sector level.

ALTERNATIVE AND CUSTOM MODELS

The reality is that there can be many other approaches to equity attribution. We've shown you three of the more commonly used
models. Some firms take these and make adjustments (as we
showed with the variation of the BHB model).

One commonly asked question regarding the BHB model (or
its variation) is why we use the index returns for sector selection,
rather than the portfolio's? This is an option you may wish to consider implementing. Let's see what happens if we make this slight
adjustment.

We've shown our earlier example, using the variation of the
BHB, in Table 3–9, with the only difference being how we derived
the industry selection effect. Table 3–10 compares the industry effects
using the index returns (from our earlier example) and portfolio returns. As you can see, while there are differences for each industry,
the total effects are equal (the fractional basis point is attributable to
rounding). It appears that this approach will work, too.

It's not unusual for firms to modify a model so that it conforms to their investment style and philosophy.

T A B L E   3–9

Variation on BHB Model, as Presented Earlier, but Using Portfolio ROR

	ROR		Weight		Market Effect	
	Portfolio	Index	Portfolio	Index	Stk. Sel.	Ind. Sel.
Basic Materials	0.25%	0.15%	10%	11%	0.010%	−0.003%
Industrials	0.50%	0.51%	11%	9%	−0.001%	0.010%
Consumer Cyclicals	1.00%	1.01%	8%	7%	−0.001%	0.010%
Utilities	−0.80%	−0.75%	12%	13%	−0.006%	0.008%
Energy	2.00%	1.95%	7%	5%	0.004%	0.040%
Financial	−0.30%	−0.31%	6%	8%	0.001%	0.006%
Healthcare	0.80%	0.79%	15%	13%	0.001%	0.016%
Technology	0.60%	0.70%	9%	10%	−0.009%	−0.006%
Telecom	−0.20%	−0.21%	13%	10%	0.001%	−0.006%
Consumer Non-Cyc.	−0.50%	−0.52%	9%	14%	0.002%	0.025%
Portfolio	0.29%	0.19%	100%	100%	0.002%	0.101%

Some firms will develop custom models for attribution. Often, these involve the analysis of several factors simultaneously. These are referred to as multifactor models.

The key is that you're consistent, that it makes sense, that it's documented, and explainable. Oh, and that it also conforms with our attribution laws!

T A B L E   3–10

Comparing Industry Selection Effects

	Industry Selection Effects	
	Using Index ROR	Using Portfolio ROR
Basic Materials	0.000%	−0.003%
Industrials	0.006%	0.010%
Consumer Cyclicals	0.008%	0.010%
Utilities	0.009%	0.008%
Energy	0.035%	0.040%
Financial	0.010%	0.006%
Healthcare	0.012%	0.016%
Technology	−0.005%	−0.006%
Telecom	−0.012%	−0.006%
Consumer Non-Cyc.	0.035%	0.025%
Portfolio	0.100%	0.101%

CHALLENGES FOR CONSULTANTS AND PLAN SPONSORS

Because of the different results we can get, depending upon which model we use, it's important that investment consultants and plan sponsors who review such reports from their managers recognize this and understand the model that's behind the numbers, especially when comparing one manager with another. Differences between managers can arise simply because of the different models that they may be using. It's important to ask for specifics—don't just look at the numbers.

Our research suggests that many plan sponsors aren't aware of the models their managers use; they should be. As we've seen, the models can provide conflicting results, so it's important that the plan sponsor understand how the manager approaches this important analytical area.

CONCLUDING REMARKS

Equity attribution has been around for quite some time. We've seen it grow from a single approach, to variations, to very different views on how to allocate the excess return. Attention should be paid to the first law of attribution when picking a model, to ensure that it meets your needs, is understandable, and explainable.

EXERCISE

Calculate the attribution effects for the portfolio in Table 3–E–1, using the three models we discuss in this chapter.

T A B L E   3–E–1

Portfolio and Benchmark Details

	Rate of Return		Weights	
	Portfolio	**Index**	**Portfolio**	**Index**
Industrials	2.00%	3.00%	40.00%	25.00%
Transportation	3.00%	2.00%	20.00%	25.00%
Utilities	4.00%	5.00%	30.00%	25.00%
Financials	5.00%	4.00%	10.00%	25.00%
	3.10%	3.50%		

Fixed Income Attribution[1]

*Both Steve Campisi & Tim Lord
make sure. Campisi a bit simpler*

While equity attribution is fairly well developed, with numerous models and many generally agreed-upon approaches, the same cannot be said for attribution of fixed income portfolios.

On the surface, this may be a bit surprising. After all, fixed income investments dwarf equities. And yet, just like many other aspects of investing, fixed income plays second fiddle to equities.[2]

There are a few reasons for this, one being that fixed income is more complex than equities; with the wide array of instruments to choose from and investigate, it's a daunting task to develop software for it. New fixed income security types crop up on a regular basis. Just the name itself, "fixed" income is misleading, as some securities actually produce "variable" income!

Secondly, the investment approach itself of the fixed income manager can often be more complex than that of an equity manager. Fixed income managers rely heavily on mathematical concepts and techniques that can be a challenge to perform, communicate, and comprehend.

---

[1]The input for this chapter comes from a variety of sources, most notably from Steve Campisi, who teaches a class on attribution with me. Steve is a fixed income portfolio manager whose knowledge of performance measurement and fixed income attribution is extensive.

[2]Another example that comes to mind is trade/order management systems. While we've had several competing products available to support the equity market, the fixed income side has had very little to choose from.

Finally, a simple model, as we show in chapter 3, won't be adequate for fixed income, since bond managers typically look simultaneously at multiple criteria. While the notion of addressing one factor at a time has some benefit, the ideal is to address them in concert.

We hope to demonstrate that while many people may use these earlier models, they're really inappropriate for fixed income attribution analysis. What we need is a "true" fixed income attribution system. We present a couple of approaches below.

FIXED INCOME INVESTING

Steve Campisi offers the following perspectives on investing. "Portfolio management is primarily about risk management, and secondarily about return enhancement. The portfolio manager's first responsibility is to identify the types and levels of risk that are appropriate for the client, and then to develop an asset allocation that delivers these risks. The manager's secondary responsibility is to implement the agreed-upon asset allocation by purchasing and maintaining appropriate securities. Finally, the manager undertakes the ongoing responsibility of monitoring the portfolio and its investments to ensure that the investment strategies are working and that the client is adequately compensated for the risk being borne."[3]

Sri Ramaswamy apparently concurs. "In broad terms, portfolio management refers to the process of

> Our portfolio can be viewed as a "basket of risk."

managing the risk of a portfolio relative to a benchmark with the purpose of either tracking or adding value."[4]

Based on this approach, our portfolio is, in essence, a "basket of risks."

OUR APPROACH FOR THIS CHAPTER

For this article, I am definitely "standing on the shoulders of giants"—in particular, Steve Campisi and Tim Lord, both of whom have written wonderful articles on fixed income attribution for *The*

---

[3]Campisi [2000], page 14.
[4]Ramaswamy [2001], page 58.

Journal of Performance Measurement.[5] I've borrowed extensively from both of their writings. Also, Steve has provided me with additional guidance in preparing this material.

We now begin by briefly contrasting bonds and stocks, and in the process hopefully show why the equity attribution models are inappropriate for fixed income.

We next introduce some theory from both Tim and Steve regarding their views on where fixed income returns come from. You'll see some similarities between their approaches, as well as some slight differences. We show you the formulas they use for their models.

We then walk through an example using Steve Campisi's model. This will give you some insight into what's actually involved when doing this kind of analysis.[6]

THE "ONE SIZE FITS ALL" APPROACH

Some software vendors have attempted to use their equity attribution models to satisfy the needs of the fixed income manager. If we try to adhere to Attribution Law #1, we quickly see that the fixed income manager doesn't manage the same way that an equity manager does.

"Sector Selection Effect"—what does this mean to a fixed income manager? Do these managers pick bonds based upon their industry? Usually not. We could use this to distinguish between *types* of bonds, but it in itself isn't enough for our analysis, since much more is taken into consideration.

"Security Selection Effect"—what does this mean for fixed income? That a manager is a "good bond picker?" This doesn't seem appropriate, since "all bonds with the same coupon and beginning market price will deliver the same income return, if held throughout the performance measurement period. All bonds with the same duration will reflect the same price effect as interest rates change. Finally, all bonds in a given sector will reflect a general change in risk premiums resulting from the market's change in required compensation for risk."[7]

---

[5]Lord [1997], Campisi [2000].

[6]Tim Lord and Steve Campisi are not alone when it comes to fixed income models for attribution. Sri Ramaswamy (Ramaswamy [2001]) and others have begun to offer their approaches to this increasingly interesting area of analysis.

[7]Campisi [2001], page 21.

How *do* fixed income managers invest? Our earlier remarks from Steve Campisi and Sri Ramaswamy referenced how risk is taken into consideration. They tend to look at multiple bond attributes, such as duration, yield, ratings, and convexity. While the price volatility of a stock may derive from sector and issue selection, a bond's will derive from duration, and rate and spread changes.

Just as an equity manager will diversify his portfolio to control risk, a bond manager will do the same. Each manager's portfolio is sensitive to a variety of risks; for example, the equity manager has to deal with systematic risk, corporate risk, and other aspects of the stock market and the economy at large. The bond world has a basket of risks, too, such as interest rate risk, credit risk, and prepayment risk. Because some of its securities have a tendency to be dependent upon the company's stock (e.g., high yield), we also have equity risk to contend with. And a country's fundamentals can effect the returns on emerging market debt.

A SIMPLISTIC APPROACH

One approach that some software developers have offered is to use their equity models, but to base the way the portfolio is viewed on criteria other than industry. For example, a bond might be sliced up into duration ranges (e.g., less than 1 year, 1–3 years, 3–5 years, 5–10 years, 10 years or more). The index that the portfolio is being measured against will be divided in a similar fashion. Thus we could assess how each of these ranges contributed to the portfolios excess return. We still have this the effect of "selection," which lumps everything else together. While such analysis might provide some insight, its overall usefulness is quite limited.

BONDS VERSUS STOCKS

Here are some critical differences between stocks and bonds.[8]

1. Bonds are temporary lending agreements, with a stated maturity, whereas stocks are permanent investments.
2. Bonds promise a fixed return, with a limited upside; stocks promise the uncertain returns and unlimited upside associated with ownership.
3. Bonds are typically purchased by institutions, which hold

[8]Campisi [2000], page 15.

them until maturity. This results in a limited secondary market for bonds. Stock investing takes place in an active secondary market. As a result, bonds are illiquid, when compared to stocks.

4. Bond performance is driven by promised income and by changes in market yields. When market yields rise above a bond's stated yield, the price of that bond falls. As a result, the relevant risk for bonds is the sensitivity to changes in yields. Stock performance is driven by the market's economic sectors, and the relevant risk for stocks is the sensitivity to the overall market, or beta.

5. Bonds are simply the promise of a cash flow annuity, and so are relatively homogenous in their pricing. For example, bonds with the same maturity and default risk will generally sell at the same price. Because of this, bonds reflect very little selection effect. Stock prices respond dramatically to company-specific conditions and reflect a very large selection effect.

The reason is that the way the fixed income market works, any bond of the same type with the same rating and the same maturity date will have roughly the same yield, and therefore the same return. The market is quite homogeneous when it comes to such things. This is clearly not the same thing with stocks where, for example, automobile company stock performance can vary quite a bit. Granted, there might be some correlation because of similar responses to the economy, interest rates, etc., but the differences are vast enough to justify our comparing one stock with another.

But when a bond manager is looking for a particular bond type and duration to add to her portfolio, there's little actual "bond picking" that goes on.

Fixed income managers have another distinction with their equity counterparts—their benchmarks. It's common for the constituent details of an equity benchmark to be made public. This is not always so in the case of fixed income benchmarks. The reason tends to be because of pricing issues.[9]

---

[9]Many of the providers of fixed income market indexes don't wish to provide the detailed pricing, which would typically be sold separately. Because most of the bonds are not traded with the frequency of stocks and there aren't widely disseminated market prices for the bonds, this pricing has some value. Thus, there is reluctance to part with the details on a regular basis.

TABLE 4–1

Bond and Stock Differences

Bonds	Stocks
Borrower	Owner
Fixed term	Permanent investment
Fixed payments	Variable dividends
Fixed return	Entitled to profits
Illiquid market	Liquid, actively traded market

   Again, unlike equities, bonds often trade outside of the ex-
changes, and individual issues trade with much less frequency.
Prices are tied to Treasury bill rates and other factors, such as duration and ratings. Many bonds are priced using "matrices,"[10]
which take into consideration common factors; the basis for the
matrices may be considered proprietary by many of the providers.
If index providers released the constituent details, they'd also be
providing pricing information that others typically pay for. Thus,
our ability to do security-level attribution for bonds is understand-
ably limited.
   Table 4–1 provides some other differences between bonds and
stocks that make using equity-based models inappropriate.
   As you are probably aware, there are two widely used approaches for corporations to raise funds: issuing bonds or issuing
stock. This book won't go into great details regarding the differences; however, suffice it to say that there are many books that do.
Bonds are debt, meaning that the corporation is *borrowing* money
from the bond holder. Stock is ownership, meaning that the buyer
is *investing* in the corporation. With new stock offerings, we have
dilution of the ownership.
   The sources of performance for fixed income securities are also
different. While stocks tend to be heavily impacted by economic conditions, bonds are driven by interest rates. (For example, in the
United States, if the Federal Reserve rate changes, it will usually impact other bond rates and have a direct effect on performance.)

[10]Referred to as "matrix pricing."

From a risk standpoint, bonds are sensitive to duration,[11] while stocks are heavily impacted by the overall market.

There are three key factors that influence bond prices, which in turn impact performance.

- *Changes in yield:* these have an inverse effect on bond prices—as rates go up, prices go down; as rates go down, prices go up.
- *Duration:* if we multiply duration by the change in rate, we can derive the change in price.
- *Spread:*[12] risky assets are less desirable, so prices fall more quickly.

A bond's yield comes from three sources.

- *The risk-free rate* (for the United States, it's typically the Treasury rate): this rate is supposed to compensate the investor for expected inflation.
- *The maturity premium:* this compensates us for unexpected inflation.
- *The risk premium:* this compensates us for the risk of default or prepayment.

With stocks, we look for stock picking and asset allocation decisions as the sources for our excess return. With bonds, we look for the manager's decisions relative to duration, rate changes, and spread changes.

WHERE DO OUR RETURNS COME FROM?

Let's think back for a moment to an equity portfolio. Where do our returns come from? I'd suggest two primary sources: income (dividends), and stock appreciation. From an attribution perspective,

---

[11]Duration measures the bond's sensitivity to interest rate changes; it's a weighted average maturity measure. Steve Campisi suggests that duration is "the systematic risk measure for bonds—analogous to beta for stocks." Campisi [2000], page 17. It's "the systematic factor representing the sensitivity or elasticity of price with respect to the component of yield change." Campisi [2002].

For those wishing to learn more about these terms and the details of the bond market, there are numerous texts available that will do a much better job than this author.

[12]This represents our compensation for risk. As perceived risk increases, spreads will "widen."

F I G U R E   4–1

Decomposing a Stock Portfolio's Return

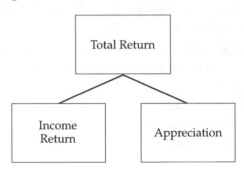

our excess return comes from our stock selection, asset allocation, and currency allocation skills. Make sense? (See Figure 4–1.)

The same kind of decomposition of return can take place in the bond world. Both Steve Campisi and Tim Lord offer their views of this, with quite a bit of similarity, as you'll see.

Figure 4–2 shows how Steve Campisi suggests we might break a bond's return up into it's underlying components.[13]

As we can see, there are two primary sources of the return: income and price changes. Price comes primarily from two sources: duration, and changes in the yield curve. Yield curve changes result from changes in the Treasury rate and spread changes. And finally, spread comes from various bond types: we've shown investment and noninvestment-grade corporates, and mortgage-backed securities.

Figure 4–3 shows where are Steve feels the returns come from for a bond. Table 4–2 shows the formulas for these returns.

Figure 4–4 shows Tim Lord's view on decomposing a bond portfolio's return.[14] As you can see, he identifies two primary sources of a bond's return: DMT total return, and excess return.

"DMT" stands for "duration-matched Treasury" bond. The DMT is a synthetic (noncallable) Treasury bond, constructed from the Treasury yield curve. The "factors of attribution consist of

[13]Campisi [2002].
[14]Lord [1997], page 47.

FIGURE 4–2

Campisi's Decomposition of a Bond's Return

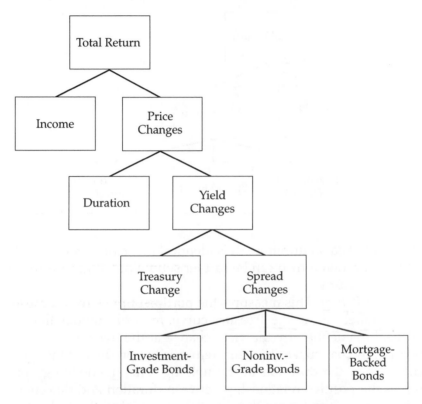

duration, yield curve distribution, sector allocation, and issue selection.[15]

Lord offers the following definitions to explain what the various returns mean.[16]

Duration Return: This is the portion of the price return that is attributable to changes in the Treasury par yield curve. It is the product of the (beginning) duration of a holding and the change in the yield of its duration-matched Treasury bond. It measures the change in market value due solely to changes in the Treasury curve

[15]Lord [1997], page 48.
[16]Lord [1997], pages 48–50. While I've done some slight paraphrasing with this material, for the most part, these are Tim's definitions.

F I G U R E   4–3

Sources of a Bond's Return, as per Steve Campisi

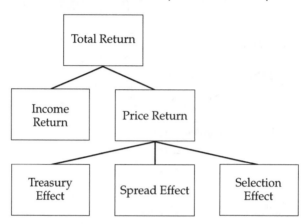

at a point of equal duration. (It is identical to the price return of the DMT.) Duration return can be further subdivided into shift return and twist return.

Shift Return: This measures the portion of price return caused by a parallel shift in the Treasury curve. In Lord's model, the parallel shift is defined by the yield change at the five-year maturity point of the par curve. The shift return is the product of that yield change and the duration of the holding. This methodology preserves the positive relationship between duration and percentage price change; the longer the duration, the higher the percentage price change for a given shift in rates.

T A B L E   4–2

Formulas for Campisi's Returns

Return	Formula
Income Effect	Coupon ÷ Price
Treasury Effect	(−Duration) × Treasury Change
Spread Effect*	(−Duration) × Average Spread Change
Selection Effect	Total Return − Income Effect − Treasury Effect − Spread Effect

*Please note that "spread effect" can be considered analogous to "allocation effect."

FIGURE 4-4

Tim Lord's Decomposition of Bond Return

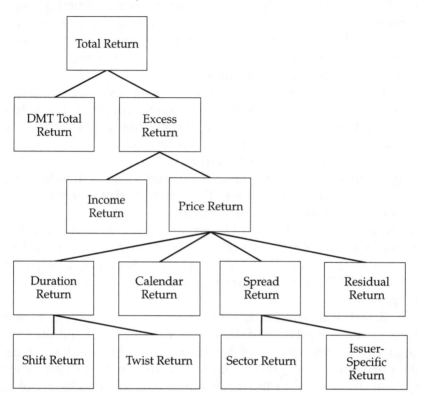

Twist Return: This measures the portion of price return attributable to nonparallel changes in the yield curve. It is the difference between the duration return and the shift return. At the security level, this difference reflects changes in the yield spread between the 5-year Treasury (which defines the parallel shift) and the DMT of the holding. For example, the twist return of a 30-year bond (an approximate duration of 12 years) is determined by the yield spread change between the 5- and 30-year points on the yield curve. At the portfolio level, twist return quantifies the impact of the yield curve distribution strategy. For example, if a portfolio is structured as a barbell (or bullet) relative to its benchmark, the twist return quantifies the effectiveness of such a strategy given the actual changes in the Treasury curve relative to a 5-year maturity Treasury note.

Spread Return: This measures the portion of price return attributable to changes in the yield spread between a bond and its DMT. The product of that change and the bond's duration measures the percentage price change due to a widening or tightening of the yield spread. This can be caused by changes in perceived credit quality, intrinsic value, or other factors. A change in spread affects long more than short-duration bonds.

The spread return of a corporate bond, mortgage, or asset-backed security can be subdivided into two components. The first is the portion due to the influence of the sector in which the bond resides; the second is due to issuer-specific features.

Sector Return: In Lord's attribution model, every bond is mapped to a sector matrix table, populated solely with index data. Corporate bonds are mapped to the corporate sector of the matrix, CMOs to the mortgage sector, private placements to the private corporate sector, and so on. The sector matrix table contains data on yield spread changes. Each cell contains the average OAS[17] (option-adjusted spread) change of all the index bonds that qualify for that cell. The matrix is subcategorized by duration and quality ranges.

Based on this matrix and the attributes of the holding, the sector return is the product of the duration of the bond and the OAS change of the relevant cell of the sector matrix. The result estimates the price return of the bond with respect to changes in sector yield spreads. By comparing the sector return of a portfolio to that of its benchmark, the model can be used to quantify the impact of a portfolio's sector allocation strategy. This illustrates one benefit of integrating index information into the attribution of portfolios.

Issuer-Specific Return: This measures the price return due to issuer-specific features, such as company announcements, earnings reports, changes in ratings, etc. It is the difference between the spread return and the sector return. Because it reflects the portion of spread return unaccounted for by sector-related factors, it provides an estimate of the value added due to issue selection. At the

---

[17]The option-adjusted spread measures the yield spread of a bond that is not attributable to imbedded options. For example, we have a callable bond that trades at a spread to Treasuries of 200 basis points; if 60 basis points are attributable to its call feature, the remaining 140 basis points can be attributed to factors such as its credit risk and liquidity. The option-adjusted spread for this bond would be 140 basis points. (Contingency Analysis [1996–2000].)

portfolio level, issuer-specific return can be compared to that of an index to assess the relative effectiveness of bond selection decisions. At the Cusip level, this factor reveals the relative performance across holdings.

The yield curve and spread factors discussed above typically explain most of the price return of a holding. There are, however, other factors that can impact price return. For example, the passage of time can impact the price of a bond, giving rise to "calendar return."

Calendar Return: This is the portion of price return due solely to the passage of time, assuming an otherwise static market. It consists of two parts: One is the accretion (or decline) of a bond's price toward par, and the other is the impact of rolling down (or up) the yield curve. For bonds trading near par, the return due to accretion/decline is negligible; however, for premium or deep discount bonds such as Treasury STRIPS (particularly those near maturity), the impact can be significant. The impact of rolling along the curve depends on its shape and the duration of the holding.

The calendar return is computed for a DMT, based on the coupon and the beginning duration of the holding and the corresponding yield of the Treasury par curve. Those variables result in an initial premium or discount price, depending on the coupon relative to the yield. The ending price is based on the same variables, adjusted only for the passage of time and the beginning shape of the curve. "Accretion" and "roll" can be complementary or mutually offsetting. They are complementary for discount securities when the yield curve is upward sloping and offsetting for premium bonds. The reverse is true when the curve is inverted. For most bonds, the calendar return is an insignificant factor in the attribution results and is typically ignored in the strategy process.

The objective of the attribution model is to explain as much of the price return as possible; what's left unexplained is called "residual."

Table 4–3 provides the formulas for the various returns in Lord's model.[18]

With Tim Lord's model, you can see that he's looking at a lot of factors simultaneously.

---

[18]Lord [1997], page 51.

T A B L E   4–3

Return Formulas Used in Tim Lord's Model

Attribution Factor	Formula	Comments
Duration return	$D_{bond} \times (_t Y_{DMT} - _{t-1} Y_{DMT})$	Holding's duration multiplied by yield change of the corresponding duration-matched Treasury bond.
Shift return	$D_{bond} \times (_t Y_{5-yr} - _{t-1} Y_{5-yr})$	Shift return is defined by the change in the five-year maturity Treasury (DMT) note.
Twist return	duration return − shift return	
Spread return	$D_{bond} \times (_t S_{DMT} - _{t-1} S_{DMT})$	Holding's duration multiplied by the change in the yield spread, defined relative to the DMT.
Sector return	$D_{bond} \times (_t OAS_i - _{t-1} OAS_i)$	Holding's duration multiplied by the change in the Option-Adjusted Spread (OAS) of the index sector in which it resides.
Issue return	spread return − sector return	
Calendar return	$\dfrac{_t P_{bond} - _{t-1} P_{bond}}{_t P_{bond}}$	Price in period t differs from that in t-1 due only to the passage of time and yield curve roll. All other factors are static.
Residual return	price return − duration return − spread return − calendar return	Typically includes effects due to convexity, inaccurate data, or model misspecification.

D = effective duration (beginning of period); Y = yield;
P = price given coupon of bond and yield of DMT; S = yield spread (bond vs. DMT)

WALKING THROUGH A FIXED INCOME ATTRIBUTION MODEL

We now use Steve Campisi's approach to demonstrate how fixed income attribution can be done. We use a portfolio that's based upon a benchmark, which is itself made up of a mix of indices.[19] As we stated earlier, a portfolio is a basket of risks, so the manager selects security types that address these risks. Our benchmark consists of:

- 6% Interest Rate Risk (U.S. Treasuries)
- 66% Investment Grade Credit Risk (an A-rated Corporate Index)
- 18% Prepayment Risk (Mortgage-Backed Securities Index)

[19]Much of what we use comes from Campisi [2000], pages 18–25. He was kind enough to share with me some additional details (e.g., further levels of precision on weights, for example), which has helped provide the material we're using. If you attempt to reconcile our analysis with the original article, you'll see some differences, which we attribute to our refined data.

FIGURE   4–5

Sector Allocation—Bond Portfolio versus Benchmark

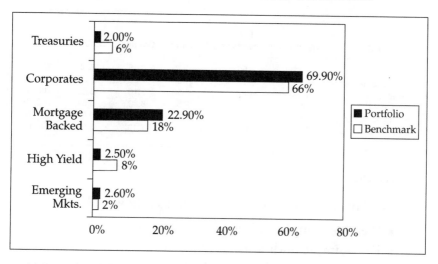

- 10% Equity-Type Risk (8% Domestic High-Yield Bonds and 2% Emerging Market Bond Indexes)

Figure 4–5 shows the breakdown of the benchmark, as well as the strategy that the manager employs.

As you can see, the manager has overweighted certain sectors while underweighting others. No surprise here.

Tables 4–4 and 4–5 show various portfolio and benchmark statistics that we turn to in our analysis.

TABLE   4–4

Portfolio Data

Sector	Weight	Par* (in millions)	Return	Coupon	Duration	Price
Treasuries	2.04%	162	−6.22	6.11	7.65	102.56
Mortgage-Backed	22.88%	1,860	2.60	7.08	4.23	99.74
A-Rated Corp.	69.92%	5,748	−1.07	7.03	5.92	98.64
High-Yield	2.53%	233	7.04	8.19	5.21	87.98
Emerging Markets	2.62%	261	15.32	8.92	6.94	91.38
Overall Portfolio	100%	8,264	0.30	7.11	5.58	98.12

*Amounts have been rounded.

TABLE   4–5

Benchmark Data

Sector	Weight	Par* (in thousands)	Return	Coupon	Duration	Price
Treasuries	6%	56	−1.75	6.45	5.02	107.19
Mortgage-Backed	18%	177	1.86	7.03	1.95	101.98
A-Rated Corp.	66%	627	−1.96	7.18	6.03	105.32
High-Yield	8%	90	2.39	8.02	4.64	88.69
Emerging Markets	2%	30	23.07	7.20	3.59	67.04
Overall Benchmark	100%	979	−0.41	7.19	5.06	102.13

*Amounts have been rounded.

The "overall" statistics are derived as follows:

- Weight—simple addition
- Par—simple addition
- Return—sum of the individual sector returns, weighted by their respective weights
- Coupon—sum of the individual sector coupon values, weighted by par[20]
- Duration—sum of the individual sector duration values, weighted by their respective weights
- Price—sum of the individual sector prices, weighted by par

We now calculate the various effects.

Treasury Effect: This is the component of our price change that results from the change in treasury rates and the sensitivity of the investment to the change in rates. Table 4–6 shows the rates and their price effects.

Figure 4–6 shows the increase in Treasury rates from 1998 to 1999. We calculate the Treasury effect using the change in these rates at the point on the curve corresponding to the duration of the investment (or portfolio).

Table 4–7 shows the sectors with their corresponding portfolio and benchmark durations, along with the equivalent Treasury change we'll use. You can see how we tie back to Table 4–6.

[20]We take the par for each sector and divide it by the total par, and use this as the multiplying factor.

TABLE 4–6

1999 Interest Rate Changes and Price Effects

Duration	Rate Change	Price Effect
0.50	1.15	−0.58
1.00	1.41	−1.41
2.00	1.70	−3.40
3.00	1.62	−4.86
3.50	1.67	−5.85
4.00	1.73	−6.90
4.50	1.78	−8.00
5.00	1.83	−9.15
5.25	1.81	−9.49
5.50	1.79	−9.82
5.75	1.76	−10.13
6.00	1.74	−10.44
6.50	1.70	−11.02
7.00	1.65	−11.55
7.50	1.68	−12.59
8.00	1.71	−13.65
9.00	1.76	−15.87
10.00	1.82	−18.20
20.00	0.98	−19.60
30.00	1.35	−40.50

FIGURE 4–6

Treasury Rates for 1998 and 1999

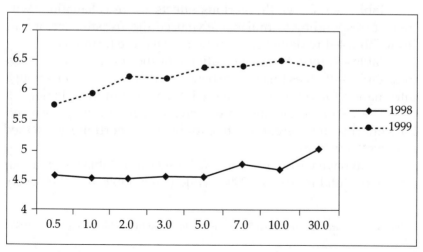

T A B L E   4–7

Treasury Change Values for Benchmark and Portfolio

Sector	Portfolio Duration	Portfolio Treasury Change	Portfolio Treasury Effect	Benchmark Duration	Benchmark Treasury Change	Benchmark Treasury Effect
Treasuries	7.65	1.68	−12.85	5.02	1.83	−9.19
Mortgage-Backed	4.23	1.73	−7.40	1.95	1.70	−3.32
A-Rated Corp.	5.92	1.74	−10.31	6.03	1.74	−10.49
High-Yield	5.21	1.81	−9.43	4.64	1.78	−8.26
Emerging Markets	6.94	1.65	−11.45	3.59	1.67	−6.00

For example, for Treasuries, our portfolio duration is 7.65, so we use the 7.5 figure from Table 4–6 and get the Treasury change of 1.68.[21] On the benchmark side, our Treasury duration is 5.02, so we use the duration of 5 in Table 4–6, picking up the Treasury change of 1.83.

Now that we have the treasury change values, we can calculate our Treasury effect, using the formula from Table 4–2:

$$- \ Duration \times TreasuryChange$$

These values are shown in Table 4–7 for our sectors, for both the benchmark and portfolio.

Table 4–8 shows the various effects we're calculating, with their corresponding formulas. We've used the Treasury sector data from Table 4–4 to demonstrate how to use these formulas.

Table 4–9 repeats the calculations for the entire portfolio's sectors; Table 4–10 does this for the benchmark's. We've given enough information for you to validate the information in these tables.

The weighted averages are derived by multiplying each sector's effect by it's weight (relative to the entire portfolio, expressed in percentage terms).

What have we done so far? We know (from Table 4–4) that our portfolio's total return is 0.30%, while (from Table 4–5) the bench-

---

[21]We use the duration value from Table 4–6 that is closest to the duration of the portfolio.

TABLE   4–8

Formulas for Campisi's Returns

Return	Formula	Portfolio's Treasuries
Income Effect*	Coupon ÷ Price	$\dfrac{6.11}{\$102.56} = 5.96\%$
Treasury Effect	(−Duration) × Treasury Change	$(-7.65) \times (1.68) = -12.85$
Spread Effect	(−Duration) × Average Spread Change	$(-7.65) \times -0.09 = 0.67$
Selection Effect**	Total Return − Income Return − Treasury Effect − Spread Effect	0.00

*You may see "income return" written; this is synonymous with "income effect."

**You'll see that we generally won't have a selection effect. As Steve Campisi informed me, "There is none for indexes. For the portfolio, it's included with the spread effect. That is, the difference in spread change can be attributed to overweighting of sectors, different style mix (subsector mix differences) and selection." Also, "the selection effect is not material, and it introduces complexity." Campisi [2002].

mark's return is −0.41%, giving us an excess return of 71 basis points. We've calculated our various effects for our portfolio and benchmark (Tables 4–9 and 4–10). Now, we want to see if we've accounted for everything.

Table 4–11 summarizes our returns and effects for the portfolio and benchmark.

Figure 4–7 graphically represents these values from Table 4–11.

TABLE   4–9

Attribution Effects for the Portfolio

	Return	Income Effect	Treasury Effect	Spread Effect	Spread Change
Treasuries	−6.22	5.96	−12.85	0.67	−0.09
Mortgage-Backed	2.60	7.10	−7.40	2.90	−0.69
A-Rated Corp.	−1.07	7.12	−10.31	2.11	−0.36
High-Yield	7.04	9.31	−9.43	7.17	−1.38
Emerging Markets	15.32	10.96	−11.45	15.81	−2.28
Weighted Averages	0.30	7.25	−9.70	2.75	−0.49

T A B L E   4–10

Attribution Effects for the Benchmark

	Return	Income Effect	Treasury Effect	Spread Effect	Spread Change
Treasuries	−1.75	6.02	−9.19	1.42	−0.28
Mortgage-Backed	1.86	6.89	−3.32	−1.72	0.88
A-Rated Corp.	−1.96	6.82	−10.49	1.71	−0.28
High-Yield	2.39	9.04	−8.26	1.61	−0.35
Emerging Markets	23.07	10.74	−6.00	18.33	−5.10
Weighted Averages	−0.41	7.04	−8.85	1.40	−0.18

We are able to account for our excess return of 71 basis points as follows:

- 21 basis points came from our income effect.
- We lost 85 basis points from our treasury effect.[22]
- We lost 31 basis points from the change in spreads.
- We gained 31 basis points from the selection effect.

One might argue that our selection effect is high. We can include in this various structural aspects such as the effects of convexity, allocation, illiquidity, timing of purchases, and concentrations within sectors (e.g., industrial sectors within the credit bucket or country weightings within emerging markets).[23]

T A B L E   4–11

Attribution Effects for the Benchmark (Note: Some rounding is taking place.)

	Returns	Income Effect	Treasury Effect	Spread Effect	Spread Change	Selection Effect
Portfolio	0.30	7.25	−9.70	2.75	−0.49	−0.19
Benchmark	−0.41	7.04	−8.85	1.40	−0.18	−0.59
Difference	0.71	0.21	−0.85	1.35	−0.31	0.31

[22]This came from having longer-duration Treasuries in a rising-rate environment. Campisi [2002].
[23]Campisi [2002].

FIGURE 4-7

Contributors to the Return

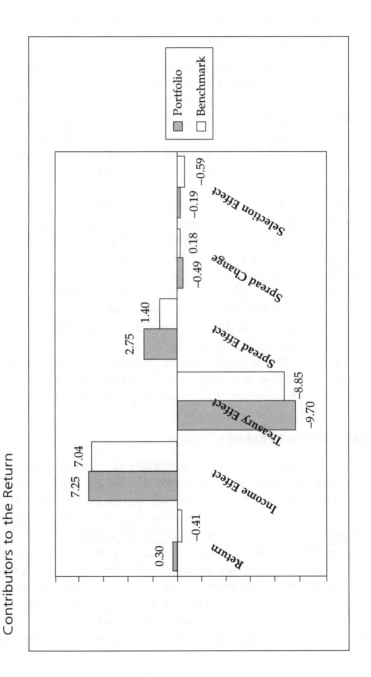

USING AN EQUITY ATTRIBUTION MODEL WITH OUR FIXED INCOME PORTFOLIO

As we stated earlier, some firms will use an equity model for their fixed income portfolios. Let's see what happens when we do this with our portfolio. We now use the Brinson-Fachler method to derive the attribution effects (the results are in Table 4–12).

First, we confirm that the sum of effects (0.71%) equals our excess return (portfolio return minus benchmark return, or 0.30% − 0.41% = 0.71%), which it does, thus satisfying our second law of attribution.[24]

Now let's look at the numbers. We see that our issue selection effect dominates our total effect (62 of the 71 basis points). You'll also notice that we don't do such a good job of picking Treasuries (having lost 9 basis points do to this selection). Does this make sense? Hopefully, not.

Nowhere in this analysis can we account for the factors that the fixed income manager is typically looking for. Instead, we attribute our superior return to our bond-picking skills, which is typically not something we're going to tout.

I hope that this brief exercise reinforces the problems we encounter with using an equity model for fixed income attribution—the results can be misleading and essentially have little value.

CONCLUDING REMARKS

This chapter has introduced you to a few fixed income concepts and to a couple of approaches to fixed income attribution. One of our goals is to demonstrate how fixed income and equity attribution differ. As you will hopefully agree, fixed income is significantly more challenging, requiring more effects to be measured and reviewed.

The world of fixed income attribution requires further research and (hopefully) the development of some common principles. We've hopefully demonstrated some of the challenges and opportunities available in this arena. And now you will probably agree that for fixed income, it's important to use a *true* fixed income attribution system, not attempt to use an equity model for this purpose.

---

[24]We've got some rounding going on here, since we show the industry selection effect (0.10%) plus issue selection (0.62%) summing to 0.71%.

TABLE 4-12

Using an Equity Attribution Model (Brinson-Fachler) for Our Fixed Income Portfolio

	Portfolio Weight	Benchmark Weight	Portfolio Return	Benchmark Return	Industry Selection Effect	Issue Selection Effect	Total Effect
Treasuries	2.04%	6%	−6.22%	−1.75%	0.07%	−0.09%	−0.02%
Mortgage-Backed	22.88%	18%	2.60%	1.86%	0.09%	0.17%	0.26%
A-Rated Corp.	69.92%	66%	−1.07%	−1.96%	−0.08%	0.62%	0.55%
High-Yield	2.53%	8%	7.04%	2.39%	−0.13%	0.12%	−0.01%
Emerging Markets	2.62%	2%	15.32%	23.07%	0.14%	−0.20%	0.06%
Overall Portfolio	100%	100%	0.30%	−0.41%	0.10%	0.62%	0.71%

EXERCISE

Using the data in Tables 4–E–1, 4–E–2, and 4–E–3, determine the attribution effects using the Campisi method we discuss in this chapter.

T A B L E   4–E–1

Portfolio Data

Sector	Weight	Par (in millions)	Return	Coupon	Duration	Price
Treasuries	3.00	162	−6.40	6.11	7.65	102.58
Mortgage-Backed	24.00	1,860	2.50	7.08	4.23	99.78
A-Rated Corp.	68.00	5,748	−1.08	7.03	5.92	98.62
High-Yield	4.00	233,400,000	7.03	8.19	5.21	87.96
Emerging Markets	1.00	261	15.40	8.92	6.94	81.40
Overall Portfolio	100.00	8,264.440	0.11	7.11	5.55	98.11

T A B L E   4–E–2

Benchmark Data

Sector	Weight	Par (in thousands)	Return	Coupon	Duration	Price
Treasuries	4.00	56	−6.37	6.45	7.55	108.00
Mortgage-Backed	22.00	177	2.48	7.03	4.30	102.31
A-Rated Corp.	66.00	627	−1.1	7.18	6.03	105.40
High-Yield	6.00	90	6.5	8.02	4.94	89.98
Emerging Markets	2.00	30	18.4	7.20	3.59	68.05
Overall Benchmark	100.00	980	0.32	7.19	5.60	102.13

T A B L E   4–E–3

1999 Interest Rate Changes and Price Effects

Duration	Rate Change	Price Effect
0.50	1.15	−0.58
1.00	1.41	−1.41
2.00	1.70	−3.40
3.00	1.62	−4.86
3.50	1.67	−5.85
4.00	1.73	−6.90
4.50	1.78	−8.00
5.00	1.83	−9.15
5.25	1.81	−9.49
5.50	1.79	−9.82
5.75	1.76	−10.13
6.00	1.74	−10.44
6.50	1.70	−11.02
7.00	1.65	−11.55
7.50	1.68	−12.59
8.00	1.71	−13.65
9.00	1.76	−15.87
10.00	1.82	−18.20
20.00	0.98	−19.60
30.00	1.35	−40.50

Global Attribution

Very good & directly applicable to US.

Fig 5-2 (p87)

As we learn in chapter 3, a domestic equity manager can vary his portfolio relative to the benchmark in two ways: by allocating funds differently across industries, and by picking different stocks. When we move to the global scene, another option arises: to allocate across countries in a manner that's different than the benchmark. And because foreign exchange rates can change from the original purchase date to the date of the sale of the securities, the realized return can be affected by more than the appreciation (or depreciation) of the underlying security. This chapter will address how we can measure the effect of currency on our portfolio's return and how to perform attribution on a global portfolio.

OUR APPROACH FOR THIS CHAPTER

We have a lot to cover in this chapter. Figure 5–1 summarizes what we'll be addressing.

We begin by an overview of the global market.

This will lead to a brief discussion on the differences between local and base returns, and a discussion on hedging.

Next, we present a fairly straightforward way to look at attribution from a currency perspective. We then move onto a presentation of the Karnosky-Singer model, which is often used for global attribution. Within this section, we also discuss how rates of returns are derived for a global portfolio.

FIGURE 5–1

Our Global Market Perspective

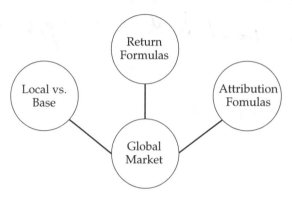

We then walk through examples of both our simple and Karnosky-Singer models to show how they're used.

A SIMPLE EXAMPLE TO SHOW WHY THIS IS IMPORTANT

Let's use a simple example to show how the currency change can affect the performance of a security.

On January 1, a portfolio manager purchases stock in the European car maker, Automax. In order to make this purchase, the

> **Base Currency:** *the currency of the client's portfolio*
> **Local Currency:** *the asset's currency*

client's money (which is in U.S. dollars) must be converted to Euros. Let's get a couple key terms out of the way:

> *Base Currency:* This is the currency of the portfolio of our client, in this case, U.S. dollars ($).
> *Local Currency:* This is the currency of the asset that we're buying, in this case, Euros (€).

At the time of the purchases, each share in Automax costs €50.00 We purchase 1000 shares, so our total cost is €50,000.[1] In

---

[1]For simplicity, we exclude commission and other transaction costs.

order to settle the trade (actually acquire the shares), we must exchange our U.S. dollars for Euro dollars. We check the exchange rate and learn that $1.00 = €1.13513. We need €50,000, so if we divide €50,000 by 1.13513, we then know how many U.S. dollars we need to make the purchase of Automax shares.

$$\frac{50,000}{1.13513} = 44,047.82$$

We therefore enter into a foreign exchange (or FX) transaction and purchase €50,000 for $44,047.82.

A year goes by and we decide to sell our Automax stock. What's happened in the meantime? Good news; Automax is up 10%. Each share now sells for €55.00. So, our 1000 shares are now valued at €55,000. And, we can easily validate our rate of return in local currency:

$$ROR_L = \frac{EMV_L - BMV_L}{BMV_L} = \frac{55,000 - 50,000}{50,000} = 10\%$$

where

ROR = Rate of return
EMV = ending market value
BMV = beginning market value
L = local

We sell our shares and now have €55,000 in cash.

But holding Euros does our U.S. client no good, unless we expect to make another purchase in Europe, so the currency has to be converted back to U.S. dollars. We need to determine what happened to the exchange rate during this time.

We find that the Euro has dropped 11% relative to the U.S. dollar. Now $1.00 gets us even more Euros. In fact, we now get €1.25999 of them for each $1.00. But we're not purchasing Euro dollars; we're purchasing U.S. dollars. To convert the other way, we divide 1.00 by 1.25999 and get 0.79365.

$$\frac{1.00}{1.25999} = 0.79365$$

For each €1.00, we'll get $0.79365. We can determine how many U.S. dollars we should get by either multiplying our

Euros by 0.79365 or dividing by 1.25999. Since we have €55,000, we end up with $43,651.14, as determined by the following arithmetic:[2]

$$\frac{55,000}{1.25999} = 43,651.14 \qquad\qquad 55,000 \times 0.79365 = 43,651.14$$

Let's now determine the return from a base[3] currency perspective, since our client wants to know how she did in U.S. dollars. We needed $44,047.82 to convert to Euros to make our purchase, and received $43,651.14 back after we sold our shares. We ended up losing $396.68. And, we find that our return in base currency is −0.90 percent.

$$ROR_b = \frac{EMV_b - BMV_b}{BMV_b} = \frac{43,651.14 - 44.047.82}{44,047.82}$$

$$= \frac{-396.68}{44,047.82} = -0.90\%$$

where

ROR = Rate of return
EMV = ending market value
BMV = beginning market value
b = base

From a local (Euro-€) perspective, we're up 10%; but from a base (U.S.-$) standpoint, we're down 90 basis points.

This chapter is about assessing the effect of currency decisions on our portfolio. While this rather simple example demonstrates that there's more at work than just the change in price of our stock, we need to go beyond this simple math in order to assess the true effect of our portfolio manager's decisions.

In global attribution, we hope to assess the effect of currency on the portfolio's return, which results from overweighting or underweighting country allocations.

---

[2]Rounding might result in slight differences, but the math does work properly. It *has* to!

[3]To avoid confusion with returns of benchmarks, when we use the subscript "B," we use the lowercase "b" for base.

HEDGING—THE SOLUTION TO THE CURRENCY CHALLENGE?

One might be tempted to say that we won't have a problem if we hedge[4] our investments. Let's see.

First, what *is* hedging? It is a process to reduce exposure to currency fluctuations by taking a market position in the currency in the opposite direction of our initial exchange. If we're selling U.S. dollars and buying Euros to make our stock purchase, then we'd simultaneously enter into a contract to sell Euros and buy U.S. dollars at some point in the future. This forward-looking transaction is supposed to be our return vehicle to get back to U.S. dollars, once we've disposed of our automobile stock.

It's not perfect for a few reasons. First, how much do we hedge? Typically, we'll hedge about the same amount of money as our investment.[5] When we're ready to sell our stock, creating Euros and looking to sell them for U.S. dollars, we may have more Euros then we need, or we may not have quite enough. We may have to make some other transaction to handle the difference.[6]

Another problem is the time frame for our contract—how far out do we go? How can we predict when we'll sell our automobile shares? We can't. So we pick a date at some point in the future. If the contract expires before we decide to sell our stock, then we have to execute before its expiration date. Alternatively, if we're selling earlier, we have options as well that can allow us to take advantage of the hedge we placed on our currency exposure.[7]

Perhaps the greatest problem is that fact that we aren't perfectly covered by this transaction. Let me explain.

---

[4]"A hedge is a risk that is taken to offset another risk." Contingency Analysis [1996–2000]. We're essentially trying to neutralize our risk by taking an offsetting position (if one goes up, the other goes down).

[5]Of course, there are currency strategies that involve partial hedging, too.

[6]Here's a simplified explanation. Using our example, we initially purchase €50,000. We could therefore have a contract to sell €50,000 at some point in the future. Since our stock went up 10%, we have an additional €5000 that we didn't account for in our forward transaction, so we'll have some exposure when we convert these to U.S. dollars. Had the stock gone down 10%, then we'd only be generating €45,000 from our sale of the stock but have a contract to sell €50,000.

[7]This is really a very overly simplified explanation; the point is that the dates of our forward contract and our actual sale of securities will likely not coincide, so some action will be necessary when we sell our stock.

First, what we're entering into when we do a hedge is a forward contract. It's also called a Forward Rate Agreement, or FRA.[8] When we do our initial transaction, we use the "spot" rate. The "forward" rate is what we expect to have at some point in the future. The problem is that the "spot" rate and "forward" rates won't usually be the same. Why not?

Let's think about this. What if you can convert your U.S. dollars into Euros, and know that in a year, you'll be able to convert back, dollar-for-dollar, at the same rate; is there any potential benefit from entering into a future contract, even if you're not looking to purchase stock in Europe? There might be. What if the interest rate in Europe is currently 6% versus 4% in the United States? Why not take our dollars, convert to Euros, make the additional 2 percent, and then come back ahead? Wouldn't everyone be looking to take advantage of this? Maybe not everyone, but surely a lot of people. This is a form of arbitrage—taking advantage of the simultaneous inconsistencies between two markets to make a gain.[9]

But what actually happens when you enter into a forward contract? The person (or firm) who sells you the contract has exposure the other way, doesn't he? He's anticipating that at some point, he's going to have to buy those Euro dollars from you. So at the initial point of the execution of the forward contract, he may have simultaneously borrowed U.S. dollars to have ready when you bring your Euros to sell. And the rate he pays will take into account interest rate differences. Actually, they're tied closely to the differences in the risk-free rates between the two regions.

The forward contract rates are, in other words, sensitive to the differences in interest rates from one country to another. The forward rate may be higher or lower than the spot rate, depending on interest rate differentials.

This doesn't mean to suggest that hedging is a waste of time; clearly, it can provide some protection from our currency rate exposure. But being aware what the rates take into consideration should help us understand what's going on.

---

[8]Laker [2002], page 3.

[9]This book isn't the place to give a detailed explanation of the effect of interest rates on foreign exchange rates and other economic implications on hedging versus nonhedging. If you want to learn more about this, we suggest you begin by reading Karnosky [1994] and then pursue other articles and books that will give much more lengthy and mathematically intense explanations.

The real point is that we can't expect to get the local return for our global investments, whether we hedge or not.

To address how to calculate global attribution, we present you with two approaches. We begin with a rather basic approach and then discuss the well-regarded Karnosky-Singer approach.

A SIMPLE APPROACH

We start with a rather simple model. In this approach, we have a separate formula to derive the effect of currency fluctuations on our portfolio:

$$CurrContrib = W_P \times (R_{P_b} - R_{P_l}) - W_B \times (R_{B_b} - R_{B_l})$$

where

W = weight
R = return
P = portfolio
B = benchmark
b = base
l = local

We begin by looking at the portfolio, by taking the beginning amount of our portfolio that's invested in the country, times the difference in base and local returns. We subtract from this the beginning weight the benchmark has in the country, times the difference in returns.

Let's use a simple example. Table 5–1 shows a portfolio that is invested in Japan. As you can see, the manager overweighted her investments relative to the benchmark (10% versus 8%).

We can see that our return is greater in base ($) than local (¥), meaning that the exchange rates moved to our benefit from the

T A B L E   5–1

Applying the Basic Approach to a Simple Example

	Portfolio	Benchmark
Weight in Japan	10%	8%
Return in Base ($)	12%	11.5%
Return in Local (¥)	11%	10.5%

time of our purchase to this point—the dollar apparently weakened relative to the Japanese yen, and we get more dollars for our yen when we convert back.

Using our attribution formula, we see that we gained two basis points by overweighting our investment in Japan, benefitting from the change in currency rates over the time of our investment.

$$CurrContrib = [0.10 \times (0.12 - .011)] - [0.08 \times (0.115 - 0.105)]$$
$$= 0.02\%$$

In reviewing this model, I think we can conclude that it appears to make intuitive sense. We'd expect to gain some benefit from the currency movement, and that's exactly what we see. It's also quite simple to apply and understand. However, this model doesn't take into consideration currency hedging, and so it is limited.

This does not mean that this model doesn't have some usefulness—it does provide some insight into what's gone on. However, as a "true" and complete global attribution model, it falls short.

COMPONENTS OF GLOBAL INVESTING

When we invest outside of our own market, we essentially are dealing with two components: the market bet and the currency bet. That is, the effect of the security we purchase going up or down, and secondarily, the effect of the currency.

Figure 5–2 decomposes our return into its primary sources. As you can see, we present two: the market and our currency strategy. As we remember learning in chapter 3, the equity portfolio's return comes principally from our allocation and selection decisions. While we still have them as contributors for our global portfolio, we also have to be sensitive to the currency side, and here we see that our strategy relative to hedging factors in.

To deal with the currency bet, we have three alternatives:

1. **No hedging:** Here, we simply convert our base currency to local (e.g., U.S. dollars to Euros), make our purchase in the other country, and then when we sell the security, convert back. Whatever has happened to the currency in the interim will be felt when we convert back. This is probably not a bad decision when going into a market where there

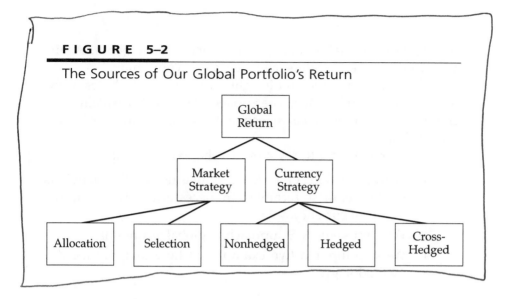

FIGURE 5–2

The Sources of Our Global Portfolio's Return

isn't expected to be much of a change, and/or where the interest rate differences are minor.

2. Hedging: When we make our purchase of the security, we simultaneously enter into a forward contract, so that we have no exposure (or minimal exposure) to the exchange rates over the period.

3. Cross-Hedging: While we're making our security purchase in one country, we simultaneously enter into a forward contract agreement, but with a third country. A manager who is doing this obviously feels that she can pick up some additional return (or reduce risk further) by using an intermediate country's currency in the hedging transaction.

KARNOSKY-SINGER APPROACH [Karnosky, 1994]-pet it!

Denis Karnosky and Brian Singer developed some basic principles about global performance attribution; their monograph should be in the library of anyone who's involved in attribution, especially at the global level. (Karnosky [1994]).

We will introduce several of the main concepts behind the Karnosky-Singer (K-S) approach. However, this section won't cover all the details presented in their monograph.

Another point: this introduction won't substitute for a course in foreign exchange markets and the role of futures. There are loads of references available that go into much greater depth. Again, you're encouraged to add such materials to your library.

Our goal is to give you insight into the key attributes of the K-S approach and how it can be applied. We will also explain some characteristics of the global investing market and how they impact the attribution analysis.

Our approach for this rest of this chapter is as follows:

#1 We discuss some of the key formulas used in the model. As you'll see, these formulas are necessarily sensitive to the effects of currency.

#2 We discuss the K-S approach to global attribution.

#3 We step through two examples of how to apply the K-S methodology.[10]

Rate-of-Return Formulas[11]

The return formulas we typically use to analyze domestic securities are not adequate for global investments since they do not take into account the effects of currency. And, since with currency we have various strategies available, we have to be sensitive to each.

We have three currency strategies that we can employ. Our simple approach is unhedged. If we're going to hedge, we have two approaches: simple hedging and cross-hedging.

The return for our unhedged component is simply:

$$Unhedged = R_i + E_{\$,i}$$

where

R_i = the local currency return
$E_{\$,i}$ = our exchange rate, from dollars into currency i

Our hedged component return is:

$$Hedged = R_i + F_{\$,i} = R_i + (C_\$ - C_i)$$

where

$F_{\$,i}$ = our forward exchange rate, from dollars into currency i

---

[10]The first of these two examples was shared with me by Kevin Terhaar, for which I'm quite grateful. He provided me with assistance as I did my research. Terhaar [2000 and 2002].
[11]Karnosky [1994], page 8.

$C_\$$ = the three-month Euro currency rate for dollars
C_i = the three-month Euro currency rate for currency i

Finally, the cross-hedged return is:

$$Cross\text{-}Hedged = R_i + F_{j,i} + E_{\$,i} = R_i + (C_j - C_i) + E_{\$,i}$$

where

$F_{j,i}$ = our forward exchange rate, from currency j into currency i
C_j = the three-month Euro currency rate for currency j

As you can see, even though our formulas call for forward exchange rates, they can be determined by subtracting the currency rates from the "to" currency from the "from" currency.

> **Global Currency Returns**
> $Unhedged = R_i + E_{\$,i}$
> $Hedged = R_i + F_{\$,i} = R_i + (C_\$ - C_i)$
> $Cross\text{-}Hedged = R_i + F_{j,i} + E_{\$,j} =$
> $R_i + (C_j - C_i) + E_{\$,i}$

Let's walk through how we can use these formulas to derive our returns.

We use a pretty basic portfolio that has investments in the United States, Germany, the United Kingdom, and Japan. Table 5–2 shows the currency rates for our portfolio.

This is all the data we need to derive our various unhedged, hedged, and cross-hedged returns for our portfolio. Let's go through a few examples:

Unhedged
For our unhedged return, we use:

$$Unhedged = R_i + E_{\$,i}$$

T A B L E 5–2

Portfolio's Currency Rates

	Local Currency Return (R_i)	Exchange Rate Return ($E_{\$,i}$)	3-Month Euro Currency Rate (C_i)
Germany	7.00%	1.00%	5.00%
U.K.	10.50%	−3.00%	11.00%
Japan	9.50%	−1.00%	8.50%
U.S.	8.00%	0.00%	7.50%

TABLE 5–3

Unhedged Returns

	Local Currency Return (R_i)	Exchange Rate Return $(E_{\$,i})$	Unhedged Market Returns
Germany	7.00%	1.00%	8.00%
U.K.	10.50%	−3.00%	7.50%
Japan	9.50%	−1.00%	8.50%

with which we can easily calculate our returns. For example:

$$Unhedged_{Germany} = 7.00 + 1.00 = 8.00$$

Table 5–3 shows all of the currency returns for the three countries without hedging.

Hedged
For our hedged returns, recall that we use:

$$Hedged = R_i + F_{\$,i} = R_i + (C_\$ - C_i)$$

As an example, our hedged return for Germany is:

$$Hedged_{Germany} = 7.00 + (7.50 - 5.00) = 9.50$$

Table 5–4 shows our hedged returns into the three countries.

TABLE 5–4

Hedged Returns

	Local Currency Return (R_i)	3-Month Euro Currency Rate $(\$)$	3-Month Euro Currency Rate (C_i)	Hedged Market Returns
Germany	7.00%	7.50%	5.00%	9.50%
U.K.	10.50%	7.50%	11.00%	7.00%
Japan	9.50%	7.50%	8.50%	8.50%

T A B L E   5–5

Cross-Hedged Returns (hedging using an
intermediate country)

	Local Currency Return (R_i)	3-Month Euro Currency Rate (C_j) (into currency)	3-Month Euro Currency Rate (C_i) (from currency)	Exchange Rate Return $(E_{\$,i})$ (into currency)	Cross-Hedged Market Returns
Cross-Hedging into Japan					
Germany	7.00%	8.50%	5.00%	−1.00%	9.50%
U.K.	10.50%	8.50%	11.00%	−1.00%	5.00%
Cross-Hedging into Germany					
U.K.	10.50%	5.00%	11.00%	1.00%	5.50%
Japan	9.50%	5.00%	8.50%	1.00%	7.00%
Cross-Hedging into the U.K.					
Germany	7.00%	11.00%	5.00%	−3.00%	10.00%
Japan	9.50%	11.00%	8.50%	−3.00%	9.00%

Cross-Hedged

With the introduction of an intermediate currency, we need to take into consideration two currency rates. The math is slightly more complex, but not by much. Again, the basic formula is:

$$Cross\text{-}Hedged = R_i + F_{j,i} + E_{\$,i} = R_i + (C_j - C_i) + E_{\$,i}$$

And, if we're investing in Germany, but cross-hedging into Japan, our return is:

$$Cross\text{-}Hedged_{Germany/Japan} = 7.00 + (8.50 - 5.00) + (-1.00) = 9.50$$

Table 5–5 provides the details for all of our combinations.

The K-S monograph provides much greater details on the actual return formulas, and you're encouraged to review this material for a more in-depth discussion.

The Attribution Model

Recall for a moment how the Brinson-Hood-Beebower model is presented in chapter 3: we use a grid system to show the components

F I G U R E   5–3

BHB Attribution Model (from chapter 3)

Selection

	Portfolio	Benchmark
Portfolio	(IV) Actual Portfolio Return	(II) Policy and Timing Return
Benchmark	(III) Policy and Security Selection Return	(I) Policy Return (Passive Portfolio Benchmark)

Timing

of our return, which leads to our attribution formulas. We've repeated that grid for comparison purposes (Figure 5–3).

Like the Brinson-Hood-Beebower model, the Karnosky-Singer model uses a grid system to describe allocation.[12] But unlike the BHB model, which relied upon a single grid, we need two grids for the K-S model because there are two sources for our returns: the market, and the currency (as we see in Figure 5–2). And the model takes these sources into consideration, so that everything is properly accounted for (see Figures 5–4 and 5–5).

Using these two grids, we can define the market returns as follows:

Market selection	$(M)II - (M)I$
Security selection	$(M)III - (M)I$
Other	$(M)IV - (M)III - (M)II + (M)I$
Total	$(M)IV - (M)I$

[12]Probably not a big surprise, given that Denis and Brian worked with Gary Brinson at Brinson Partners (now UBS Global Asset Management).

F I G U R E   5–4

Market Components

	Security Selection	
	Actual	Passive
Actual (Market Selection)	(M)IV Actual, Local-Currency Return Premium *Active Weights,* *Active Returns*	(M)II Policy and Active Allocation, Local-Currency Return Premium *Active Weights,* *Passive Returns*
Passive (Market Selection)	(M)III Policy and Security, Selection, Local-Currency Return Premium *Passive Weights,* *Active Returns*	(M)I Policy, Local-Currency Return Premium *Passive Weights,* *Passive Returns*

Likewise, currency selection derives as:

Currency selection	$(C)II - (C)I$
Hedge selection	$(C)III - (C)I$
Other	$(C)IV - (C)III - (C)II + (C)I$
Total	$(C)IV - (C)I$

If we refer back to chapter 3, we see that the returns match up with the Brinson-Hood-Beebower approach. Here's what we show in chapter 3:

Timing (Market Selection)	$II - I$
Stock Selection	$III - I$
Other	$IV - III - II + I$
Total	$IV - I$

F I G U R E   5–5

Currency Components

Hedge Selection

	Actual	Passive
Actual	(C)IV Actual, Base-Currency Eurodeposit Premium *Active Weights,* *Active Returns*	(C)II Policy and Active Allocation, Base-Currency Eurodeposit Return Premium *Active Weights,* *Passive Returns*
Passive	(C)III Policy and Hedge, Selection, Base-Currency Eurodeposit Return Premium *Passive Weights,* *Active Returns*	(C)I Policy, Base-Currency Eurodeposit Return *Passive Weights,* *Passive Returns*

Currency Selection

The Grids and What They Provide

Let's briefly discuss these grids. We start with the market grid.

Our lower right-hand quadrant ((M)I), as with the BHB model, represents our passive (or benchmark) position (passive weights and returns). Quadrant (M)IV (upper left) provides our portfolio return, or the result of our active decisions (active weights and returns).

Like our earlier BHB model, our market return is simply quadrant (M)IV minus quadrant (M)I. This represents the contribution to our return across and within asset markets and is based on local currency return premiums.

TABLE 5-6

Portfolio and Benchmark Returns and Weights

	Benchmark Weight	Passive Local Currency Return	Risk Premium	Portfolio Market Weight	Passive Exchange Rate Return	Cash Return (in $)	Portfolio Currency Weight
Germany	25%	7.00%	2.00%	60%	1.00%	6.00%	10%
U.K.	25%	10.50%	−0.50%	10%	−3.00%	8.00%	45%
Japan	25%	9.50%	1.00%	10%	−1.00%	7.50%	25%
U.S.	25%	8.00%	0.50%	20%	0.00%	7.50%	20%
Total	100%			100%			100%

Our currency grid runs parallel with the market grid. Our lower right quadrant (C)I provides the passive "Eurodeposit"[13] return for the benchmark, in base currency (again, passive weights and returns). Quadrant (C)IV (upper left) provides our active decisions regarding currency (active weights and returns). And, the difference ((C)IV − (C)I) provides our contribution to return as a result of these decisions.

We now want to derive our portfolio and benchmark returns. There are two components of each: the return from the market and the return from currency. Table 5–6 shows the data we'll use.

Our formulas are pretty simple. For example, for our benchmark return, it's the sum of the product of our passive (benchmark) weights and returns. For our benchmark returns using the market grid, we get:

$$BenchmarkMktRtn = \sum_{i=1}^{n} W_{Bi} \times RP_{Bi}$$
$$= (0.25 \times 0.02) + (0.25 \times (-0.50)) + (0.25 \times 0.01)$$
$$+ (0.25 \times 0.005) = 0.75\%$$

where

W_{B_i} = Benchmark weight for country "i"
RP_{B_i} = Risk premium return for country "i"

[13]These are the "cash rates available to investors depositing funds from another currency." Laker [2002], page 4.

If we repeat this same algebra for our other factors, we obtain the data in Table 5–7, which provides us with our returns.

Now that you've seen how we create the key data for our model, we're ready to try our hand at the actual attribution analysis.

We see from the table that the portfolio return is the sum of our market and currency returns. When we subtract the benchmark's return from our portfolio's, we obtain a 93-basis-point difference, which we intend to account for in our attribution analysis.

To simplify our analysis, we've picked a portfolio that did not alter the security selection from the benchmark (i.e., the manager employed a passive security selection strategy). Consequently, we won't be dealing with the security selection effect.

Our table shows our benchmark weight, which is the same for the currency and market. The manager has altered the weights, as shown in the "Portfolio Market Weight" and "Portfolio Currency Weight" columns (Table 5–6).

We can now use the attribution formulas for our two grids (Figures 5–4 and 5–5) to derive our market allocation and currency allocation effects.

First, recall that market allocation is derived by subtracting quadrant (M)I from (M)II in the "Market Components" grid (Figure 5–4). We have the ingredients for this, as shown in Table 5–8.

Market allocation is therefore 0.60% (1.35 − 0.75).

Currency allocation is derived in a similar fashion: Quadrant (C)II − (C)I. Table 5–9 shows these details.

You should notice that for these effects, we use the passive returns for both the market (risk premium) and currency (cash re-

T A B L E 5–7

Portfolio and Benchmark Returns

	Market-Weighted Risk Premium (Market Return)	Currency-Weighted Cash Return ($) (Currency Return)	U.S. Dollar Returns
Portfolio Return	1.35%	7.58%	8.93%
Benchmark Return	0.75%	7.25%	8.00%
Excess Return	0.60%	0.33%	0.93%

TABLE 5–8

Deriving the Market Allocation Effect Quadrants

	Quadrant (M)II		Quadrant (M)I	
	Active Weights	Passive Returns	Passive Weights	Passive Returns
Germany	60%	2.00%	25%	2.00%
U.K.	10%	−0.50%	25%	−0.50%
Japan	10%	1.00%	25%	1.00%
U.S.	20%	0.50%	25%	0.50%
Total		1.35%		0.75%

turn). The only difference is the way we've allocated the portfolio relative to the benchmark. Currency allocation is 0.33% (7.58 − 7.25).

When we add our market allocation (0.60%) to our currency allocation (0.33%) effect, we obtain 0.93%, which is our excess return.

We can break our effects down by country, as well, by using the same formula. Table 5–10 shows these details.

As you can see, we've accounted for all of the excess return and can determine where we benefitted and where we were penalized, as a result of our allocation decisions. For example, our market allocation decisions provided us with 60 basis points overall,

TABLE 5–9

Deriving the Currency Allocation Effect Quadrants

	Quadrant (C)II		Quadrant (C)I	
	Active Weights	Passive Returns	Passive Weights	Passive Returns
Germany	10%	6.00%	25%	6.00%
U.K.	45%	8.00%	25%	8.00%
Japan	25%	7.50%	25%	7.50%
U.S.	20%	7.50%	25%	7.50%
Total		7.58%		7.25%

TABLE   5–10

Attribution Effects by Country

	Market Allocation	Currency Allocation	Total
Germany	0.70%	−0.90%	−0.20%
U.K.	0.08%	1.60%	1.68%
Japan	−0.15%	0.00%	−0.15%
U.S.	−0.03%	−0.38%	−0.40%
Total	0.60%	0.33%	0.93%

while we gained an additional 33 basis points from our currency allocation decisions. We benefited greatly from our investing in the U.K., where we got 8 basis points from our market allocation and another 160 basis points from our currency allocation. However, we didn't do as well in Germany, where we lost 20 basis points overall, clearly as a result of our currency decisions. In fact, we see that the U.K. was our only overall winner because we lost 15 basis points in Japan and another 40 basis points in the United States.

Another Example

Let's expand upon our last example by introducing some variability into our security selection.

Table 5–11 shows our portfolio statistics, while Table 5–12 shows the statistics for our benchmark.

TABLE   5–11

Portfolio Data

	Market Weights	Local Currency Return	Risk Premium	Currency Weight	Exchange Rate Return	Cash Return (in $)
Germany	60%	7.10%	2.10%	10%	1.00%	5.90%
U.K.	10%	10.60%	−0.45%	45%	−3.00%	8.05%
Japan	10%	9.55%	1.10%	25%	−1.00%	7.45%
U.S.	20%	8.10%	0.60%	20%	0.00%	7.55%
Total	100%		1.45%	100%		

T A B L E   5–12

Benchmark Data

	Market Weights	Local Currency Return	Risk Premium	Currency Weight	Exchange Rate Return	Cash Return (in $)
Germany	25%	7.00%	2.00%	25%	1.00%	6.00%
U.K.	25%	10.50%	−0.50%	25%	−3.00%	8.00%
Japan	25%	9.50%	1.00%	25%	−1.00%	7.50%
U.S.	25%	8.00%	0.50%	25%	0.00%	7.50%
Total	100%		0.75%	100%		

Table 5–13 shows the return calculations, using the same formulas as before. For example, our benchmark market return remains the same:

$$BenchmarkMktRtn = \sum_{i=1}^{n} W_{B_i} \times RP_{B_i} = (0.25 \times 0.02)$$
$$+ (0.25 \times (-0.50)) + (0.25 \times 0.01) + (0.25 \times 0.005) = 0.75\%$$

We have enough data to derive our quadrant values, as shown in Tables 5–14 and 5–15.

Using these quadrant values, we can derive our various effects, as reported in Table 5–16.

As you see, the sum of our attribution effects (1.03%) equals our excess return (9.03% − 8.00% = 1.03%), thus we were able to satisfy our second law of attribution.

T A B L E   5–13

Portfolio and Benchmark Returns

	Market-Weighted Risk Premium (Market Return)	Currency-Weighted Cash Return ($) (Currency Return)	U.S. Dollar Returns
Portfolio Return	1.45%	7.58%	9.02%
Benchmark Return	0.75%	7.25%	8.00%
Excess Return	0.70%	0.32%	1.03%

T A B L E 5–14

Market Quadrant Values

	Quadrant (M)I		Quadrant (M)II		Quadrant (M)III		Quadrant (M)IV	
	Passive Weights	Passive Returns	Active Weights	Passive Returns	Passive Weights	Active Returns	Active Weights	Active Returns
Germany	25%	2.00%	60%	2.00%	25%	2.10%	60%	2.10%
U.K.	25%	−0.50%	10%	−0.50%	25%	−0.45%	10%	−0.45%
Japan	25%	1.00%	10%	1.00%	25%	1.10%	10%	1.10%
U.S.	25%	0.50%	20%	0.50%	25%	0.60%	20%	0.60%
Total		0.75%		1.35%		0.84%		1.45%

TABLE 5-15

Currency Quadrant Values

	Quadrant (C)I		Quadrant (C)II		Quadrant (C)III		Quadrant (C)IV	
	Passive Weights	Passive Returns	Active Weights	Passive Returns	Passive Weights	Active Returns	Active Weights	Active Returns
Germany	25%	6.00%	10%	6.00%	25%	5.90%	10%	5.90%
U.K.	25%	8.00%	45%	8.00%	25%	8.05%	45%	8.05%
Japan	25%	7.50%	25%	7.50%	25%	7.45%	25%	7.45%
U.S.	25%	7.50%	20%	7.50%	25%	7.55%	20%	7.55%
Total		7.25%		7.58%		7.24%		7.59%

TABLE 5–16

Market and Currency Attribution Effects

Market Selection	(M)II − (M)I	0.60%
Security Selection	(M)III − (M)I	0.09%
Other Market Effects	(M)IV − (M)III − (M)II + (M)I	0.01%
Total Market Effects	Sum [also, (M)IV − (M)I]	0.70%
Currency Selection	(C)II − (C)I	0.32%
Hedge Selection	(C)III − (C)I	−0.01%
Other Currency Effects	(C)IV − (C)III − (C)II + (C)I	0.02%
Total Currency Effects	Sum [also, (C)IV − (C)I]	0.33%
Total Effects		1.03%

SUMMARY

In this chapter, we provided you with some insight into global investing and attribution. We demonstrated that our return calculation formulas must be changed in order to address the effect of our currency strategy. We also demonstrated how the Karnosky-Singer model can be used to account for the various attribution effects.

EXERCISES

1. Using Table 5–E–1, derive the unhedged, hedged, and cross-hedged returns.
2. Using the portfolio data in Table 5–E–2 and benchmark data in Table 5–E–3, derive the rates of return and attribution effects.

TABLE 5–E–1

Portfolio's Currency Rates

	Local Currency Return (R_i)	Exchange Rate Return $(E_{\$,i})$	3-Month Euro Currency Rate (C_i)
Germany	5.00%	2.00%	4.50%
U.K.	11.00%	−2.50%	9.00%
Japan	9.00%	−1.50%	7.50%
U.S.	7.00%	0.00%	8.00%

TABLE 5–E–2

Portfolio Data

	Market Weights	Local Currency Return	Risk Premium	Currency Weight	Exchange Rate Return	Cash Return (in $)
Germany	50%	7.10%	2.10%	20%	1.00%	5.90%
U.K.	20%	10.60%	−0.45%	35%	−3.00%	8.05%
Japan	15%	9.55%	1.10%	15%	−1.00%	7.45%
U.S.	15%	8.10%	0.60%	30%	0.00%	7.55%
Total	100%			100%		

T A B L E   5–E–3

Benchmark Data

	Market Weights	Local Currency Return	Risk Premium	Currency Weight	Exchange Rate Return	Cash Return (in $)
Germany	35%	7.00%	2.00%	25%	1.00%	6.00%
U.K.	15%	10.50%	−0.50%	25%	−3.00%	8.00%
Japan	20%	9.50%	1.00%	25%	−1.00%	7.50%
U.S.	30%	8.00%	0.50%	25%	0.00%	7.50%
Total	100%			100%		

Geometric Attribution[1]

You may recall from chapter 1 that there are two ways to calculate excess return: arithmetic and geometric. Arithmetic is the difference between the portfolio and benchmark returns, while geometric uses a fraction.

$$ER_A = R_P - R_B \qquad ER_G = \frac{1 + R_P}{1 + R_B} - 1$$

where

ER = excess return
R = return
P = portfolio
B = benchmark
A = arithmetic
G = geometric

The models we introduce in chapter 3 are all examples of *arithmetic* attribution (also called "additive"). They are based on the arithmetic view of excess return.

[1]Much of what I discuss in this chapter comes from information I learned from my friend, Carl Bacon. I have referred to Carl as the "crusader for geometric attribution," as he constantly promotes the benefits of this approach over arithmetic. He spent a great deal of time and showed a great deal of patience with me, clarifying the formulas involved with this method, for which I'm very grateful. I hope that this chapter does justice to Carl's philosophy and views.

In this chapter, we discuss *geometric* attribution, which uses the geometric approach to derive excess return. Geometric attribution is also referred to as "multiplicative," since many of the numbers we encounter are multiplied together rather than added.

The arithmetic approach represents excess return as the profit in excess of the benchmark return. That is, the profit we received versus what we could have gotten had our monies been invested in the benchmark.

For example, we have a portfolio that starts with a market value of $1000. It grows by 7%, ending the period at $1070. The corresponding benchmark's return was 5%. Had our $1000 been invested in the benchmark, it would have grown to $1050. Our excess return, from the arithmetic view, would therefore be 2% (7% minus 5%). Another way to look at this is to compare the difference in profits ($70 versus $50). If we take the difference and divide it by our starting value, we also get 2%:

$$\frac{70-50}{1000} = \frac{20}{1000} = 2\%$$

Now let's look at these numbers from the geometric perspective.

First, let's calculate the excess return using our earlier formula by simply looking at the two returns:

$$ER_G = \frac{1+R_P}{1+R_b} - 1 = \frac{1+0.07}{1+0.05} - 1 = \frac{1.07}{1.05} - 1 = 1.9\%$$

We can also look at the geometric excess return from the perspective of the profit we got. But instead of comparing the profit to our starting value, we look at the profit relative to what we would have gotten had we been in the benchmark:

$$\frac{\$20}{\$1050} = 1.9\%$$

The geometric excess return looks at the *added value* we get by being in the portfolio, relative to the benchmark. That is, "how much more money do I have than I would have had, had I invested in the benchmark. I have $20 more, hence I have $20/$1050 more than at the end of the period, hence 1.9% more."[2]

[2]Bacon [2002].

CONVERTIBILITY

One of the benefits of the geometric approach is that it reports the same excess return, regardless of the currency.

For example, let's say on January 1, our portfolio starts out at U.S.$100. On that date, the conversion rate to Euro was 1.13305 (i.e., for $1, we get €1.1305). Our conversion to Pounds Sterling is £0.696676. (so, for our $1, we get roughly 69 pence, or less than one pound, or £0.696676.)

If we convert our $100 into these currencies and we get:

to Euros   €113.31
to Pounds Sterling   £69.67

Twelve months go by, and our U.S. portfolio has gone up 10%, to $110. If we want to compare our return in these other currencies, we now must check the current FX or foreign exchange rates. In doing this, we find the following:

$1 = €1.18970
$1 = £0.710610

This means that to convert our $110 into these currencies we have:

to Euros   €130.87
to Pounds Sterling   £78.17

Our benchmark (in U.S. dollars) has gone up 8% during this time. If we were to apply this increase to our portfolio ($100) it would rise to $108. Likewise, we can apply the same increase to our other currencies.

Table 6–1 shows the starting and ending values in the three currencies for the portfolio and benchmark. We also show the returns. We also show the excess returns.

Please note that regardless of the currency, the geometric excess return remains the same: 1.85%. Mathematically, we have:

$$ER_{G\$} = \left(\frac{1.10}{1.08}\right) - 1 = 1.85\%$$

$$ER_{G€} = \left(\frac{1.1550}{1.1340}\right) - 1 = 1.85\%$$

$$ER_{G£} = \left(\frac{1.1220}{1.1016}\right) - 1 = 1.85\%$$

TABLE 6-1

Convertibility Holds for Geometric

	Starting Values		Ending Value		Return		Excess Return	
	Portfolio	Index	Portfolio	Index	Portfolio	Index	Arithmetic	Geometric
U.S. $	$100	$100	$110	$108	10.0%	8.00%	2.00%	1.85%
Euros	€113.31	€113.31	€130.87	€128.49	15.50%	13.40%	2.10%	1.85%
Pounds	£69.67	£69.67	£78.17	£76.75	12.20%	10.16%	2.04%	1.85%

As this table shows, our arithmetic excess return varies from country to country because of the exchange rate differences. The fact that the geometric excess return shows the same value regardless of the exchange is considered an advantage, especially for firms that market internationally.

PROPORTIONATE

One advantage to geometric excess returns is that it takes into consideration the magnitude of the individual returns. That is, it provides some dimension to what's going on.

For example, let's say our portfolio had a return of 11% versus a benchmark of 10%. Arithmetically, we'd have an excess return of 1%. Likewise, if our portfolio was 25% versus a 24% benchmark, we'd show an excess return of 1%. Right?

Geometrically, we get different numbers:

$$\frac{0.11 + 1}{0.10 + 1} - 1 = \frac{1.11}{1.10} - 1 = 0.91\%$$

$$\frac{0.25 + 1}{0.24 + 1} - 1 = \frac{1.25}{1.24} - 1 = 0.81\%$$

The differences occur because the 1% addition earned relative to 10% counts a whole lot more than it does relative to 24%. Make sense?

Here's my metaphorical attempt to explain the difference. Let's say that you and I bump into each other in an appliance store, where you're about to spend $500 on a television. I tell you that I saw the exact same model, just a mile away, for just $400. You'll save $100 if you make the trip. Will you go? Probably.

A few weeks later, I see you at a new car dealer, where you're about to spend $29,800 for a new car. I tell you that the exact same car, with the same equipment, can be bought for just $29,700 just a mile away. Will you go? Probably not.

Why not? You'll save the same $100! Well, $100 relative to $500 sounds a whole lot better (and more) than it does relative to $29,800, doesn't it? And we have the same situation with that 1%— it counts for more relative to 10% than it does relative to 24%. Geometric excess return acknowledges and reflects this; arithmetic doesn't.

THE INGREDIENTS TO THE GEOMETRIC ATTRIBUTION MODEL

Let's begin the model definition by seeing what our input variables are. First, our portfolio rate of return:

$$R_P = \sum W_{P_i} \times R_{P_i}$$

Now the benchmark return:

$$R_B = \sum W_{B_i} \times R_{B_i}$$

And finally, we have something that blends the two together, that takes into account the *weight* of the portfolio and the *return* of the benchmark. We first encountered this in the Brinson, Hood, Beebower model—the Quadrant II value. If we consider the benchmark to be our *notional* value (what would provide our profit if we were to invest in it), then by using its return coupled with the weight of the portfolio, we can call it the *seminotional* return.

$$R_S = \sum W_{P_i} \times R_{B_i}$$

The attribution effects use these three returns. First, stock selection:

$$StkSel = \frac{1 + R_P}{1 + R_S} - 1$$

where

R = return
S = seminotional
P = portfolio

This effect takes the portfolio return and essentially divides it by the seminotional return (i.e., keeping the weights the same but using the returns from the portfolio and benchmark) in a manner quite similar to the actual geometric excess return formula.

And now, we discuss asset allocation.

$$AssetAlloc = \frac{1 + R_S}{1 + R_B} - 1$$

where

S = seminotional
B = benchmark

Again, we use the seminotional return, along with the bench-mark return.

If we compound the stock selection with asset allocation, we get our excess return.

$$\frac{1 + R_P}{1 + R_B} = \frac{1 + R_P}{1 + R_S} \times \frac{1 + R_S}{1 + R_B}$$

The above formulas work for the overall portfolio. For the individual sector effects, we need slight variations on these.[3]

Let's start with stock selection:

$$StkSel = W_p \times \left(\frac{(1 + R_p)}{(1 + R_b)} - 1\right) \times \left(\frac{1 + R_b}{1 + R_S}\right)$$

where

W_p = individual sector portfolio weight
R_P = individual sector portfolio return
R_b = benchmark return for the individual sector
R_S = overall seminotional return

This formula resembles, to some degree, the formula we show in chapter 3 for stock selection for the Brinson models:

$$\Sigma W_P \times (R_P - R_B)$$

In words, we're multiplying the portfolio weight for the individual sector times the sector's geometric excess return, and then times the benchmark return for the sector divided by the overall seminotional return.

---

[3]I asked Carl how he developed this logic, and he explained: "It took a while to reach this point in reality. I've always been completely convinced geometric excess returns are best, therefore I need a geometric attribution methodology. The leap forward for me was realizing the formula works [the one we showed above, using the portfolio benchmark, and semi-notional returns]. I just needed a formula for each ratio that adds up and looks like the above. I basically worked it out from first principles. The asset allocation dropped out correct the first time [as we note above, it is essentially what we have with the Brinson models]. The intellectual challenge was to then work out why you need this term (the arithmetic certainly works, but what is the logic behind it): (1 + sector benchmark return)/(1 + overall portfolio semi-notional return). This is the ratio of the sector return over the semi-notional return (in reality, a small effect). In the end, I understood—in dollars and cents it matters which sector you outperform within a portfolio. Remember in geometric excess return you are calculating how much you've added relative to the end value—this factor makes the appropriate adjustment." (Bacon [2002].)

For asset allocation we have:

$$AssetAlloc = (W_p - W_b) \times \left(\frac{1 + R_b}{1 + R_B} - 1 \right)$$

where

W_b = individual sector benchmark weight
R_B = overall benchmark return

This formula matches up quite well with the Brinson-Fachler formula we show in chapter 3:

$$\sum (R_b - R_B) \times (W_P - W_B)$$

Let's apply the geometric model to the sample portfolio we use in chapter 3 (see Table 6–2).

Let's now calculate our three returns: portfolio, benchmark, and seminotional, for the industries. Table 6–3 shows these returns.

We calculate our excess return geometrically:

$$ER_G = \left(\frac{1 + R_P}{1 + R_B} \right) - 1 = \left(\frac{1.0029}{1.0019} \right) - 1 = 0.10$$

T A B L E   6–2

Sample Portfolio

	ROR		Weight	
	Portfolio	**Index**	**Portfolio**	**Index**
Basic Materials	0.25%	0.15%	10%	11%
Industrials	0.50%	0.51%	11%	9%
Consumer Cyclicals	1.00%	1.01%	8%	7%
Utilities	−0.80%	−0.75%	12%	13%
Energy	2.00%	1.95%	7%	5%
Financial	−0.30%	−0.31%	6%	8%
Healthcare	0.80%	0.79%	15%	13%
Technology	0.60%	0.70%	9%	10%
Telecom	−0.20%	−0.21%	13%	10%
Consumer Non-Cyc.	−0.50%	−0.52%	9%	14%
Portfolio	0.29%	0.19%	100%	100%

TABLE 6-3

Calculating the Returns

	ROR		Weight		Returns		
	Portfolio	Index	Portfolio	Index	R_p	R_b	R_s
Basic Materials	0.25%	0.15%	10%	11%	0.025%	0.017%	0.015%
Industrials	0.50%	0.51%	11%	9%	0.055%	0.046%	0.056%
Consumer Cyclicals	1.00%	1.01%	8%	7%	0.080%	0.071%	0.081%
Utilities	-0.80%	-0.75%	12%	13%	-0.096%	-0.098%	-0.090%
Energy	2.00%	1.95%	7%	5%	0.140%	0.098%	0.137%
Financial	-0.30%	-0.31%	6%	8%	-0.018%	-0.025%	-0.019%
Healthcare	0.80%	0.79%	15%	13%	0.120%	0.103%	0.119%
Technology	0.60%	0.70%	9%	10%	0.054%	0.070%	0.063%
Telecom	-0.20%	-0.21%	13%	10%	-0.026%	-0.021%	-0.027%
Consumer Non-Cyc.	-0.50%	-0.52%	9%	14%	-0.045%	-0.073%	-0.047%
Portfolio	0.29%	0.19%	100%	100%	0.289%	0.187%	0.287%

T A B L E   6–4

Calculating the Effects

	R_p	R_b	R_s	Stk Sel	Asset Alloc	Excess ROR
Basic Materials	0.025%	0.017%	0.015%	0.010%	0.000%	0.008%
Industrials	0.055%	0.046%	0.056%	−0.001%	0.006%	0.009%
Cons Cyc	0.080%	0.071%	0.081%	−0.001%	0.008%	0.009%
Utilities	−0.096%	−0.098%	−0.090%	−0.006%	0.009%	0.002%
Energy	0.140%	0.098%	0.137%	0.003%	0.035%	0.042%
Financial	−0.018%	−0.025%	−0.019%	0.001%	0.010%	0.007%
Healthcare	0.120%	0.103%	0.119%	0.001%	0.012%	0.017%
Technology	0.054%	0.070%	0.063%	−0.009%	−0.005%	−0.016%
Telecom	−0.026%	−0.021%	−0.027%	0.001%	−0.012%	−0.005%
Cons Non-Cyc	−0.045%	−0.073%	−0.047%	0.002%	0.035%	0.028%
Portfolio	0.289%	0.187%	0.287%	0.002%	0.100%	0.102%

The product of our attribution effects should equal 10 basis points,[4] in accordance with our second law of attribution.[5]

Now that we have the returns, we can derive the attribution effects, as shown in Table 6–4.

The overall portfolio effects can be derived in two ways. We can either sum the individual sector effects, or use the formulas that have been introduced:

$$StkSel = \frac{1 + R_P}{1 + R_S} - 1 \qquad AssetAlloc = \frac{1 + R_S}{1 + R_B} - 1$$

It's not a bad idea to do both, as a check to confirm that our math is correct.

Table 6–5 compares the attribution effects we got geometrically with those we got earlier using the arithmetic models.

[4]We get the same excess return as we did arithmetically because the returns are so small.

[5]This law, as we define it in chapter 1, states that the sum of the attribution effects should equal the excess return. That's from the arithmetic perspective. Because we're now discussing the geometric approach to attribution, the proper wording is that the "product" should equate to the excess return, since we actually multiply the effects together (actually, the individual effects, plus one, and then substrate the one).

TABLE 6-5

Comparing the Geometric and Arithmetic Effects

	Stock Selection			Asset Allocation			
	B-F/BHBV	BHB	Geo.	B-F	BHB/BHBV	Geo.	Other BHB
Basic Materials	0.010%	0.011%	0.010%	0.000%	-0.002%	0.000%	-0.001%
Industrials	-0.001%	-0.001%	-0.001%	0.006%	0.010%	0.006%	0.000%
Consumer Cyclicals	-0.001%	-0.001%	-0.001%	0.008%	0.010%	0.008%	0.000%
Utilities	-0.006%	-0.007%	-0.006%	0.009%	0.008%	0.009%	0.001%
Energy	0.004%	0.003%	0.003%	0.035%	0.039%	0.035%	0.001%
Financial	0.001%	0.001%	0.001%	0.010%	0.006%	0.010%	0.000%
Healthcare	0.001%	0.001%	0.001%	0.012%	0.016%	0.012%	0.000%
Technology	-0.009%	-0.010%	-0.009%	-0.005%	-0.007%	-0.005%	0.001%
Telecom	0.001%	0.001%	0.001%	-0.012%	-0.006%	-0.012%	0.000%
Consumer Non-Cyc.	0.002%	0.003%	0.002%	0.035%	0.026%	0.035%	-0.001%
Portfolio	0.002%	0.001%	0.002%	0.100%	0.100%	0.100%	0.000%

As you can see, our results are quite similar. "It is only for large returns over multiple periods that you begin to see the difference."[6]

NO RESIDUAL WHEN LINKING ACROSS PERIODS

We haven't yet addressed the issue of linking, but it's important to touch on it briefly here (we discuss arithmetic linking in detail in chapter 7 and geometric linking in chapter 8). We often have the need to link attribution effects across time periods. Arithmetic linking offers several challenges, as we soon find out. Because geometric attribution effects "naturally link," we don't have the same challenges. I prefer not to go into this in any detail right now, since we have a whole chapter devoted to the subject.

CONCLUDING REMARKS

Geometric attribution has some clear advantages over its arithmetic counterpart: convertibility, proportionality, and simpler linking, which naturally eliminates residuals. The challenge is that geometric excess return is not as intuitive as arithmetic. People generally expect us to address excess return as the portfolio return minus the benchmark; to see it presented in a fractional manner is not easy to comprehend. Nevertheless, we are beginning to see greater interest in this approach to attribution analysis.

[6]Bacon [2002].

EXERCISE

Calculate the geometric attribution effects for the portfolio shown in Table 6–E–1.

T A B L E   6–E–1

Portfolio and Benchmark Details

	Rate of Return		Weights	
	Portfolio	Index	Portfolio	Index
Industrials	2.00%	3.00%	40.00%	25.00%
Transportation	3.00%	2.00%	20.00%	25.00%
Utilities	4.00%	5.00%	30.00%	25.00%
Financials	5.00%	4.00%	10.00%	25.00%
Total	3.10%	3.50%		

Linking Across Time— Arithmetic

1) very difficult to do intuitively
2) Geometric & smoothing might work, but can
*   yield to very counter intuitive results (p143)*

"O holy simplicity."
John Huss

Having attribution effects monthly is generally an adequate time period. However, some people would like the monthly effects linked to produce quarterly or even annual effects. Also, for those who prefer to do daily attribution, we need somehow to link the daily numbers together to obtain the monthly effects.

What do we mean by this? Well, let's start with the monthly. We have attribution effects for January, February, and March. We want to know the effects for the first quarter. Or we have daily and want to derive the monthly effects. How do we do this? How do we get daily numbers to link to arrive at monthly, or monthly to link to get to quarterly or annual?

> **Third Law of Performance Attribution**
> *The sum of the linked attribution effects must equal the sum of the linked excess return.*

If we're dealing with geometric attribution, it's quite simple (please refer to chapter 8). However, if you're doing arithmetic attribution, you have a challenge. Actually, quite a challenge.[1]

---

[1]To say that this topic is controversial is a fairly significant understatement. As you see in this rather long chapter, I've introduced a variety of methods. Owen Davies and Damien Laker (Davies, 2001) provide additional insights, which, for brevity's sake and the pressure to get this material completed, I elected not to include. Also, Andrew Frongello has recently offered a new approach that I was not able to include. However, you're encouraged to investigate their views for yet other perspectives.

Let's start with the third law of performance attribution:

THE THIRD LAW OF PERFORMANCE ATTRIBUTION

The sum of the linked attribution effects must equal the sum of the linked excess return.[2]

Mathematically, this appears as:

$$\sum_{i=1}^{n} LAE_i = LR_P - LR_B$$

where

LAE = linked attribution effects
LR = linked return
B = benchmark
P = portfolio
i = individual effect
n = number of effects

This "law" states that the sums of the linked attribution effects (*LAE*) must equal the difference between the sum of the linked returns for the portfolio, minus the linked returns for the benchmark (i.e., that we must account for 100% of the excess return for the period across which we're linking).

This makes sense, doesn't it? After all, if we believe in the justification for the Second Law of Performance Attribution (see chapter 1), then this law is a logical extension.

But getting this law to hold can be difficult.[3] We go through several of the optional methodologies available to us to achieve multiperiod linking.

The Example We Use

We use the portfolio and index information in Table 7–1 for our starting example, which we use to demonstrate all of our ap-

[2]This law, like our second law, is presented in the form consistent with arithmetic attribution. It also holds for geometric models, albeit the geometric view of excess return would be in order (i.e., we wouldn't sum our effects but would essentially take their products).

[3]As you soon see, there is often a "gap" between the linked excess return and the linked effects, which is often referred to as "residue."

TABLE 7–1

Portfolio and Index Weights and Returns, and
Attribution Effects

	ROR		Weight		Market Effects	
	Portfolio	**Index**	**Portfolio**	**Index**	**Stk. Sel.**	**Ind. Sel**
Equities	7.00%	8.00%	70%	60%	−0.70%	0.80%
Bonds	7.50%	6.00%	20%	40%	0.30%	−1.20%
Cash	6.00%	5.00%	10%	0%	0.10%	0.50%
Portfolio	7.00%	7.20%	100%	100%	−0.30%	0.10%

proaches. As you can see, we've broken our portfolio and index up by security type, which is about as simple a breakdown as we can employ. Hopefully, this will help explain how the approaches work. To make the process even simpler, we're keeping the same monthly data for the next two months; i.e., we have three months in a row of identical results. While this is a highly unlikely possibility, it should succeed in demonstrating how each method works.[4]

Using the monthly data, let's derive the excess return for the three months. Table 7–2 shows the monthly returns for the portfolio and benchmark, the linked quarterly return, and the excess return for the quarter.

We obtain the quarterly portfolio return by using the standard geometric linking[5] formula. For example, for the portfolio returns we get:

Step 1: Convert returns to decimal equivalent by dividing by 100.

$$7.00 \div 100 = 0.070$$
$$7.00 \div 100 = 0.070$$
$$7.00 \div 100 = 0.070$$

[4]We're actually using a portfolio and index situation that David Cariño uses in his Dietz Award-winning article (Cariño, [1999]).

[5]It's interesting that *so* many people, when they think about "geometric attribution," think we're talking about the same thing as "geometric linking," since this is a standard part of performance measurement (see Spaulding [1997], page 34). We're obviously not.

TABLE 7–2

Monthly and Quarterly Returns; Excess Return for Quarter

Month 1		Month 2		Month 3		Quarter (linked)	
Portfolio	Index	Portfolio	Index	Portfolio	Index	Portfolio	Index
7.00%	7.20%	7.00%	7.20%	7.00%	7.20%	22.50%	23.19%
				Quarterly Excess Return			−0.69%

Step 2: Add 1.

$$.0700 + 1 = 1.0700$$
$$.0700 + 1 = 1.0700$$
$$.0700 + 1 = 1.0700$$

Step 3: Multiply

$$1.0700 \times 1.0700 \times 1.0700 = 1.2250$$

Step 4: Subtract 1.

$$1.2250 - 1 = .2250$$

Step 5: Multiply by 100, to convert decimal to a percent.

$$.2250 \times 100 = 22.50\%$$

When we repeat these steps for the index return, we get 23.19%. So the linked portfolio return for this three-month period is 22.50%, and the index has a return of 23.19%. Taking the difference yields a linked excess return of −0.69% or −69 basis points. This is the amount we wish to arrive at by linking the individual attribution effects across this three-month period.

We now present a variety of ways to attempt to link the monthly effects, to derive corresponding quarterly effects, in an attempt to satisfy the third law of attribution.

METHOD #1—ARITHMETIC LINKING

Let's start with the simplest approach available to us: arithmetic linking. Here, we simply add the three months' effects. The formula for this is:

$$\sum_{i=1}^{n} \sum_{t=1}^{m} AE_{i,t} \stackrel{?}{=} LR_P - LR_B$$

where

AE = attribution effect
LR = linked return
P = portfolio
B = benchmark
i = individual effect
t = time period
n = number of effects
m = number of time periods

This formula is asking if the simple arithmetic sum of the individual attribution effects equals the difference between the linked return for the portfolio and the linked return for the benchmark (i.e., the excess return for the period). To test, let's add the individual effects of the three months for these sectors. This is shown in Table 7–3.

The linked stock selection effect is −0.90%, while industry selection links to 0.30% for the quarter; these values sum to a net effect of −0.60%. So we can conclude that this approach doesn't work, since we needed to get −0.69%. Therefore,

$$\sum_{i=1}^{n} \sum_{t=1}^{m} AE_{i,t} \neq LR_P - LR_B$$

> Arithmetic linking fails to satisfy our third law of attribution. Well, let's try another approach.

METHOD #2—GEOMETRIC LINKING

Geometric linking is familiar to us from basis performance measurement:

Step 1: Convert period returns to decimals.
Step 2: Add 1.
Step 3: Multiply the numbers together.
Step 4: Subtract 1.
Step 5: Convert to a percent.

TABLE 7-3

Applying Arithmetic Linking to Our Portfolio

	Month 1		Month 2		Month 3		Quarter	
	Stk. Sel.	Ind. Sel.	Stk. Sel.	Ind. Sel.	Stk. Sel.	Ind. Sel.	Stk. Sel.	Ind. Sel.
Equities	-0.70%	0.80%	-0.70%	0.80%	-0.70%	0.80%	-2.10%	2.40%
Bonds	0.30%	-1.20%	0.30%	-1.20%	0.30%	-1.20%	0.90%	-3.60%
Cash	0.10%	0.50%	0.10%	0.50%	0.10%	0.50%	0.30%	1.50%
Portfolio	-0.30%	0.10%	-0.30%	0.10%	-0.30%	0.10%	-0.90%	0.30%
Net Effects		-0.20%		-0.20%		-0.20%		-0.60%

Let's see if geometric linking works for attribution. This approach can be represented by the following formula:[6]

$$\left[\sum_{i=1}^{n} \prod_{t=1}^{m} (AE_{i,t} + 1) \right] - 1 \stackrel{?}{=} LR_P - LR_B$$

Table 7–4 shows the results of geometrically linking our attribution effects.

Coincidentally, we get the linked number −0.60%. We obtain this whether we link the net effects of each of the three months or sum the linked effects of the portfolio. The portfolio's linked effects can be obtained by linking the monthly effects (going across) or summing the stock selection and industry selection effects (coming downward).

Unfortunately, we're forced to conclude that geometric linking apparently doesn't work.

$$\left[\sum_{i=1}^{n} \prod_{t=1}^{m} (AE_{i,t} + 1) \right] - 1 \neq LR_P - LR_B$$

Arithmetic and geometric can be viewed as rather simple approaches to linking, and neither works. Now, we have to consider more complex models to link the period returns. These other models use what we may call an "agent" to get the linked effects to equal the linked excess return.

We'll begin with the logarithmic approach.

METHOD #3—LOGARITHMIC LINKING   *works, but strange*

The logarithmic model for linking was first described by Dietz Award-winning Author, David Cariño, as the system that his firm, Frank Russell Company, used. The approach distributes a small residual proportionately among all of the effects calculated for the period. I now attempt to describe the process for you. You're invited to go directly to the source (Cariño [1999]) for further elaboration.

Table 7–5 shows our portfolio and the key formulas used in this approach. We'll review each of these formulas as we proceed

---

[6]This formula is slightly different than what we show in chapter 8 for linking geometric attribution. Here, we sum the products; in chapter 8, we multiply the products. For this chapter, the math works better if we sum, so that's what I've chosen to do.

TABLE 7-4

Applying Geometric Linking to Our Portfolio

	Month 1		Month 2		Month 3		Quarter	
	Stk. Sel.	Ind. Sel.	Stk. Sel.	Ind. Sel.	Stk. Sel.	Ind. Sel.	Stk. Sel.	Ind. Sel.
Equities	−0.70%	0.80%	−0.70%	0.80%	−0.70%	0.80%	−2.09%	2.42%
Bonds	0.30%	−1.20%	0.30%	−1.20%	0.30%	−1.20%	0.90%	−3.56%
Cash	0.10%	0.50%	0.10%	0.50%	0.10%	0.50%	0.30%	0.30%
Portfolio	−0.30%	0.10%	−0.30%	0.10%	−0.30%	0.10%	−0.90%	0.30%
Net Effects		−0.20%		−0.20%		−0.20%		−0.60%

TABLE 7–5

Applying the Cariño Linking Methodology to Our Portfolio

	Portfolio	Index	Excess Return
Month 1	7.00%	7.20%	
Month 2	7.00%	7.20%	
Month 3	7.00%	7.20%	
	22.50%	23.19%	−0.69%
k_1	0.9337		
k_2	0.9337		
k_3	0.9337		
K	0.8140		
beta1	1.15		−0.0023
beta2	1.15	Individual	−0.0023
beta3	1.15	Beta (Rp−Rb)	−0.0023
			−0.69%

$$k_t = \frac{\ln\left(1 + R_{P_t}\right) - \ln\left(1 + R_{B_T}\right)}{R_{P_t} - R_{B_t}}$$

$$k = \frac{\ln\left(1 + R_P\right) - \ln\left(1 + R_B\right)}{R_P - R_B}$$

$$\beta_t^{Log} = \frac{k_t}{k}$$

$$\sum_t \beta_t^{Log}\left(Rp_t - Rb_t\right)$$

through the model. Our goal with this approach is to discover "k-factors," which are used to adjust the attribution effects so that the result satisfies our third law.

We begin by finding k_t factors for each period:

$$k_t = \frac{\ln(1 + R_{P_t}) - \ln(1 + R_{B_t})}{R_{P_t} - R_{B_t}}$$

This factor is calculated for each period, t, and uses the natural log (ln) function. In this formula, we're essentially seeing the excess return for each period in the numerator (portfolio return minus benchmark return), but in the form of natural logs. The denominator has the monthly excess return.

In our case, we have three months, so we need three separate k_t factors. We have a separate k factor for each month, which is

based on that month's portfolio and benchmark returns. Our table
shows these factors.[7]

We next calculate a k factor for the entire three-month period,
which uses the linked portfolio and benchmark returns. You should
notice that the formula is exactly like the formula used for the k_t factors, except that it uses the linked returns for the full period.

$$k = \frac{\ln(1 + R_P) - \ln(1 + R_B)}{R_P - R_B}$$

Again, our table shows the results (0.8140).

Now that we have both the k and k_t factors, we can derive our
beta factors. The formula is simply:

$$\beta_t^{Log} = \frac{k_t}{k}$$

Since our data is identical for each of the months, we therefore
arrive at identical *beta* factors for each period (1.15).

David's approach provides us with a midpoint check, to validate
that we're proceeding in the correct direction. We can validate that our
math has worked properly so far by doing the following calculation:

$$\sum_t \beta_t^{Log} (Rp_t - Rb_t) \stackrel{?}{=} R_P - R_B$$

That is, we multiply the individual *beta* factors by their respective period's excess return. In our case, we get the same results
(−0.0023). We next sum these results. The sum should equal the
linked excess return. And, as we show, it does equal −0.69%. This
confirms that we've derived the proper k factors (individual period
and across period), so we're now ready to apply these factors to our
attribution effects, which is the next step in this process.

Table 7–6 shows the actual derivation of the attribution effects.

For reference purposes, I reshow the individual monthly effects here.

We use the individual k_t factors from Table 7–5, times each
month's attribution effects, to obtain adjusted effects.

$$k_t \times A_{i,t}$$

The A term stands for the individual attribution effect. The
subscripts (i,t) are for the individual period and effect. Since we

[7]In this example, they all equal 0.9337.

T A B L E   7–6

Calculating the Attribution Effects

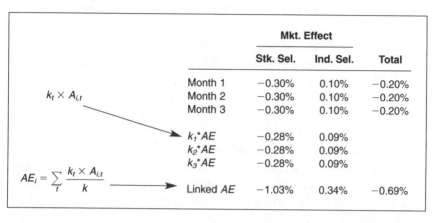

		Mkt. Effect		
		Stk. Sel.	Ind. Sel.	Total
	Month 1	−0.30%	0.10%	−0.20%
$k_t \times A_{i,t}$	Month 2	−0.30%	0.10%	−0.20%
	Month 3	−0.30%	0.10%	−0.20%
	$k_1{}^*AE$	−0.28%	0.09%	
	$k_2{}^*AE$	−0.28%	0.09%	
	$k_3{}^*AE$	−0.28%	0.09%	
$AE_i = \sum_t \dfrac{k_t \times A_{i,t}}{k}$	Linked AE	−1.03%	0.34%	−0.69%

have three periods, i goes from 1 to 3; since we have two effects, t goes from 1 to 2; so, we have six combinations (1,1; 1,2; 2,1; 2,2; 3,1; 3,2), which encompass all the combinations of effects and periods.

Our final equation sums these factors and divides by our linked period k factor.

$$AE_i = \sum_t \frac{k_t \times A_{i,t}}{k}$$

This yields the adjusted three-month period effects.

We show a linked attribution effect for stock selection of −1.03% and for industry selection of 0.34%. When combined, we get −0.69%, which is our excess return for the period. Thus, we have shown that Cariño's multistep method works and results in linked period effects that satisfy our third law!

METHOD #4—OPTIMIZED APPROACH

The fourth method was developed by Jose Menchero and is referred to as the "Optimized Approach."[8] It's similar to the logarithmic

---

[8]Jose pointed out that this method "rests on the fact that there is a natural scaling (as given by A) that scales the active return from the single period to the multiperiod case, i.e., every basis point of relative performance in the single period case scales into A basis points of relative performance over the multi-period case. The natural scaling is purely a result of geometric compounding. The alphas are constructed to be minimally small, thus minimizing any distortions that result from deviations from this natural scaling." Menchero [2002].

method in its mathematical complexity. It has similar calculations to Cariño's method. Instead of finding k factors, we are going to find *beta* factors, which will then be used to adjust our attribution effects.

Table 7–7 demonstrates how we derive the *beta* factor.

We begin by calculating the A term, which is based on the following formula:

$$A = \frac{1}{T} \times \left[\frac{(R_P - R_B)}{(1 + R_P)^{1/T} - (1 + R_B)^{1/T}} \right]$$

The T represents the number of periods; in our case, it's 3, so the fraction is $1/3$. By raising the values in the denominator to the $1/3$ power, that's equivalent to taking the cube root of the numbers. Our numerator shows the excess return for the period, while the denominator resembles the excess return. We calculate A to be 1.1468.

Our next step involves using this A term to derive individual *alpha* terms.

$$\alpha_t = \left[\frac{R_P - R_B - A\sum_{j=1}^{T} (R_{P_J} - R_{B_J})}{\sum_{j=1}^{T} (R_{P_J} - R_{B_J})^2} \right] \times (R_{P_t} - R_{B_t})$$

I think it's interesting that this expression, while to be used to derive the three individual sets of *alpha* terms, actually uses the monthly figures for all three months! You can see this in the denominator, where we see the Riemann sum expression. Each alpha is calculated to be 0.0002.

As in the case of the Cariño model, we have a midpoint test (referred to as a "constraint") to validate that we're doing the math correctly and proceeding along properly. This test uses the following expression:

$$R_P - R_B = \sum_{t=1}^{T} (A + \alpha_t) \times (R_{P_t} - R_{B_t})$$

In the table, I've shown the calculation of the three individual monthly values, of the A term plus the respective *alpha*, then times

TABLE 7-7

Creating the Beta Factor—Optimized Approach

	Portfolio	Index	Excess Return
Month 1	7.00%	7.20%	
Month 2	7.00%	7.20%	
Month 3	7.00%	7.20%	−0.69%
	22.50%	23.19%	
A term	1.1468		
alpha1 (α_1)	0.0002		
alpha2 (α_2)	0.0002		
alpha3 (α_3)	0.0002		
Test	(0.0023)		
	(0.0023)		
	(0.0023)		
Constraint	−0.69%		
BetaOpt1	1.1470		
BetaOpt2	1.1470		
BetaOpt3	1.1470		

$$A = \frac{1}{T} \times \left[\frac{\left(R_p - R_B\right)}{\left(1 + R_P\right)^{1/T} - \left(1 + R_B\right)^{1/T}} \right]$$

$$\alpha_t = \left[\frac{R_P - R_B - A \sum_{j=1}^{T}\left(R_{P_J} - R_{B_J}\right)}{\sum_{j=1}^{T}\left(R_{P_J} - R_{B_J}\right)^2} \right] \times \left(R_{P_t} - R_{B_t}\right)$$

$$R_P - R_B = \sum_{i=1}^{T}\left(A + \alpha_t\right) \times \left(R_{P_t} - R_{B_T}\right)$$

$$\beta_t^{Opt} = A + \alpha_t$$

the monthly excess return, which results in -0.0023. We also show
the summation that is equal the excess return for the three-month
period. As you can see, we passed this test (since we were able to
derive our excess return (-0.69%))! This test essentially validates
that our A term and individual *alphas* are accurate.

We can now calculate the three monthly optimized *beta* terms,
which are simply the sum of the A term with the individual *alphas*.

$$\beta_t^{Opt} = A + \alpha_t$$

Now that we have the individual optimized *betas*, we can
move to the final step, to derive the attribution effects. This work is
shown in Table 7–8.

We begin by adjusting the monthly attribution effects, using
the optimized *beta* values from Table 7–7. I refer to these values in
the equation, both below and in Table 7–8, as "adjusted" (-0.34%
and 0.11%).

$$Adj'\,dAE_t = \beta_t^{Opt} \times AE_t$$

We simply multiply each month's effects by its respective optimized *beta* (β^{Opt}) value.

Finally, we sum these values to derive the linked effects
(-1.03% and 0.34%).

$$AE_t = \sum \beta_t^{Opt} \times AE_{i,t}$$

TABLE 7–8

Calculating the Attribution Effects for the
Optimized Approach

		Mkt. Effect		Excess Return
		Stk. Sel.	Ind. Sel.	
	Month 1	-0.30%	0.10%	-0.20%
	Month 2	-0.30%	0.10%	0.20%
	Month 3	-0.30%	0.10%	-0.20%
$Adj'\,dAE_t = \beta_t^{Opt} \times AE_t \longrightarrow$	betaOpt*AE1	-0.34%	0.11%	
	betaOpt*AE2	-0.34%	0.11%	
	betaOpt*AE2	-0.34%	0.11%	
$AE_i = \sum \beta_t^{Opt} \times AE_{i,t} \longrightarrow$	Sum'd AE	-1.03%	0.34%	-0.69%

Summing the stock selection (−1.03%) and industry allocation (0.34%) effects, we get −0.69%. Thus, we have demonstrated that Menchero's optimized approach, like David Cariño's logarithmic method, yields results that satisfy our third law of attribution.[9]

COMPARING THE FOUR METHODS

Table 7–9 shows the linked effects as we obtain them using these four methods.

At this point, it's worth pondering the benefits that we obtained from the much more mathematically rigorous logarithmic and optimized approaches. Was this additional precision worth the cost?

Granted, we've completely accounted for the linked period excess return (−0.69%) rather than be short 6 basis points by using the geometric or arithmetic methods, but I think you grant me that the approaches are rather complex.

Of course, building a program to apply either Menchero's or Cariño's method shouldn't be overly onerous. But we should at least consider what other vendors have apparently been doing.

From our unpublished research, it appears that many attribution vendors typically use the geometric method to link the subperiod effects. I think they do this for a few reasons. First, it's simple and easy to comprehend. Second, the more sophisticated methods were developed by their competitors; do they want to use a method designed by a competitor? Often the answer is "no." Third, to develop a similarly complex method would require some intense analysis. When you realize that both Jose Menchero and David Cariño have Ph.D.'s, I think you begin to respect the amount of intense mental horsepower one needs to develop such a method. And finally, I think vendors feel that the geometric method comes "close enough" to be satisfactory for most users.[10]

Do these vendors allow their systems to report results that don't match the linked excess return (i.e., do they violate attribution

[9]This is a special case of three identical periods linked together, so we'd expect the logarithmic and optimized approaches to yield the same results. In general, they will not be equal.

[10]There is actually yet another school of thought, which we don't address in this text: whether the numbers *should* in fact equal? That is, whether or not our third law of attribution is a valid one. Some believe that to expect our attribution effects to sum is contrary to what the effects represent. That unlike returns, they shouldn't compound. Suffice it to say, this school of thought doesn't have as many followers as the ones who support our third law, so we pass on spending any further time discussing it.

T A B L E   7–9

Comparing the Linked Effects

| | Linked Attribution Effects | | |
	Stk. Sel.	Ind. Sel.	Total
Arithmetic	−0.90%	0.30%	−0.60%
Geometric	−0.90%	0.30%	−0.60%
Logarithmic	−1.03%	0.34%	−0.69%
Optimized	−1.03%	0.34%	−0.69%

law #3)? In some cases, yes. But, I believe many (if not most) typically engage in a *smoothing* exercise to force the numbers to equal. Some people refer to this as applying a "fudge factor."

Fixed income portfolio manager Steve Campisi uses smoothing techniques based on the geometric results and comes up with pretty respectable results.[11] He essentially determines the ratios of the effects and adjusts accordingly. Steve offers two approaches.

- Use the ratio of the linked excess return to the sum of the linked effects, and adjust each attribution factor.
- Calculate the ratio of each attribution effect to the sum of the attribution effects, and apply this to the linked excess return.

Both methods produce the same results, since they are mathematically equivalent. I prefer the first method, since it's easier to visualize. In summary, this method is simple, intuitive, and it often does the job: the sum of the attribution effects always equals the linked excess return, spot on.

Table 7–10 shows the results we obtained earlier using geometric linking of the attribution effects. At the time, we pointed out that the difference (0.75 versus 0.78) violated our third law of attribution.

We will now use Steve Campisi's smoothing method to eliminate the difference.

The first method is quite straightforward. First, calculate the ratio of the excess return divided by the total attribution effect (in

TABLE 7–10

Geometrically Linked Results

Industry Selection Effect	0.30%
Stock Selection Effect	−0.90%
Total Attribution Effect	−0.60%
Linked Excess Return	−0.69%
Difference	−0.09%

our case, it's (−0.69) ÷ (−0.60), which yields 1.15). This is in essence the *smoothing factor*. We multiply this by both of our effects to obtain our adjusted effects (0.30 industry selection and −0.90 for stock selection). The linked industry selection for the period becomes 0.345%, while the linked stock selection effect is −1.035%. Adding these linked effects together, we find that our results equal our excess return, thus satisfying our second law. Table 7–11 shows the details of this approach.

The second method approaches the problem from a slightly different angle. Essentially, we want to determine what the ratio is of the two linked effects that we have obtained, to the total effect, and then apply this ratio against the linked excess return to determine the corresponding ratio, which becomes the linked effects.

Our first step is simply to determine these ratios by dividing the two linked effects by the total attribution. Next we multiply each of these ratios by the excess return. Adding the adjusted effects together, we once again obtain our excess return and also see that we have the exact same results as we obtained using the first approach.

TABLE 7–11

Campisi Smoothing Method 1

Ratio of Actual to Calculated	(−0.69) / (−0.60)	1.15
Adjusted Industry Selection Effect	1.15 × 0.30	0.345
Adjusted Stock Selection Effect	1.15 × (−0.90)	−1.035
Adjusted Total	0.345 + (−1.035)	−0.69

T A B L E   7–12

Campisi Smoothing Method 2

Proportion from Ind. Selection	0.30 / (−0.60)	−0.50
Proportion from Stk. Selection	−0.90 / (−0.60)	1.5
Adjusted Ind. Selection	−0.50 × (−0.69)	0.345
Adjusted Stk. Selection	1.5 × (−0.69)	−1.035
Adjusted Total	0.345 + (−1.035)	−0.69

If we now add Campisi's results to our earlier Table 7–9, we find that his method also satisfies our third law. (See Tables 7-12 and 7-13).

Since we obtain essentially the same results as the two mathematically intense approaches, we may ask if all this mathematical rigor is really necessary? Let's do a couple more examples before we draw any conclusion.

A MORE ROBUST EXAMPLE

Now let's apply these same methods to a more complex portfolio scenario to show that they work equally well. In our earlier example, we use a portfolio that is broken down only to the asset class level; we now drop down to industry. We also vary the data from period to period. We use the three months of portfolio returns, as described in Tables 7–14 through 7–16.

T A B L E   7–13

All Five Approaches

	Linked Attribution Effects		
	Stk. Sel.	Ind. Sel.	Total
Arithmetic	−0.90%	0.30%	−0.60%
Geometric	−0.90%	0.30%	−0.60%
Logarithmic	−1.03%	0.34%	−0.69%
Optimized	−1.03%	0.34%	−0.69%
Campisi	−1.035%	0.345%	−0.69%

TABLE 7-14

Month 1 Details

	ROR		Weight		Mkt. Effect	
	Portfolio	Index	Portfolio	Index	Stk. Sel.	Ind. Sel.
Basic Materials	3.84%	3.75%	8%	6%	0.01%	0.08%
Industrials	−11.52%	−14%	14%	9%	0.35%	−0.70%
Consumer Cyclicals	5.09%	5.21%	12%	11%	−0.01%	0.05%
Utilities	6.57%	6.20%	7%	10%	0.03%	−0.19%
Energy	8.30%	8%	15%	12%	0.05%	0.24%
Financial	4.75%	4.50%	9%	8%	0.02%	0.05%
Healthcare	−11.60%	−12%	11%	12%	0.04%	0.12%
Technology	3.50%	3.10%	6%	9%	0.02%	−0.09%
Telecom	14.06%	10.11%	10%	13%	0.40%	−0.30%
Consumer Non-Cyc.	6.85%	5.50%	8%	10%	0.11%	−0.11%
Portfolio	2.33%	2.18%	100%	100%	1.00%	−0.86%
Excess ROR		0.14%				0.14%

T A B L E 7-15

Month 2 Details

	ROR		Weight		Mkt. Effect	
	Portfolio	Index	Portfolio	Index	Stk. Sel.	Ind. Sel.
Basic Materials	3.00%	2.70%	7%	6%	0.02%	0.03%
Industrials	-5.21%	-4.80%	12%	9%	-0.05%	-0.14%
Consumer Cyclicals	5.13%	4.15%	11%	11%	0.11%	0.00%
Utilities	5.11%	5.12%	9%	10%	0.00%	-0.05%
Energy	7.21%	6.90%	14%	12%	0.04%	0.14%
Financial	-1.13%	-1.01%	8%	8%	-0.01%	0.00%
Healthcare	2.50%	1.18%	11%	12%	0.15%	-0.01%
Technology	3.01%	2.99%	7%	9%	0.00%	-0.06%
Telecom	3.10%	2.61%	11%	13%	0.05%	-0.05%
Consumer Non-Cyc.	8.30%	8.10%	10%	10%	0.02%	0.00%
Portfolio	3.18%	3.01%	100%	100%	0.33%	-0.15%
Excess ROR		0.18%				0.18%

TABLE 7-16

Month 3 Details

	ROR		Weight		Mkt. Effect	
	Portfolio	Index	Portfolio	Index	Stk. Sel.	Ind. Sel.
Basic Materials	1.30%	0.50%	8%	6%	0.06%	0.01%
Industrials	-3.80%	-3.90%	12%	9%	0.01%	-0.12%
Consumer Cyclicals	3.12%	2.10%	12%	11%	0.12%	0.02%
Utilities	0.11%	4.10%	10%	10%	-0.40%	0.00%
Energy	0.21%	2.30%	9%	12%	-0.19%	-0.07%
Financial	0.31%	3.20%	9%	8%	-0.26%	0.03%
Healthcare	2.20%	1.31%	10%	12%	0.09%	-0.03%
Technology	1.01%	0.30%	8%	9%	0.06%	0.00%
Telecom	-0.50%	-6.10%	11%	13%	0.62%	0.12%
Consumer Non-Cyc.	4.00%	1.01%	11%	10%	0.33%	0.01%
Portfolio	0.77%	0.34%	100%	100%	0.44%	-0.02%
Excess ROR		0.42%				0.42%

Using the monthly data, let's derive the excess return for the three months. Table 7–17 shows the monthly returns for the portfolio and benchmark, the linked quarterly return, and the excess return for the quarter.

As we have done earlier, we geometrically link the monthly data to arrive at our quarterly values.

Step 1: Convert returns to decimal equivalent by dividing by 100.

$$2.33\% \div 100 = .0233$$
$$3.18\% \div 100 = .0318$$
$$0.77\% \div 100 = .0077$$

Step 2: Add 1.

$$.0233 + 1 = 1.0233$$
$$.0318 + 1 = 1.0318$$
$$.0077 + 1 = 1.0077$$

Step 3: Multiply.

$$1.0233 \times 1.0318 \times 1.0077 = 1.0639$$

Step 4: Subtract 1.

$$1.0639 - 1 = .0639$$

Step 5: Multiply by 100, to convert decimal to a percent.

$$.0639 \times 100 = 6.39\%.$$

When we repeat these steps for the benchmark return, we get 5.61%.

TABLE 7–17

Monthly and Quarterly Returns; Excess Return for Quarter

Month 1		Month 2		Month 3		Quarter (linked)	
Portfolio	Index	Portfolio	Index	Portfolio	Index	Portfolio	Index
2.33%	2.18%	3.18%	3.01%	0.77%	0.34%	6.39%	5.61%
					Quarterly Excess Return		0.78%

The linked portfolio return for this three-month period is 6.39%, and the index has a return of 5.61%. The difference yields a linked excess return of .78%, or 78 basis points. This is the amount we want to arrive at by linking the individual attribution effects across this three-month period (i.e., to satisfy our third law of attribution).

METHOD #1—ARITHMETIC LINKING

We begin with the arithmetic approach. Again, the formula is simply:

$$\sum_{i=1}^{n}\sum_{t=1}^{m} AE_{i,t} \overset{?}{=} LR_P - LR_B$$

And our question is whether or not it will satisfy our third law.

We add the individual effects of the three months for these sectors, which is shown in Table 7–18.

The linked attribution effects yield 0.75% rather than the 0.78% we need. So, once again we conclude that the arithmetic approach to linking simply doesn't work.

$$\sum_{i=1}^{n}\sum_{t=1}^{m} AE_{i,t} \neq LR_P - LR_B$$

METHOD #2—GEOMETRIC LINKING

We'll try geometric linking again, as represented by this formula:

$$\left[\sum_{i=1}^{n}\prod_{t=1}^{m} (AE_{i,t} + 1)\right] - 1 \overset{?}{=} LR_P - LR_B$$

Table 7–19 shows the results of geometrically linking the period attribution effects.

We get the linked number, 0.75%. And we are once again forced to conclude that geometric linking will not satisfy our need to account for the period's excess return.

$$\left[\sum_{i=1}^{n}\prod_{t=1}^{m} (AE_{i,t} + 1)\right] - 1 \neq LR_P - LR_B$$

TABLE 7–18

Applying Arithmetic Linking to Our Portfolio

	Month 1		Month 2		Month 3		Quarter	
	Stk. Sel.	Ind. Sel.	Stk. Sel.	Ind. Sel.	Stk. Sel.	Ind. Sel.	Stk. Sel.	Ind. Sel.
	0.01%	0.08%	0.02%	0.03%	0.06%	0.01%	0.09%	0.11%
	0.35%	−0.70%	−0.05%	−0.14%	0.01%	−0.12%	0.31%	−0.96%
	−0.01%	0.05%	0.11%	0.00%	0.12%	0.02%	0.22%	0.07%
	0.03%	−0.19%	0.00%	−0.05%	−0.40%	0.00%	−0.37%	−0.24%
	0.05%	0.24%	0.04%	0.14%	−0.19%	−0.07%	−0.10%	0.31%
	0.02%	0.05%	−0.01%	0.00%	−0.26%	0.03%	−0.25%	0.08%
	0.04%	0.12%	0.15%	−0.01%	0.09%	−0.03%	0.28%	0.08%
	0.02%	−0.09%	0.00%	−0.06%	0.06%	0.00%	0.08%	−0.16%
	0.40%	−0.30%	0.05%	−0.05%	0.62%	0.12%	1.06%	−0.23%
	0.11%	−0.11%	0.02%	0.00%	0.33%	0.01%	0.46%	−0.10%
		−0.86%		−0.15%		−0.02%		−1.03%
	1.00%	0.14%	0.33%	0.18%	0.44%	0.42%	1.78%	0.75%

TABLE 7-19

Applying Geometric Linking to Our Portfolio

Month 1		Month 2		Month 3		Quarter	
Stk. Sel.	Ind. Sel.	Stk. Sel.	Ind. Sel.	Stk. Sel.	Ind. Sel.	Stk. Sel.	Ind. Sel.
0.01%	0.08%	0.02%	0.03%	0.06%	0.01%	0.09%	0.11%
0.35%	-0.70%	-0.05%	-0.14%	0.01%	-0.12%	0.31%	-0.96%
-0.01%	0.05%	0.11%	0.00%	0.12%	0.02%	0.22%	0.07%
0.03%	-0.19%	0.00%	-0.05%	-0.40%	0.00%	-0.37%	-0.24%
0.05%	0.24%	0.04%	0.14%	-0.19%	-0.07%	-0.10%	0.31%
0.02%	0.05%	-0.01%	0.00%	-0.26%	0.03%	-0.25%	0.08%
0.04%	0.12%	0.15%	-0.01%	0.09%	-0.03%	0.28%	0.08%
0.02%	-0.09%	0.00%	-0.06%	0.06%	0.00%	0.08%	-0.16%
0.40%	-0.30%	0.05%	-0.05%	0.62%	0.12%	1.07%	-0.23%
0.11%	-0.11%	0.02%	0.00%	0.33%	0.01%	0.46%	-0.10%
1.00%	-0.86%	0.33%	-0.15%	0.44%	-0.02%	1.78%	-1.03%
	0.14%		0.18%		0.42%		0.75%

METHOD #3—LOGARITHMIC LINKING

We now try the slightly more challenging Cariño method, or logarithmic linking.

Table 7–20 shows the derivation of the k factors and the key formulas used in this approach. Table 7–21 shows the application of the k factors to our attribution effects. We don't go over the formulas in detail as we have done earlier.

We show a linked attribution effect for stock selection of 1.84%, and for industry selection of −1.07%. When combined, we get 0.78%.

TABLE 7–20

Applying the Cariño Linking Methodology to Our Portfolio

		Portfolio	Index	Excess Return
$k_t = \dfrac{\ln\left(1+R_{P_t}\right) - \ln\left(1+R_{B_T}\right)}{R_{P_t} - R_{B_t}}$	Month 1	2.33%	2.18%	
	Month 2	3.18%	3.01%	
	Month 3	0.77%	0.34%	
		6.40%	5.61%	0.78%
$k = \dfrac{\ln\left(1+R_P\right) - \ln\left(1+R_B\right)}{R_P - R_B}$	k_1	0.9779		
	k_2	0.9700		
	k_3	0.9945		
	k	0.9434		
$\beta_t^{Log} = \dfrac{k_t}{k}$				Test
	beta1	1.04		−0.0016
	beta2	1.03		−0.0017
$\sum_t \beta_t^{Log}\left(Rp_t - Rb_t\right) = R_P - R$	beta3	1.05		−0.0045
				−0.78%

T A B L E   7–21

Calculating the Attribution Effects

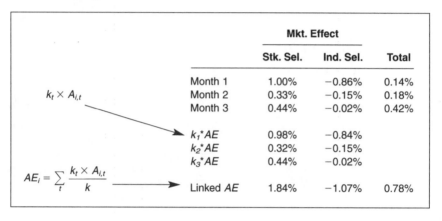

		Mkt. Effect		
		Stk. Sel.	Ind. Sel.	Total
$k_t \times A_{i,t}$	Month 1	1.00%	−0.86%	0.14%
	Month 2	0.33%	−0.15%	0.18%
	Month 3	0.44%	−0.02%	0.42%
	$k_1{}^*AE$	0.98%	−0.84%	
	$k_2{}^*AE$	0.32%	−0.15%	
	$k_3{}^*AE$	0.44%	−0.02%	
$AE_i = \sum_t \dfrac{k_t \times A_{i,t}}{k}$	Linked AE	1.84%	−1.07%	0.78%

METHOD #4—OPTIMIZED APPROACH

Now let's try the optimized approach that Jose Menchero developed. Table 7–22 shows the derivation of the beta factors, and Table 7–23 shows their application to the attribution effects.

Summing the stock selection and industry allocation effects, we get 0.78%, thus satisfying our "law."

METHOD #5—SMOOTHING

Now let's try those smoothing methods we have discussed.

Table 7–24 shows the results we obtained earlier using geometric linking of the attribution effects. At the time, we pointed out that the difference (0.75 versus 0.78) violates our third law of attribution.

We now use our smoothing method to eliminate the difference.

We start with the first method. Again, we calculate the ratio of the excess return divided by the total attribution effect (in our case, it's 0.78 ÷ 0.75, which yields 1.04). This is our *smoothing factor*. We multiply this factor by both of our effects to obtain our adjusted effects (−1.07 for sector allocation, and 1.85 for stock selection).

TABLE 7-22

Creating the Beta Factor—Optimized Approach

	Portfolio	Benchmk.	Excess Return
Month 1	2.33%	2.18%	
Month 2	3.18%	3.01%	
Month 3	0.77%	0.34%	
	6.40%	5.61%	**Excess Return** 0.78%
A term	1.0396		
alpha1 (α_1)	0.0010		
alpha2 (α_2)	0.0012		
alpha3 (α_3)	0.0030		
	0.0016		
	0.0018		
Test	0.0045		
Constraint	0.78%		
BetaOpt1	1.0407		
BetaOpt2	1.0408		
BetaOpt3	1.0426		

$$A = \frac{1}{T} \times \left[\frac{(R_p - R_B)}{(1+R_P)^{1/T} - (1+R_B)^{1/T}} \right]$$

$$\alpha_t = \left[\frac{R_P - R_B - A \sum_{j=1}^{T}\left(R_{P_J} - R_{B_J}\right)}{\sum_{j=1}^{T}\left(R_{P_J} - R_{B_J}\right)^2} \right] \times \left(R_{P_t} - R_{B_t}\right)$$

$$R_P - R_B = \sum_{j=1}^{T}\left(A + \alpha_t\right) \times \left(R_{P_t} - R_{B_T}\right)$$

$$\beta_t^{Opt} = A + \alpha_t$$

TABLE 7–23

Calculating the Attribution Effects for the
Optimized Approach

		Mkt. Effect		Excess Return
		Stk. Sel.	Ind. Sel.	
	Month 1	1.00%	−0.86%	0.14%
	Month 2	0.33%	−0.15%	0.18%
	Month 3	0.44%	−0.02%	0.42%
$Adj'\ dAE_t = \beta_t^{Opt} \times AE_t \longrightarrow$	betaOpt*AE1	1.04%	−0.89%	
	betaOpt*AE2	0.34%	−0.16%	
	betaOpt*AE3	0.46%	−0.02%	
				Total
$AE_t = \sum \beta_t^{Opt} \times AE_{i,t} \longrightarrow$	Sum'd AE	1.84%	−1.07%	0.78%

Adding them together, we find that our effects equal our excess return, thus satisfying our third law. Table 7–25 shows the details of this approach.

Table 7–26 shows our application of the second method. We begin by determining the ratios, by dividing the two linked effects by the total attribution. Next we multiply each of these ratios by the excess return. Adding the adjusted effects together, we once again obtain our excess return and also see that we have the exact same results as we obtain using the first approach.

Table 7–27 shows the results of all of our methods.

TABLE 7–24

Geometrically Linked Results

Sector Allocation Effect	−1.03%
Stock Selection Effect	1.78%
Total Attribution Effect	0.75%
Linked Excess Return	0.78%
Difference	−0.03%

T A B L E　7–25

Campisi Smoothing Method 1

Ratio of Actual to Calculated	0.78 / 0.75	1.04
Adjusted Sector Allocation Effect	1.04 × (−1.03)	−1.07
Adjusted Stock Selection Effect	1.04 × 1.78	1.85
Adjusted Total	(−1.07) + 1.85	0.78

Since we have successfully achieved our goal of completely accounting for the attribution effects using the "smoothing" approach, we're probably tempted to conclude once again that this approach is comparable to the logarithmic and optimized methods. Well, let's try one more example.

SMOOTHING AND POSSIBLE COUNTERINTUITIVE RESULTS

While there is a tremendous appeal to the smoothing methods that we have introduced above, this approach may not always yield intuitive results. They may, in a matter of speaking, provide "counterintuitive" effects that completely negate their mathematical simplicity.

I am greatly indebted to Jose Menchero who provided me with the following scenario that demonstrates the possible shortcoming of the smoothing approach.[12]

T A B L E　7–26

Campisi Smoothing Method 2

Proportion from Allocation	−1.03 / 0.75	−1.37
Proportion from Selection	1.78 / 0.75	2.37
Adjusted Allocation	−1.37 × 0.78	−1.07
Adjusted Selection	2.37 × 0.78	1.85
Adjusted Total	(−1.07) + 1.85	0.78

[12]Jose and I had a chance to discuss these approaches at a conference we both spoke at in Zurich in April, 2002, as I was wrapping up this book. He was challenged by the results I had produced and took this as an opportunity to demonstrate the shortcomings of the smoothing techniques. I'd suggest that he succeeded.

T A B L E   7–27

All Five Approaches

	Linked Attribution Effect		
	Stk. Sel.	**Ind. Sel.**	**Total**
Arithmetic	1.78%	−1.03%	0.75%
Geometric	1.78%	−1.03%	0.75%
Logarithmic	1.84%	−1.07%	0.78%
Optimized	1.84%	−1.07%	0.78%
Campisi	1.84%	−1.07%	0.78%

Table 7–28 shows the portfolio and benchmark details for two months.

Table 7–29 shows the attribution effects for the two months. We see that we've accounted for 100% of the excess return for both months. One thing that's painfully obvious: our manager isn't very good at sector selection. In the first month, when we beat the benchmark, our sector selection cost us 200 basis points. In the second month, when we fell short of the benchmark, neither our stock or sector selection helped, but once again we lost 200 basis points for sector selection.

When we apply the smoothing technique, what do we find? We find that our manager apparently obtained 200 basis points for sector selection for this two-month period, a complete reversal of what we saw in the two months individually! Since we've successfully complied with the third law, we're tempted to think that this approach has worked properly, but clearly it hasn't.

T A B L E   7–28

Portfolio and Benchmark Data for Counterintuitive Example

	Portfolio ROR	**Benchmark ROR**	**Excess Return**
Month 1	10.0%	5.1%	4.9%
Month 2	10.0%	15.0%	−5.0%
Two-Month Period	21.0%	20.87%	0.14%

T A B L E   7–29

Attribution Effects

	Stock Selection	Sector Selection	Total Effects
Month 1	6.9%	−2.0%	4.9%
Month 2	−3.0%	−2.0%	−5.0%
Smoothing	−1.87%	2.00%	0.14%
Menchero	4.53%	−4.04%	0.14%

Jose Menchero's method provides much more reasonable results, don't you agree?[13]

So while the smoothing approach makes intuitive sense and has a lot of appeal, it's subject to producing some counterintuitive results, which can be quite misleading. If you're going to use it, you have to be cautious. My recommendation: adopt either Jose Menchero's, David Cariño's, or a similar approach to link your arithmetically derived attribution effects.

CONCLUDING REMARKS

Some will argue that whether we use a multistep, mathematically robust approach like the logarithmic or optimized approach, or a much less elegant smoothing method, we are, in essence, attempting to adjust our linked attribution effects so that we satisfy our third law. Whether these terms go by the names of k factors, *beta* factors, or fudge factors, we are, in essence, filling those gaps in.

People like to see things add up, and that's our goal with these approaches: to get our multiperiod attribution effects to add up.

As the industry moves to shorter and shorter measurement periods, while maintaining the desire for relatively long reporting periods (months, quarters, years), the challenge of linking will always be with us.

---

[13]While I didn't calculate the results using David Cariño's approach, I'm confident that his method would have yielded comparative results to Jose's model, further validating the benefits of these more mathematically rigorous approaches.

Will another Ph.D. derive a mathematically elegant method to link our subperiods properly? It's highly possible.[14] But it's the end user of the system who really needs to feel comfortable with the approach used.[15]

Linking is only a problem with arithmetic attribution models. (I guess we can say that they're "linking challenged.") The geometric approach doesn't have such problems, as we show in our next chapter.

---

[14]I applaud both Frank Russell (David Cariño) and Vestek (Jose Menchero) for sharing their models. Other vendors have revealed to me that they employ similar mathematically rigorous approaches but have been reluctant to reveal the details. Hopefully they'll follow the lead of these other vendors.

[15]As noted earlier, Andrew Frongello recently offered an approach which we are not able to address here. (Frongello, 2002).

EXERCISES

1. We have a portfolio and index that have the same returns and weights for three months in a row, as shown Table 7–E-1.

   Derive the linked attribution effects using the arithmetic, geometric, logarithmic, optimized, and smoothing methods, as described above.

2. Our portfolio has had the performance results, relative to its index, and market effects for the three months shown in Tables 7–E-2 through 7–E-4.

   Find the linked attribution effects using the arithmetic, geometric, logarithmic, optimized, and smoothing methods, as described earlier.

TABLE 7-E-1

Portfolio and Index Weights and Returns, and Attribution Effects

	ROR		Weight		Market Effects	
	Portfolio	Index	Portfolio	Index	Stk. Sel.	Ind. Sel.
Equities	6.00%	5.50%	75%	70%	0.38%	0.28%
Bonds	4.00%	4.20%	20%	30%	−0.04%	−0.42%
Cash	1.00%	1.00%	5%	0%	0.0%	0.05%
Portfolio	5.35%	5.11%	100%	100%	0.34%	−0.09%

T A B L E 7–E-2

Month #1 Data

	ROR		Weight		Mkt. Effect	
	Portfolio	Index	Portfolio	Index	Stk. Sel.	Ind. Sel.
Basic Materials	3.66%	2.01%	12%	10%	0.20%	0.04%
Industrials	4.52%	2.15%	10%	13%	0.24%	-0.06%
Consumer Cyclicals	2.45%	2.12%	11%	12%	0.04%	-0.02%
Utilities	1.73%	-0.31%	11%	10%	0.22%	0.00%
Energy	-0.85%	-0.83%	10%	10%	0.00%	0.00%
Financial	2.88%	1.04%	12%	10%	0.22%	0.02%
Healthcare	0.45%	0.37%	8%	10%	0.01%	-0.01%
Technology	2.02%	1.09%	9%	8%	0.08%	0.01%
Telecom	2.17%	1.10%	9%	8%	0.10%	0.01%
Consumer Non-Cyc.	1.15%	-0.82%	8%	9%	0.16%	-0.01%
Portfolio	2.12%	0.86%	100%	100%	1.26%	
Excess ROR		1.25%				1.25%

TABLE 7-E-3

Month #2 Data

	ROR		Weight		Mkt. Effect.	
	Portfolio	Index	Portfolio	Index	Stk. Sel.	Ind. Sel.
Basic Materials	1.50%	1.35%	10%	10%	0.02%	0.00%
Industrials	1.30%	1.20%	8%	13%	0.01%	-0.06%
Consumer Cyclicals	-0.80%	-0.95%	12%	12%	0.02%	0.00%
Utilities	0.04%	0.12%	10%	10%	-0.01%	0.00%
Energy	0.08%	0.15%	10%	10%	-0.01%	0.00%
Financial	0.07%	-0.30%	12%	10%	0.04%	-0.01%
Healthcare	1.20%	1.00%	10%	10%	0.02%	0.00%
Technology	2.30%	2.45%	9%	8%	-0.01%	0.02%
Telecom	-0.80%	-0.50%	9%	8%	-0.03%	-0.01%
Consumer Non-Cyc.	2.30%	2.10%	10%	9%	0.02%	0.02%
Portfolio	0.66%	0.62%	100%	100%	0.07%	-0.03%
Excess ROR		0.04%				0.04%

155

TABLE 7-E-4

Month #3 Data

	ROR		Weight		Mkt. Effect.	
	Portfolio	Index	Portfolio	Index	Stk. Sel.	Ind. Sel.
Basic Materials	-0.80%	-0.95%	10%	10%	0.02%	0.00%
Industrials	-0.80%	-0.50%	8%	13%	-0.02%	0.03%
Consumer Cyclicals	0.04%	-0.30%	12%	12%	0.04%	0.00%
Utilities	0.07%	0.12%	10%	10%	-0.01%	0.00%
Energy	0.08%	0.15%	10%	10%	-0.01%	0.00%
Financial	1.20%	1.00%	12%	10%	0.02%	0.02%
Healthcare	1.30%	1.20%	10%	10%	0.01%	0.00%
Technology	1.50%	1.35%	9%	8%	0.01%	0.01%
Telecom	2.30%	2.10%	9%	8%	0.02%	0.02%
Consumer Non-Cyc.	2.30%	2.45%	10%	9%	-0.02%	0.02%
Portfolio	0.72%	0.55%	100%	100%	0.07%	0.10%
Excess ROR		0.17%				0.17%

Linking Across Time—
Geometric

Easy, intuitive & straightforward

Chapter 7 deals with the challenge of linking attribution effects over time for arithmetic models. Geometric attribution isn't as "linking challenged" as arithmetic. This is because of the way that the geometric approach derives excess return (see chapter 6).

In our earlier chapter, we learn that a *smoothing* of sorts must take place in order to fulfill the third law of performance attribution. A benefit of the geometric approach to attribution is that linking works out just fine—no "smoothing" is necessary, as the numbers naturally sum up properly.

Because of the different approaches to excess return, we get some differences in our results. But this is to be expected. Again, the benefit is that we can link attribution effects and have the numbers balance when we're done.

OUR BASIC EXAMPLE

We now begin with the first example that we also use in chapter 7. Recall that we have a scenario where the portfolio and index returns remain constant for three successive periods.

Table 8–1 shows the portfolio and index data as provided in chapter 7.

Now, using the process we have learned in chapter 6, we derive the geometric attribution effects for our portfolio. Table 8–2

TABLE 8–1

Portfolio and Index Weights and Returns, and Arithmetic
Attribution Effects

	ROR		Weight		Market Effects	
	Portfolio	**Index**	**Portfolio**	**Index**	**Stk. Sel.**	**Ind. Sel.**
Equities	7.00%	8.00%	70%	60%	−0.70%	0.80%
Bonds	7.50%	6.00%	20%	40%	0.30%	−1.20%
Cash	6.00%	5.00%	10%	0%	0.10%	0.50%
Portfolio	7.00%	7.20%	100%	100%	−0.30%	0.10%

shows the initial step in this process—deriving the portfolio,
benchmark, and seminotional returns. Table 8–3 picks up on this
and uses these returns to derive the respective effects.[1]

We can derive our portfolio's geometric excess return, as we
present in chapter 6:

$$\left(\frac{1 + 0.070}{1 + 0.072}\right) - 1 = -0.19\%$$

TABLE 8–2

Calculating the Returns

	ROR		Weight		Returns		
	Portfolio	**Index**	**Portfolio**	**Index**	R_p	R_b	R_s
Equities	7.00%	8.00%	70%	60%	4.90%	4.80%	5.60%
Bonds	7.50%	6.00%	20%	40%	1.50%	2.40%	1.20%
Cash	6.00%	5.00%	10%	0%	0.60%	0.00%	0.50%
Portfolio	7.00%	7.20%	100%	100%	7.00%	7.20%	7.30%

[1]It's probably important to recall that we are always geometrically linking with this approach; e.g., to derive the combined effect, we geometrically link the stock selection and industry selection effects.

T A B L E 8–3

Calculating the Effects

	R_p	R_b	R_s	Stk. Sel.	Ind. Sel.	Combined
Equities	4.90%	4.80%	5.60%	−0.652%	0.075%	−0.58%
Bonds	1.50%	2.40%	1.20%	0.280%	0.224%	0.50%
Cash	0.60%	0.00%	0.50%	0.093%	−0.205%	−0.11%
Portfolio	7.00%	7.20%	7.30%	−0.28%	0.09%	0.19%

Note that for the month, the combined attribution effect (−0.19%) equals the excess return, in compliance with our second law of attribution.

We geometrically link the three monthly returns for the portfolio and index to obtain their respective quarterly returns: 22.50% for the portfolio and 23.19% for the index. Using these results, we can apply the geometric approach to derive excess return; we obtain a result of −0.56% for the quarter.

$$ER_G = \frac{(1 + R_P)}{(1 + R_B)} - 1 = \frac{(1 + 0.2250)}{(1 + 0.2319)} - 1 = -0.56\%$$

Table 8–4 shows the linked quarterly returns, along with our excess return.

T A B L E 8–4

Monthly and Quarterly Returns; Geometric Excess Return for Quarter

Month 1		Month 2		Month 3		Quarter (linked)	
Portfolio	Index	Portfolio	Index	Portfolio	Index	Portfolio	Index
7.00%	7.20%	7.00%	7.20%	7.00%	7.20%	22.50%	23.19%
						Quarterly geometric excess return	−0.56%

TABLE 8–5

Monthly and Quarterly Attribution Effects

	Stock Selection	Industry Selection	Combined Effect
Month 1	−0.28%	0.09%	−0.19%
Month 2	−0.28%	0.09%	−0.19%
Month 3	−0.28%	0.09%	−0.19%
Quarter	−0.84%	0.28%	−0.56%

Recall that in chapter 7, using the arithmetic approach to excess return, our result is −0.69%.

Now that we have the attribution effects for each month and their linked quarterly values, we can test to see if we have achieved our goal of satisfying the third law of performance attribution.

We now link (using the standard geometric method of linking, as described in chapter 7) the quarterly attribution effects to get the combined attribution effect for the quarter.

$$(-0.0084 + 1) \times (0.0028 + 1) - 1 = -0.0056 = -0.56\%$$

And we immediately find that we've satisfied the third law: our total attribution effect *does* equal our geometric excess return.

Table 8–5 shows the monthly and quarterly effects.

OUR MORE CHALLENGING EXAMPLE

Now let's tackle the slightly more complex example from chapter 7, which involves breaking our portfolio down by industry sector and having different sets of returns for our three months.

We calculate the geometric attribution effects for each of these monthly numbers and then go through the exercise of linking them.

Tables 8–6, 8–8, and 8–10 show the calculation of the portfolio, benchmark, and seminotional returns for the three months. Tables 8–7, 8–9, and 8–11 show the calculation of the respective geometric attribution effects.

TABLE 8–6

Calculation of Returns for Month 1

	ROR		Weight		Returns		
	Portfolio	Index	Portfolio	Index	R_p	R_b	R_s
Basic Materials	3.84%	3.75%	8%	6%	0.307%	0.225%	0.300%
Industrials	−11.52%	−14.00%	14%	9%	−1.613%	−1.260%	−1.960%
Consumer Cyclicals	5.09%	5.21%	12%	11%	0.611%	0.573%	0.625%
Utilities	6.57%	6.20%	7%	10%	0.460%	0.620%	0.434%
Energy	8.30%	8.00%	15%	12%	1.245%	0.960%	1.200%
Financial	4.75%	4.50%	9%	8%	0.428%	0.360%	0.405%
Healthcare	−11.60%	−12.00%	11%	12%	−1.276%	−1.440%	−1.320%
Technology	3.50%	3.10%	6%	9%	0.210%	0.279%	0.186%
Telecom	14.06%	10.11%	10%	13%	1.406%	1.314%	1.011%
Consumer Non-Cyc.	6.85%	5.50%	8%	10%	0.548%	0.550%	0.440%
Portfolio	2.33%	2.18%	100%	100%	2.326%	2.181%	1.321%
Excess ROR		0.14%					

TABLE 8–7

Calculation of Attribution Effects for Month 1

	R_p	R_b	R_s	Stk. Sel.	Ind. Sel.
Basic Materials	0.307%	0.225%	0.300%	0.007%	0.031%
Industrials	−1.613%	−1.260%	−1.960%	0.343%	−0.792%
Consumer Cyclicals	0.611%	0.573%	0.625%	−0.014%	−0.030%
Utilities	0.460%	0.620%	0.434%	0.026%	−0.118%
Energy	1.245%	0.960%	1.200%	0.044%	0.171%
Financial	0.428%	0.360%	0.405%	0.022%	0.023%
Healthcare	−1.276%	−1.440%	−1.320%	0.043%	0.139%
Technology	0.210%	0.279%	0.186%	0.024%	−0.027%
Telecom	1.406%	1.314%	1.011%	0.390%	−0.233%
Consumer Non-Cyc.	0.548%	0.550%	0.440%	0.107%	−0.065%
Portfolio	2.326%	2.181%	1.321%	0.991%	−0.842%

TABLE 8–8

Calculation of Returns for Month 2

	ROR		Weight		Returns		
	Portfolio	Index	Portfolio	Index	R_p	R_b	R_s
Basic Materials	3.00%	2.70%	7%	6%	0.210%	0.162%	0.189%
Industrials	−5.21%	−4.80%	12%	9%	−0.625%	−0.432%	−0.576%
Consumer Cyclicals	5.13%	4.15%	11%	11%	0.564%	0.457%	0.457%
Utilities	5.11%	5.12%	9%	10%	0.460%	0.512%	0.461%
Energy	7.21%	6.90%	14%	12%	1.009%	0.828%	0.966%
Financial	−1.13%	−1.01%	8%	8%	−0.090%	−0.081%	−0.081%
Healthcare	2.50%	1.18%	11%	12%	0.275%	0.142%	0.130%
Technology	3.01%	2.99%	7%	9%	0.211%	0.269%	0.209%
Telecom	3.10%	2.61%	11%	13%	0.341%	0.339%	0.287%
Consumer Non-Cyc.	8.30%	8.10%	10%	10%	0.830%	0.810%	0.810%
Portfolio	3.18%	3.01%	100%	100%	3.185%	3.006%	2.852%
Excess ROR		0.17%					

TABLE 8–9

Calculation of Attribution Effects for Month 2

	R_p	R_b	R_s	Stk. Sel.	Ind. Sel.
Basic Materials	0.210%	0.162%	0.189%	0.020%	−0.003%
Industrials	−0.625%	−0.432%	−0.576%	−0.048%	−0.227%
Consumer Cyclicals	0.564%	0.457%	0.457%	0.105%	0.000%
Utilities	0.460%	0.512%	0.461%	−0.001%	−0.021%
Energy	1.009%	0.828%	0.966%	0.042%	0.076%
Financial	−0.090%	−0.081%	−0.081%	−0.009%	0.000%
Healthcare	0.275%	0.142%	0.130%	0.141%	0.018%
Technology	0.211%	0.269%	0.209%	0.001%	0.000%
Telecom	0.341%	0.339%	0.287%	0.052%	0.008%
Consumer Non-Cyc.	0.830%	0.810%	0.810%	0.019%	0.000%
Portfolio	3.185%	3.006%	2.852%	0.324%	−0.150%

T A B L E   8–10

Calculation of Returns for Month 3

	ROR		Weight		Returns		
	Portfolio	Index	Portfolio	Index	R_p	R_b	R_s
Basic Materials	1.30%	0.50%	8%	6%	0.104%	0.030%	0.040%
Industrials	−3.80%	−3.90%	12%	9%	−0.456%	−0.351%	−0.468%
Consumer Cyclicals	3.12%	2.10%	12%	11%	0.374%	0.231%	0.252%
Utilities	0.11%	4.10%	10%	10%	0.011%	0.410%	0.410%
Energy	0.21%	2.30%	9%	12%	0.019%	0.276%	0.207%
Financial	0.31%	3.20%	9%	8%	0.028%	0.256%	0.288%
Healthcare	2.20%	1.31%	10%	12%	0.220%	0.157%	0.131%
Technology	1.01%	0.30%	8%	9%	0.081%	0.027%	0.024%
Telecom	−0.50%	−6.10%	11%	13%	−0.055%	−0.793%	−0.671%
Consumer Non-Cyc.	4.00%	1.01%	11%	10%	0.440%	0.101%	0.111%
Portfolio	0.77%	0.34%	100%	100%	0.766%	0.344%	0.324%
Excess ROR		0.42%					

T A B L E   8–11

Calculation of Attribution Effects for Month 3

	R_p	R_b	R_s	Stk. Sel.	Ind. Sel.
Basic Materials	0.104%	0.030%	0.040%	0.064%	0.003%
Industrials	−0.456%	−0.351%	−0.468%	0.012%	−0.127%
Consumer Cyclicals	0.374%	0.231%	0.252%	0.122%	0.017%
Utilities	0.011%	0.410%	0.410%	−0.398%	0.000%
Energy	0.019%	0.276%	0.207%	−0.187%	−0.058%
Financial	0.028%	0.256%	0.288%	−0.259%	0.028%
Healthcare	0.220%	0.157%	0.131%	0.089%	−0.019%
Technology	0.081%	0.027%	0.024%	0.057%	0.000%
Telecom	−0.055%	−0.793%	−0.671%	0.614%	0.128%
Consumer Non-Cyc.	0.440%	0.101%	0.111%	0.328%	0.007%
Portfolio	0.766%	0.344%	0.324%	0.440%	−0.020%

T A B L E   8–12

Monthly and Quarterly Returns; Geometric Excess
Return for Quarter

Month 1		Month 2		Month 3		Quarter (Linked)	
Portfolio	Index	Portfolio	Index	Portfolio	Index	Portfolio	Index
2.33%	2.18%	3.18%	3.01%	0.77%	0.34%	6.39%	5.61%
				Quarterly Geometric Excess Return			0.74%

Table 8–12 shows the calculation of the quarterly returns. We
find that our geometric excess return for the quarter is 0.74%.

$$\frac{(.0639 + 1)}{(.0561 + 1)} - 1 = \frac{1.0639}{1.0561} - 1 = 0.74\%$$

Table 8–13 shows the monthly geometric attribution effects
(taken from Tables 8–7, 8–9, and 8–11), and the combined attribution effect for each of the three individual months and the quarter.

Recall that our arithmetic excess return was 0.78%. Again, because of the different approach to deriving excess return, we're ex-
pecting to have a different result.

We now link the quarterly attribution effects to get the combined attribution effect for the quarter.

$$(0.1765 + 1) \times (-0.010 + 1) - 1 = 0.74\%$$

T A B L E   8–13

Monthly and Quarterly Attribution Effects

	Stock Selection	Ind. Selection	Combined Effect
Month 1	0.991%	−0.842%	0.141%
Month 2	0.324%	−0.150%	0.177%
Month 3	0.440%	−0.020%	0.416%
Quarter	1.765%	−1.010%	0.737%

We find that we've satisfied the third law: our total attribution effect *does* equal our geometric excess return.[2]

As we first state in chapter 6, we can see that the geometric approach has yet another benefit over arithmetic: we can link over time and can account for 100% of the linked excess return without using a "smoothing" algorithm or agent.

CONCLUDING REMARKS

As Carl Bacon would point out, the appeals of geometric attribution are many. The rather simplified linking, which accounts for the entire excess return, and therefore satisfies our third law of attribution, is simply one of them.

The challenge, of course, remains with getting people used to its approach to excess return, which is probably its greatest stumbling block to acceptance. Only time will tell if the geometric approach's allure gains more converts.

---

[2]As we suggested in chapter 6, it's worthwhile to double-check our math, by not only summing the individual sector effects (to determine the overall portfolio effects), but also to derive the effects by using the formulas we present in that chapter.

EXERCISES

1. We have a portfolio and index that have the same returns and weights for three months in a row, as shown in Table 8–E–1.

   Derive the linked attribution effects using the geometric attribution approach.

2. Our portfolio has had the performance results, relative to its index, and market effects for the three months shown in Tables 8–E–2 through 8–E–4.

   Find the linked attribution effects using the geometric attribution approach to linking.

TABLE 8–E–1

Portfolio and Index Weights and Returns, and
Attribution Effects

	ROR		Weight		Market Effects	
	Portfolio	Index	Portfolio	Index	Stk. Sel.	Ind. Sel.
Equities	6.00%	5.50%	75%	70%	0.38%	0.28%
Bonds	4.00%	4.20%	20%	30%	−0.04%	−0.42%
Cash	1.00%	1.00%	5%	0%	0.0%	0.05%
Portfolio	5.35%	5.11%	100%	100%	0.34%	−0.09%

T A B L E   8–E–2

Month #1 Data

	ROR		Weight		Mkt. Effect	
	Portfolio	Index	Portfolio	Index	Stk. Sel.	Ind. Sel.
Basic Materials	3.66%	2.01%	12%	10%	0.20%	0.04%
Industrials	4.52%	2.15%	10%	13%	0.24%	−0.06%
Consumer Cyclicals	2.45%	2.12%	11%	12%	0.04%	−0.02%
Utilities	1.73%	−0.31%	11%	10%	0.22%	0.00%
Energy	−0.85%	−0.83%	10%	10%	0.00%	0.00%
Financial	2.88%	1.04%	12%	10%	0.22%	0.02%
Healthcare	0.45%	0.37%	8%	10%	0.01%	−0.01%
Technology	2.02%	1.09%	9%	8%	0.08%	0.01%
Telecom	2.17%	1.10%	9%	8%	0.10%	0.01%
Consumer Non-Cyc.	1.15%	−0.82%	8%	9%	0.16%	0.01%
Portfolio	2.12%	0.86%	100%	100%	1.26%	−0.01%
Excess ROR		1.25%				1.25%

T A B L E   8–E–3

Month #2 Data

	ROR		Weight		Mkt. Effect	
	Portfolio	Index	Portfolio	Index	Stk. Sel.	Ind. Sel.
Basic Materials	1.50%	1.35%	10%	10%	0.02%	0.00%
Industrials	1.30%	1.20%	8%	13%	0.01%	−0.06%
Consumer Cyclicals	−0.80%	−0.95%	12%	12%	0.02%	0.00%
Utilities	0.04%	0.12%	10%	10%	−0.01%	0.00%
Energy	0.08%	0.15%	10%	10%	−0.01%	0.00%
Financial	0.07%	−0.30%	12%	10%	0.04%	−0.01%
Healthcare	1.20%	1.00%	10%	10%	0.02%	0.00%
Technology	2.30%	2.45%	9%	8%	−0.01%	0.02%
Telecom	-0.80%	−0.50%	9%	8%	−0.03%	−0.01%
Consumer Non-Cyc.	2.30%	2.10%	10%	9%	0.02%	0.02%
Portfolio	0.66%	0.62%	100%	100%	0.07%	−0.03%
Excess ROR		0.04%				0.04%

T A B L E   8–E–4

Month #3 Data

	ROR		Weight		Mkt. Effect	
	Portfolio	Index	Portfolio	Index	Stk. Sel.	Ind. Sel.
Basic Materials	−0.80%	−0.95%	10%	10%	0.02%	0.00%
Industrials	−0.80%	−0.50%	8%	13%	−0.02%	0.03%
Consumer Cyclicals	0.04%	−0.30%	12%	12%	0.04%	0.00%
Utilities	0.07%	0.12%	10%	10%	−0.01%	0.00%
Energy	0.08%	0.15%	10%	10%	−0.01%	0.00%
Financial	1.20%	1.00%	12%	10%	0.02%	0.02%
Healthcare	1.30%	1.20%	10%	10%	0.01%	0.00%
Technology	1.50%	1.35%	9%	8%	0.01%	0.01%
Telecom	2.30%	2.10%	9%	8%	0.02%	0.02%
Consumer Non-Cyc.	2.30%	2.45%	10%	9%	−0.02%	0.02%
Portfolio	0.72%	0.55%	100%	100%	0.07%	0.10%
Excess ROR		0.17%				0.17%

CHAPTER 9

Other Attribution Concepts

— Monthly → Daily

— How to manage security selection
  — not that easy!!

While we've covered a fair amount of material already, there are still some other issues to consider when conducting analysis. This chapter will introduce some of these to you.

HOLDINGS-BASED VERSUS TRANSACTION-BASED ATTRIBUTION

In the industry's never-ending quest to enhance the accuracy of the information we calculate, we have two general approaches to how we look at the underlying details that go into the analysis: holdings or transaction based.

When we use the holdings-based method, we're essentially basing our returns and benchmark/portfolio differences using the starting period allocations. It's a reasonable approach for firms that (a) tend to be long-term investors, (b) don't have much intraperiod activity, and (c) don't typically rebalance within measurement periods.

This approach is contrasted with the transactions-based method, which takes into consideration the buys and sells that go on within the measurement period in order to attempt to capture as much detail and accuracy as possible.

The attribution methods that we have already introduced are of the holdings-based variety. While there are various models available for the analysis, they all presume that the starting weights are constant.

Unfortunately, very little has been written on transaction-based methodologies. Let me restate this—virtually nothing has been written, which makes it difficult to present much detail at this time.

In fact, there are varying views as to whether much benefit will be derived from going into this additional level of detail.[1] To our knowledge, even though intuitively we'd expect to see some benefit, no concrete analysis has yet been done to demonstrate fully and justify the benefits of transactions-based attribution. Nevertheless, it's an area that's gaining interest as firms want to account for virtually every basis point.

Some people appear to accomplish "transaction" attribution simply by ensuring that the returns take into consideration activity during the period. There's another view that says that at the point of any transaction, the system should ascertain the return relative to the benchmark at that point, which means real-time benchmark data has to be available—not an easy task for many of the market indices being used.

As with the case of daily versus monthly (see below), there is a cost element to consider. There will no doubt be additional cost to achieve transaction-based attribution. In the end, the user must determine whether or not this additional cost is warranted. If the firm tends to operate in a buy-and-hold style, then it very most likely won't be, as the results will probably be quite similar to holdings-based. However, if the trading volume is high and this results in changes in the asset allocation, then we would expect to see significant variances occur.

It makes intuitive sense that this additional level of analysis should yield improved results. However, until we see specific models and approaches documented, as well as supporting analytical results detailing the benefits vis-a-vis holdings-based models, there isn't much more to be said. Sorry. We will no doubt expand considerably on this topic in our second edition.

---

[1]Two of this book's reviewers, for instance, have offered me completely opposing views on the benefits of going to transaction-based methodology. Damien Laker provided the following observation: "My perception is simply that it is not a matter of research, it is simply a matter of how long people will keep tolerating attribution reports that are hundreds of basis points in error." (Laker (2002].)

DAILY VERSUS MONTHLY ATTRIBUTION

We've already discussed how moving from holdings- to transaction-based attribution is viewed as a way to enhance the accuracy of the analysis. Another way is to shorten the measurement period.

While it's not inconceivable that some firms measure attribution on a quarterly basis (using beginning-of-quarter weights and the returns for the quarter), it's unlikely that this is widespread. So we're assuming that the comparison is between monthly and daily.

The formulas we introduce in chapter 3 will suffice for this approach. The only difference is that we're using start-of-day weights and the daily returns.

In order to more effectively move to daily attribution and carry out the calculations correctly, you need to ensure the following:

- The daily portfolio data is accurate.
- The benchmark data is accurate.
- Benchmark details are available (such as industry and/or security returns and weights).

What does it mean for daily portfolio data to be accurate? It means the following:

- All positions are accurate.
- Corporate actions have been processed.
- Pricing is correct.

Since the "official books and records" are typically reflected in the custodian's position, it is appropriate to reconcile the manager's view of the client's holdings with the custodian's. This is typically done once a month, a week or two following the month's end. One immediate question should come to mind: when do we do this analysis if we're reconciling after the end of the month?

Perhaps a more precise question is, "what do we intend to do with the daily attribution information?"

I would suggest that daily attribution information should not be used for management reporting. We wouldn't expect managers to view daily attribution details. First, we know there's a question as to the accuracy of the information, given the potential for changes to be needed following the monthly reconciliation. Also, this level of frequency would serve very little purpose—the time period is simply too short to have much meaning. So the purpose of the daily attribution is for its eventual linking into monthly and/or quarterly attribution details: we measure daily but will actually report monthly (and quarterly, etc.).

If the firm does measure attribution on a daily basis, they should expect to go back and make adjustments following their monthly reconciliation, to make any necessary corrections in the underlying data. Otherwise, the results are potentially spurious.

Once we have daily attribution data, we can link it to provide results for longer periods (see chapters 7 and 8).

In deciding whether or not to employ daily attribution, the firm should ask the following questions:

1. Is the accuracy worth the increased cost?
2. Do we have the staff to support making adjustments to previously calculated (and possibly reported) results?
3. Is the increased *desired* accuracy achievable?

The final point is worth touching on. While we believe that we're going to achieve a much greater level of accuracy, can we actually accomplish this, given the "noise" that typically takes place in our portfolio and/or benchmark? There are often problems, which detract from the accuracy of our data, that sometimes cannot be easily addressed. Our perception of accuracy may therefore not be achievable.

SECURITY-LEVEL VERSUS SECTOR-LEVEL ATTRIBUTION

Our earlier examples of attribution generally looked at the portfolio from a sector perspective, to see if our overweighting or underweighting of sectors hurt or benefitted the portfolio.

We can break the portfolio down further and do the analysis at the security level. Our earlier discussion on contribution (see chapter 2) is one way to look at how securities contribute to the portfolio's return. With security-level attribution, we're refining the attribution analysis and looking to see how each security effected our excess return.

A challenge in moving to this level of analysis is the availability of the details in the benchmark. While equity index providers typically make such information available, the same cannot be said for fixed income indexes. Unless we have the constituent details, such analysis can be limited.

In doing the analysis, we have a choice: to compare security-to-security or security-to-industry. Often our portfolio will have many fewer securities in it than we find in the portfolio. For example, rather than invest in 500 securities (like the S&P 500®), the manager may choose 20–30 or so. There may be some industries in which the portfolio has no stocks at all, while others might have one, two, or three stocks.

If we do a security-to-security comparison between, say our 30-security portfolio and the S&P 500, then there will be at least 470 securities from the index that will have no representation in our portfolio, while the representation of our 30 securities will be proportionally much greater than the individual securities in the index. One might wonder what benefit such analysis will offer.

An alternative is the security-to-industry or sector approach, where we match up securities to their respective sectors. For example, let's say that we have two bank stocks in our portfolio, one (XYZ) representing 2%, and the other (ABC) 3% of the overall asset allocation. The banking sector of the index has six securities, and represents 7% of the index. How do we match these up? Table 9–1 shows the weights and returns for our securities and sector.

Since 2% of our portfolio consists of XYZ, and 3% consists of ABC, we know that 5% of the total portfolio is invested in banks. This also means that 40% of our investments in banks is represented by XYZ and the remaining 60% by ABC.[2] We see that XYZ is also held by the benchmark, but none of ABC is. Overall, the index had a return of 1.06%, meaning that our two banks outperformed the index's six. We now attempt to derive the attribution effects for these two banks.

One question should come to mind: what weight do we use for the benchmark versus the banks? Seven percent for both? This wouldn't be appropriate, would it? In fact, it would be misleading. Since XYZ represents 40% of the portfolio's banks and the manager apparently intended to underweight this sector (since only 5% of the portfolio is in banks versus 7% of the index), we should use 40% of 7% (or 2.8%) for the benchmark's weight, and 60% of 7% (the balance, or 4.2%) to represent ABC's part. The return for the benchmark will be the same.

---

[2]Since 2% divided by our total 5% invested in banks equals 40% of the banking dollars sitting with XYZ; the balance (3% divided by 5%, or 60%) is in ABC

T A B L E   9–1

Bank Stocks in Portfolio versus Banking Sector of Benchmark

	Weights		Returns	
	Portfolio	**Index**	**Portfolio**	**Index**
XYZ Bank	2.0%	.05%	1.03%	1.03%
ABC Bank	3.0%	—	1.12%	—
Banking Sector	5.0%	7.0%	1.08%	1.06%

Table 9–2 shows the attribution effects for each security as well as the overall banking sector.

We're using the Brinson-Fachler method, which we introduce in chapter 3. Our portfolio outperformed the benchmark overall, 1.50% to 1.40%. Since the banking sector underperformed the overall benchmark return (1.06% versus 1.40%), our decision to underweight this sector (5% versus 7%) was deemed to be a good thing, and the industry selection effect for the sector provided a total of 0.7 basis points. Because of the proportion that each stock represents relative to the banking sector, we are again rewarded for each of these stocks. Note that their total (0.003% and 0.004%) sums to the banking sector, which we would expect to see. Since XYZ underperformed the banking sector (1.03% versus 1.06%), we lose 0.1 basis points for stock selection. ABC, however, outperformed the sector (1.12% versus 1.06%), so we're rewarded by 0.2 basis points. Overall, we provided 0.8 basis points from our banking investment.

T A B L E   9–2

Attribution Effects

	Returns		Weights		Mkt. Effect	
	Portfolio	**Index**	**Portfolio**	**Index**	**Stk. Sel.**	**Ind. Sel.**
XYZ Bank	1.03%	1.06%	2.00%	2.80%	−0.001%	0.003%
ABC Bank	1.12%	1.06%	3.00%	4.20%	0.002%	0.004%
Banking Sector	1.08%	1.06%	5.00%	7.00%	0.001%	0.007%
Total	1.50%	1.40%				

TABLE 9–3

Security-Level Attribution Results

	ROR		Weight		Market Effect	
	Portfolio	Index	Portfolio	Index	Stk. Sel.	Ind. Sel.
XYZ Pharm.	0.25%	0.20%	10%	11%	0.005%	−0.001%
ABC Chem.	0.50%	0.51%	11%	9%	−0.001%	0.008%
Cntl Steel	1.00%		8%	0%	0.080%	−0.010%
Sin Stocks		−0.75%	0%	13%	0.000%	0.113%
Flmg Nat'l	2.00%	1.95%	12%	5%	0.006%	0.128%
Cty Stores	−0.30%	−0.31%	13%	13%	0.001%	0.000%
IT Cmptr	0.80%	0.79%	15%	13%	0.001%	0.013%
XYZ Telephone	0.60%	0.70%	9%	12%	−0.009%	−0.017%
MQZ Fin'l	−0.20%	−0.21%	13%	10%	0.001%	−0.010%
NYT Publishing	−0.50%	−0.52%	9%	14%	0.002%	0.032%
Portfolio	0.46%	0.12%	100%	100%	0.087%	0.257%

Table 9–3 shows a portfolio whose assets are broken down by security. Because our portfolio only has nine securities in it, each tied to a different industry, we are matching the securities up to their respective industry. Note that our index is invested in "sin stocks"—possibly alcohol, tobacco, and/or gambling. This particular portfolio is "sin-stock free," so we show a weight of zero percent. Likewise, our portfolio is invested in the steel industry while our benchmark isn't. Again, we're using the Brinson-Fachler model, and you can see that the model handles the case where a weight will be zero.

Our portfolio's excess return is 34 basis points (0.46 − 0.12), which completely account for with our market effects (0.087 + 0.257 = 34 basis points).

With this approach, we can see how each security contributed to the overall performance relative to our benchmark.

CONCLUSION

We are able to go beyond the approach we represent earlier in this book by enhancing the accuracy, by addressing intraday transactions, by shortening the time period from monthly to daily, and by focusing at a lower level of the portfolio by looking at individual securities.

Attribution Challenges

1) Data
2) Methodology differences
3) Interpreting the 'other' effect

As more and more firms get involved with performance attribution, we uncover challenges to its effective implementation. This chapter highlights some of these challenges.

WHAT MODEL TO USE

There are several models available to measure attribution. Some can yield conflicting results. For example, when measuring the effect of sector selection, there are two widely used approaches:

$$SSE_1 = R_{BS} \times (W_{PS} - W_{BS})$$
$$SSE_2 = (R_{BS} - R_B) \times (W_{PS} - W_{BS})$$

where

SSE = sector selection effect
R $\quad$ = return
W $\quad$ = weight
BS $\quad$ = benchmark sector
PS $\quad$ = portfolio sector
B $\quad$ = overall benchmark

In the first formula, the benchmark's return for each sector is multiplied by the difference between the portfolio's and benchmark's weights for the respective sector. If the portfolio has overweighted the sector and the return of the sector is positive, we get a positive effect.[1] If the portfolio has overweighted the sector and the return is negative, the effect will be negative.[2] Likewise, an under-weighted portfolio with a positive return will yield a negative effect.[3] Finally, if the portfolio is underweighted in the sector and the return is negative, then the effect will be positive.[4]

Here, the return is relative to zero. A positive return (i.e., greater than zero) is deemed good, while a negative return (less than zero) is deemed bad. We could also say that it's based on the absolute return: a positive number is good; a negative number is bad.

Contrast these results with how the second model works. With this approach, the sign of the sector selection is relative to the overall benchmark return. If the sector return is higher than the overall benchmark and the manager overweighted the sector, then a positive effect will result. Here, the manager is rewarded for overweighting a sector that outperformed the overall benchmark.

If, however, the manager overweighted and the sector didn't do as well as the overall benchmark, then the effect will be negative. Here, the manager is penalized because she chose to over-weight a sector that didn't contribute to the portfolio beating the benchmark, since the return is less than the benchmark.

If the manager underweighted and the sector return was greater than the overall benchmark, then the effect is negative. This is because the manager chose to place more money into a sector that didn't help the portfolio outperform the benchmark.

Finally, if the manager underweighted and the sector's return was greater than the benchmark, then the effect is positive, meaning that the decision to overweight was good, since the sector

---

[1]Recall that a positive number multiplied by a positive number yields a positive number. Here, the manager gets a positive effect because she overweighted a sector (i.e., put more of the client's money in the sector than the benchmark would have) at a time when the return is greater than zero.

[2]A negative number multiplied by a positive number yields a negative number. The manager erred because he put more money into the sector than the benchmark would have had, but the return was negative—i.e., he overweighted at a time when the return was less than zero, so he's penalized.

[3]Here, the manager is penalized for underweighting (i.e., having less of the client's money invested in the sector than the benchmark would have had) when the return was positive, thus the negative effect.

[4]A negative times a negative yields a positive. This means that the manager will be rewarded for underweighting a sector that had a negative return (i.e., the manager did a good job because she chose to underweight at a time when the return is less than zero percent).

outperformed the benchmark and thus contributed to an overall outperformance.

Table 10–1 summarizes these differences.

Although it may not be obvious, these different models can yield conflicting results. For example:

Benchmark Weight for Technology = 10%
Portfolio Weight for Technology = 12%
Benchmark's Technology ROR = 2%
Benchmark's Overall ROR = 4%.

Here, the manager overweighted the technology sector (12% versus 10%). Because the sector's return (2%) is positive, the first model yields a positive sector effect:

$$SSE_1 = 0.02 \times (0.12 - 0.10) = (0.02) \times (0.02) = 0.04\%$$

This translates as the manager being rewarded with a 4-basis-point sector selection effect, because he overweighted a positively performing sector.

However, let's see what the second model yields:

$$SSE_2 = (0.02 - 0.04) \times (0.12 - 0.10) = (-0.02) \times (+0.02)$$
$$= -0.04\%$$

The effect is the same size (4 basis points), but the sign is negative, not positive. This is because the manager is *penalized* for overweighting a sector that underperformed the overall benchmark; i.e., it didn't contribute to the portfolio's outperforming the benchmark.

T A B L E   10–1

Comparing the Industry Selection Signs of the BHB and B-F Attribution Models

	Model 1 $SSE_1 = R_{BS} \times (W_{PS} - W_{BS})$		Model 2 $SSE_2 = (R_{BS} - R_B) \times (W_{PS} - W_{BS})$	
	Sector ROR > 0	Sector ROR < 0	Sector ROR > Index ROR	Sector ROR > Index ROR
Overweight	Positive	Negative	Positive	Negative
Underweight	Negative	Positive	Negative	Positive

Let's try another example:

Benchmark Weight for Technology = 10%
Portfolio Weight for Technology = 12%
Benchmark's Technology ROR = −2%
Benchmark's Overall ROR = −4%.

The first model yields:

$$SSE_1 = (−0.02) \times (0.12 − 0.10) = (−0.02) \times (+0.02) = −0.04\%$$

Since the manager overweighted a sector with a negative return, she's penalized.

Now, the second model:

$$SSE_2 = (−0.02 − (−0.04)) \times (0.12 − 0.10) = (+0.02) \times (+0.02)$$
$$= +0.04\%$$

This model rewards the manager because she overweighted a sector that outperformed the overall benchmark. The fact that the return is negative isn't the issue; what's relevant here is the sector's relative performance to the overall benchmark, and since the return was higher, it contributed to outperformance.

Which model is preferred? It's up to you.

I personally like the second model because it's my belief that managers are supposed to outperform the benchmark; overweighting a sector that doesn't outperform the overall benchmark won't contribute to this goal, so simply having a positive number would be inappropriate. And penalizing a manager for a negative return, even when it was higher than the benchmark, seems inappropriate. But that's me. You may like the idea of the absolute approach, which is fine. Just keep in mind that the sign can flip from negative to positive, depending on which model you go with.

GETTING THE DATA

You can only do attribution if you have the respective underlying information for the benchmark. For example, if you're doing sector-level attribution, you need the returns and weights for the sectors in the benchmark; without these details, no attribution can be calculated.

Some benchmarks have these values available daily, while others only publish them monthly. And some don't ever provide these details.

The accuracy and availability of the portfolio data is also critical. Having the data but questioning its accuracy doesn't help.

Often, the intramonth numbers are unaudited, so their accuracy is questionable, and the numbers are subject to change. If you're doing daily attribution, then you'll probably want to be able to get back into the data after you've reconciled the portfolio with the custodial statement (the "official books and records for the account"), make the necessary adjustments, and then rerun the attribution.

TIME ZONE ISSUES

Another challenge that many firms face is dealing with time zone differences between their portfolios and the benchmarks they use. We first became aware of this challenge when working with clients in Switzerland who had developed quite a sophisticated attribution system. Their portfolio managers wouldn't use the system because of the significant differences in pricing between their close of business and the close for the New York City-based market indexes they used. We also are aware that managers based in Australia have this problem magnified given not only the time difference but also the international date line.

How do we handle this problem? One possibility is to price the index at the same close as their local market. This would require getting the constituent data into the system and using the same pricing. The problems are several: first, getting the data; as we discuss in chapter 4, this isn't always possible. Second, what happens when we try to compare ourselves with the index's real closing value? It won't work.

Okay, maybe we reprice our portfolio at the closing prices for the index? This is a problem, too, since our managers didn't have knowledge of changing prices after they retired for the day and thus weren't afforded the opportunity to make adjustments, if necessary, to their portfolio.

How about requiring the use of only locally priced indexes? This can work in some cases, but clearly not others. And, in some cases, it may not even be possible.

The solution? It's not clear, but one thing is clear: we need to figure out a way to deal with this.

The 'other' term in
THIS THING CALLED INTERACTION *the B−F(BHB formulas)*

As we discuss in chapters 3 and 4, we may have something left over from our arithmetic[5] attribution models. We may call this "other," "interaction," or any number of other terms. They all mean the same thing: an unaccounted-for attribution effect. Or, perhaps more correctly, an effect that can't be easily traced to its source.

What is interaction? Peter Higgs and Stephen Goode defined the interaction effect as "the benefit to returns at the fund level by being overweighted in the asset class with the relatively better active return. Of course, the interaction effect can be negative. This would occur if we were overweighted in the asset class with the less attractive active return, or underweighted in the asset class with the better active return." They also say it "measures the effect on return of the interaction of the active asset allocation and stock selection decisions." They go on to say that "the interaction effect is often aggregated with stock selection by the agencies that conduct surveys on fund performance," and reference surveys by Towers, Perrin, Forster, and Crosby to support this statement.[6] I'd suggest that this doesn't fully explain what the effect means; it shows what the numbers might be, but does it help us really grasp the meaning?

Some people suggest that it's the result of the sector allocation and security selection working together—the "interaction" of these two effects. For example, "Interaction is a defined factor in early (classical) attribution models. It represents the combined impact (or cross product) of stock and asset selection."[7] Or it represents how well you overweighted sectors where you have positive stock selection.

Steve Campisi's suggests in his article[8] that "the small, unexplained residual[9] is the selection effect," while Tim Lord says, "Analysis of residuals often reveals useful information about the

[5]Geometric models don't have this problem.
[6]Higgs [1993], page 78.
[7]EIPC [2001], page 3.
[8]Campisi [2000], page 15.
[9]I have attempted not to use the term "residue" or "residual," so as not to confuse it with the amount that's typically unaccounted for with arithmetic linking (see chapter 7). However, it's clear that others use this term to refer to what we call "other" or "interaction."

input data as well as the effectiveness of the model."[10] He goes on to say that the residual return "typically includes effects due to convexity, inaccurate data or model mis-specification."

Damien Laker wrote an article for *The Journal of Performance Measurement* on this very topic, where he argued that there's value in this effect.[11]

On the other hand, I've heard Carl Bacon make a very good argument in opposition to it. He has essentially suggested that we typically might have someone in the firm who's responsible for stock selection, another person responsible for asset allocation, but who's responsible for interaction? Of course, Carl is a big fan of the geometric approach that doesn't experience interaction, and he uses this as just another reason why firms should not use arithmetic attribution.[12]

Some folks look at the presence of an interaction effect as a flaw in the model.

The bottom line: it's controversial; there is no consensus on this. I think that Steve Campisi and Tim Lord's agreement as to what can be contributing to a fixed income portfolio's residue makes sense; their models account for a lot of what's going on, but not everything. Perhaps this is the right attitude. Our models aren't perfect. This "other" term picks up what we can't identify. Ideally, it's small.

CONCLUDING REMARKS

As we spend more and more time on attribution, we discover more challenges. And these also increase as we attempt to enhance the precision of our analysis.

Attribution, unlike any other aspect of performance measurement, has a lot of controversy. Even though it's been around for quite some time, there's still not enough definition. While we've attempted to establish some "laws" within this text, much more is needed. And, while we may agree that we won't agree on everything, there are certain aspects of this science that we should all come to grips with.

---

[10]Lord [1997], page 50.

[11]Laker [2000]. If it's true that there *should* be an interaction effect, then we're inclined to ask if its absence from the geometric approach indicates a shortcoming. I'll let Carl Bacon address this one.

[12]He also has suggested to me that for those who want to see an interaction effect, one can be built into a geometric model.

CHAPTER 11

Using the Information

fd EIPC document (European, Investment Performance Committee) Content: p 186 ff

NOW THAT YOU HAVE THE RESULTS, WHAT DO YOU DO WITH THEM?

The whole point of having analytical tools is to help do analysis, right? In our case, we want to use the results of exercising our attribution model to analyze the sources of our return—to help us better understand where the return came from—why the portfolio manager beat (or failed to beat) the benchmark.

Since we have different audiences looking at the numbers, we might expect to have different needs. Let's start with the portfolio manager.

PORTFOLIO MANAGERS AND ATTRIBUTION ANALYSIS

Portfolio managers typically look for ways to enhance their clients' returns relative to the benchmark they're being measured against. So they will engage in various investment strategies. We discussed some of these in chapter 1 when we talked about asset allocation and stock picking. Part of the attribution analysis will obviously be used to validate the success of those strategies. For example:

- Did my overweighting of the technology sector help?
- Did my underweighting of pharmaceutical help?

- Was I successful in picking better banking stocks than were in the benchmark?
- Was my overweighting of Japan and underweighting of Singapore advantageous?

The analysis can also help us analyze the input we got from others. Often, portfolio managers rely upon security analysts to give them advice. In some cases, these are from other firms; perhaps the brokers they're dealing with. In other cases, they may be internal resources. Wouldn't it be helpful to ascertain whether the advice worked as promised? Attribution analysis can help here. So if an analyst suggested a particular stock, we can measure the success of this recommendation. If someone suggested underweighting a sector because of bad economic times ahead, we can determine if this was a good move.

We may reward people based upon their recommendations. In the case of internal resources, we can track our analysts over time and determine whether or not they're doing the job we hired them for. For outside analysts, we can determine whether or not the price we're paying for their advice is worth it.[1]

PLAN SPONSORS AND CONSULTANTS, AND HOW TO USE THE INFORMATION

Larger pension funds typically utilize many portfolio managers to handle various parts of the plans' asset allocation strategies. More and more, we find these plans (and/or their consultants) asking for attribution details. But what do (or should) the recipients do with the information?

Tim Lord suggested that "a consultant or plan sponsor may be primarily interested in what attribution can reveal about the performance results of a particular asset allocation strategy or management style." And "a portfolio manager may want to know how a duration bet or sector allocation decision contributes to portfolio return."[2]

---

[1]Often, in the case of outside research, we "pay" for the advice by way of commission soft dollars—trade flow that we direct their way. In some cases, the research has a specific price tag associated with it; in other cases, we're expected to do a certain amount (albeit, perhaps not defined in detail) of business with the firm providing the research in return for the advice.
[2]Lord [1997], pages 45–46.

Before they even get the information, they need to know what they might be getting. As we discuss in chapter 3, there are various models available to conduct the attribution analysis. Depending on which ones the manager chooses to use, they may get conflicting results. It's very important that plan sponsors and consultants understand the various models and their advantages and disadvantages. When asking for attribution results, they need to ask what model(s) the manager will employ. They can then determine if there are any hidden biases within the model that might favor or hinder the manager's presentation.

It's also possible that different managers will use different models. So to compare the results from one manager to another could prove a challenge. An alternative would be for the plan sponsor or consultant either to have the managers use the same model(s) or to calculate the information themselves. While this approach may be costly and time-consuming, it would ensure that you're looking at the information the same way.

Given that our first law of attribution calls for the model to match the investment style of the manager, it's important for the plan sponsor to recognize that the model she uses might conflict with the manager's investment style.

In the end, we're more likely to see different models being used. So being aware of the underpinnings of the models will help in analyzing the manager.

A Top-Down Manager—What to Expect

If our manager uses a top-down approach, we'd expect the model to present attribution statistics for asset allocation and stock selection, at a minimum. If our manager is a global manager, than we'd expect global attributes to be reported on, too.

When we look at the results, we should never focus on a single time period to draw a conclusion. For example, let's say our top-down manager reports that his 2% excess return came as follows: 2.10% from stock picking, and −0.10% from asset allocation. You'd be quick to be concerned perhaps that his alleged asset allocation skills are coming up short. So do you fire the manager? Well, the manager beat the benchmark, right? That's a good thing. But he beat it not by asset allocation skills, but by stock picking. Should this concern you?

If the manager touts his asset allocation strengths but the numbers don't prove this out for a single period, it only serves as a single snapshot in time. Monitor the situation.

Figure 11–1 might help explain how you might do this.

If we were looking at May's report, we'd see that asset allocation cost us 54 basis points while we picked up 108 basis points from stock selection. We might want to criticize the manager for poor asset allocation decisions. Then we get the June report and see that it's gotten worse, with the asset allocation costing us 102 basis points while gaining 196 basis points from stock selection. Rather than rushing to judgement, let's wait and see what else happens. Sure enough, our manager's asset allocation decisions turned around, and for the year, were positive 9 out of the 12 months. So how much do we fault the manager? Do we expect the manager to be perfect? Given that the manager has consistently beaten the benchmark, the source generally favors asset allocation, although stock picking has helped, too.

Now contrast this situation with our second portfolio, shown in Figure 11–2. Here we get our first glimpse of a problem in April, when our top-down manager lost 48 basis points to asset allocation. Not wanting to get alarmed, we do the right thing and monitor. The

F I G U R E   11–1

Sample Asset Allocation Graph

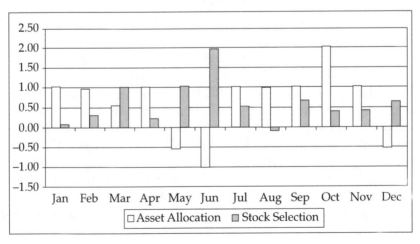

following month, we are told that we lost 54 basis points to the manager's asset allocation decisions. Continuing through the year, we continue to see poor marks for asset allocation. I'd suggest that this pattern should warrant attention and a review of polices and the manager's investment process. What's happened to contribute to this downturn? While we often see positive marks for stock picking, we would expect to see a more superior set of numbers for asset allocation—not seeing this should be a cause for a review.

Misusing the Information

Let's say that we got the report shown in Figure 11–2 from our bottom-up manager. Should we be alarmed?

Given that the manager uses a bottom-up approach, she probably doesn't spend much time doing asset allocation; rather, her investment decisions are based on which stocks to include in the benchmark. _Any_ effect from asset allocation is coincidental, right? It's not directly attributable to actual asset allocation decisions. To attempt to judge the manager on these numbers would probably be inappropriate. This is an example of why it's important that we use a model that fulfills the first law of attribution.

L Fit the managers style.

FIGURE   11–2

A Deteriorating Asset Allocation Portfolio

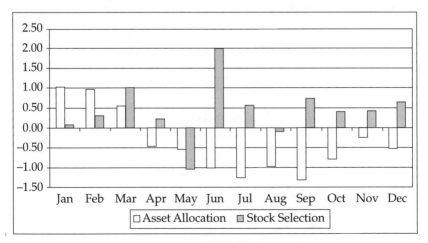

LOOKING AT THE UNINTENDED CONSEQUENCES

As we show in chapter 1, it's appropriate not only to satisfy the first law, but also to consider looking at the portfolio from different viewpoints.

Even though the manager may not use industry selection as part of the investment decision process, he might find it useful to see what effect the allocation differences have on the return. Likewise, market capitalization, P/E ratio, and other metrics can be used to *slice and dice* the portfolio and provide the manager with insights into the various sources of return—intended and unintended. Figure 11–3 graphically depicts the idea of looking at the relationship between the portfolio and the benchmark from different angles and perspectives.

GOING BEYOND THE OBVIOUS

Attribution analysis can involve some extensive digging, not unlike what an investigator does when looking into a crime scene. Just as investigators are taught not to limit their conclusions to the obvious, attribution analysts can delve in further or view the results from different perspectives to uncover some interesting points.

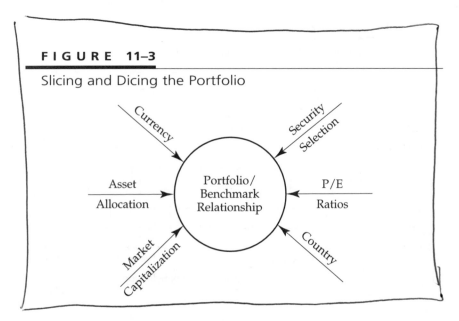

FIGURE   11–3

Slicing and Dicing the Portfolio

T A B L E   11–1

Portfolio/Benchmark by Country

	France	Germany
Benchmark weight	50%	50%
Portfolio weight	53%	47%
Benchmark return	6.0%	6.7%

Let's take this sample international portfolio to show how this might be done.[3] Table 11–1 shows the benchmark that our portfolio is measured against—a very simple one in which our assets are split evenly across two countries.

Let's assume that there is no effect from currency. Our benchmark's return can be derived quite easily, by multiplying the weight by the return, yielding a return of 6.35%.

$$ROR_B = \sum W_B \times R_B = (0.50 \times 0.06) + (0.50 \times 0.067) = 6.35\%$$

While we don't show the details, the portfolio return for this period is 6.45%. We therefore want to account for this 10-basis-point excess return (6.45% − 6.35%).

As we can see from this table, the manager overweighted France by 3%, which is offset by an underweighting of Germany by 3%. The effect from country allocation can be derived quite simply:[4]

$$CntryAlloc'n = \sum (W_P - W_B) \times R_B$$
$$= [(0.53 - 0.50) \times 6.0] + [(0.47 - 0.50) \times 6.7]$$
$$= 0.03 \times 6.0 + (-0.03) \times 6.7 = -0.021\%$$

We can conclude that we lost 2 basis points because of our country allocation decisions.

Since, as stated earlier, there is no effect from currency, our only other contributor to the 10-basis-point excess return must, by

[3]Terhaar [2000].

[4]Please note that we are using the industry allocation formula from the Brinson, Hood, Beebower model (see chapter 3).

T A B L E   11–2

Returns and Effects from Country View

Benchmark return	6.35%
Portfolio return	6.45%
Excess return	0.10%
Country allocation	−0.02%
Stock selection	0.12%

default, be stock selection, in order to fulfill the second rule of attribution (accounting for 100% of the excess return). Thus we have the results in Table 11–2.

Seems reasonable, right? We need to account for 10 basis points; we have −2 basis points from country selection, so our stock selection *must* come from 12 basis points. Well, let's see.

Let's now look at the portfolio by industry (see Table 11–3). Again, our allocation is quite simple, limiting the distribution to only two industries. Our benchmark return is computed, as we would expect, to be 6.35%.

$$ROR_B = \sum W_B \times R_B = (.40 \times 0.0475) + (.60 \times 0.0742) = 6.35\%$$

Our manager chose to overweight autos by 2% and underweight computers by 2%. When we calculate the industry allocation effect, we see that we lost 5 basis points from our allocation decisions.

T A B L E   11–3

Portfolio/Benchmark by Industry

	Autos	Computers
Benchmark weight	40%	60%
Portfolio weight	42%	58%
Benchmark return	4.75%	7.42%

T A B L E   11–4

Returns and Effects from Industry View

Benchmark return	6.35%
Portfolio return	6.45%
Excess return	0.10%
Industry allocation	−0.05%
Stock selection	0.15%

$$IndAlloc'n = \sum (W_P - W_B) \times R_B = [(0.42 - 0.40) \times 4.75]$$
$$+ [(0.58 - 0.60) \times 7.42]$$
$$= 0.02 \times 4.75 + (-0.02) \times 7.42 = -0.0534\%$$

Table 11–4, like Table 11–2, applies our industry allocation effect and concludes that the we have to have gotten 15 basis points from stock selection in order to account for our 10 basis points of excess return.

We can delve a little deeper into our portfolio and see how the returns break down by industry within each country. Table 11–5 shows the returns while Table 11–6 shows the allocation of the benchmark assets.

Using the combination of weights and returns, we can validate our benchmark's return:

$$R_B = \sum W_{B_i} \times R_{B_i}$$
$$= (.04 \times .25) + (.08 \times .25) + (.06 \times .15) + (.07 \times .35) = 6.35\%$$

T A B L E   11–5

Returns Broken Down Further

	France	Germany	Industry
Autos	4.00%	6.00%	4.75%
Computers	8.00%	7.00%	7.42%
Country	6.00%	6.70%	6.35%

TABLE 11–6

Weights Broken Down Further

	France	Germany	Industry
Autos	25%	15%	40%
Computers	25%	35%	60%
Country	50%	50%	100%

Now let's look at the manager's allocation of assets. Table 11–7 shows the allocation by percent, while Table 11–8 shows the manager's active bets.[5]

We can apply the manager's weights to the benchmark's returns to determine the allocation effect, which we've done in Table 11–9.

Thus we are able to account for 100% of the portfolio's return by looking at the combination of country and security allocation. Therefore we obtained no benefit from stock selection.

This says a few things. First, we can't be too quick to judge, even though the evidence may suggest something. Second, where we have multiple factors working simultaneously, a simple attribution model (for example, one that only looks at country or industry) might not suffice.

[5]We're showing the net weight differences (i.e., the portfolio weight minus the benchmark weight), which reflects the manager's decision to *overweight* or *underweight* by a certain amount.

TABLE 11–7

The Portfolio Manager's Allocation

	France	Germany	Industry
Autos	22%	20%	42%
Computers	31%	27%	58%
Country	53%	47%	

T A B L E   11–8

The Portfolio Manager's Active Bets

	France	Germany	Industry
Autos	−3%	+5%	+2%
Computers	+6%	−8%	−2%
Country	+3%	−3%	

THE EIPC'S RECOMMENDATIONS

The European Investment Performance Committee (EIPC) is working on guidelines for users of attribution analysis. This document is still in draft, but I'd like to summarize some of their key points.[6]

They state at the beginning that, "Return Attribution is a technique used to analyse [sic][7] the sources of excess returns of a portfolio against its benchmark into the active decisions of the investment management process."[8] This is consistent with what we describe in chapter 1.

"The following list of questions have been provided to assist the user of attribution analysis to gain the maximum value from the presentation."[9]

[6]EIPC [2001].
[7]This is a European document and so uses the British version of English.
[8]EIPC [2001], page 1.
[9]Ibid.

T A B L E   11–9

Applying Manager Weights and Benchmark Returns

	France	Germany	Industry
Autos	(22% × 4.0) + (20% × 6.0)		2.08%
Computers	(31% × 8.0) + (27% × 7.0)		+4.37%
Country	3.36% + 3.09%		6.45%

You'll find that these questions agree with some of our laws and other comments discussed above.

"1. Does the attribution model follow the investment decision process of the asset manager?"[10]

Clearly, this is in line with our first law of attribution.

"2. Is the benchmark appropriate to the investment strategy?

3. Has the benchmark or investment style changed during the period of analysis?

4. Has the attribution model changed during the period of analysis?"[11]

This is an interesting point, isn't it? Our research suggests that many plan sponsors don't even know what model is being used, let alone that it may have changed. Good suggestion, I'd say.

"5. Does the model generate an unexplained performance residual?"[12]

This goes back to our earlier discussion on interaction and residuals (chapter 10). As you'll see, they distinguish between "residuals" and "interaction." They offer a comment with this question: "Residuals may bring into question the quality of the analysis and bring into doubt any conclusions that may be drawn from it."[13] Continuing with this point, they ask:

"6. If a residual is generated is it:

    i. Shown separately as a residual, balancing, timing or transaction item?

    ii. Ignored?

    iii. Allocated between other factors?"[14]

They suggest that "it is not a good practice to ignore residuals."[15] The challenge, of course, is understanding what they mean.

"7. Is the interaction specifically calculated?"[16]

As promised above, here's where they draw a distinction between "residual" and "interaction." They say that interaction "represents the combined impact (or cross product) of stock and asset selection."[17] I would suggest that the distinction is if it's

[10]Ibid, page 2.
[11]Ibid.
[12]Ibid.
[13]Ibid.
[14]Ibid, page 3.
[15]Ibid.
[16]Ibid.
[17]Ibid.

defined as part of the model, it's interaction; if it's unexplained, it's residual.

"8. If Interaction is calculated, is it:
   i. Shown separately?
   ii. Ignored?
   iii. Allocated to another factor?
   iv. Allocated to other factors consistently?

   9. Is the attribution model arithmetic or geometric (multiplicative)?

   10. If the model used is arithmetic, has a smoothing algorithm been used to allocate residuals to other factors?"[18]

We, of course, discuss this point in chapter 7.

   "11. Is the attribution based on buy/hold snap shorts or are transactions included?

   12. How are weights of the elements of attribution defined?"[19]

They discuss this further by pointing out that "only weight measures that ensure the weighted sum of returns is equal to the portfolio return will be accurate." Our "contribution rule #1" discusses this very point (see chapter 2).

   "13. Is the model genuinely multi-currency? What FX rates are used for the portfolio and benchmark?

   14. How are asset allocation decisions outside of the benchmark treated?

   15. Are transaction costs included within stock selection or asset allocation, or are transaction costs treated as a separate attributable factor?

   16. Are the returns to be attributed to net or gross of fees."[20]

This is an interesting point that we don't touch upon: whether we're dealing with net- or gross-of-fee returns. A positively performing account can become underperforming after the fees are removed.

   "17. Is cash specifically included in the attribution? If so has a cash benchmark been determined?

   18. Does the attribution include gearing or leverage and if so is the attribution based on all cash analysis?"[21]

---

[18]Ibid, pages 3–4.
[19]Ibid, page 4.
[20]Ibid, pages 4–5.
[21]Ibid, page 5. "Gearing" and "leverage" are synonymous.

"19. Are derivatives included in the analysis? If yes, how?

20. Is the attribution derived directly from the asset manager's records? Is there is a difference between the return used in the attribution and the formal portfolio return?"[22]

Here, the point is simply that returns and attribution analysis may be coming from multiple sources, so the returns represented may be different. This is a valid point to be aware of.

"21. Which methodology is used to calculate portfolio returns?

22. If the attribution base is not a benchmark, what is the rationale for this choice?"[23]

They point out that attribution "may be performed against composites, representative accounts, model funds, carve-outs, and peer groups."[24] We have not addressed attribution against these other groupings, and it's unclear what the analysis would look like. Clearly, it runs contrary to our view that attribution is against a benchmark and measures the active decisions of the manager. This doesn't mean that such other analysis doesn't have merit, but there clearly have to be different perspectives applied.

These 22 questions are quite good and should be considered when looking at attribution reports.

CONCLUSION

If we give someone a box of carpenter tools without any instructions, they may attempt to hammer a nail in with a screwdriver— or worse. Likewise, if we give a portfolio manager or plan sponsor client attribution analysis tools without instructions, they, too, might use them improperly.

Analysis, like carpentry, requires skill. Having the tools is only part of the process. We also need to know how to use them.

Hopefully, we've demonstrated some of the key issues involved in using this important information.

[22]Ibid, pages 5–6.
[23]Ibid, page 6.
[24]Ibid.

CHAPTER 12

Searching for an Attribution System

[handwritten notes:]

1) Great step by step procedure

2) List of Vendors : ◦ Performance measured,
Technology supplement, volume 6

When it comes to considering an attribution system, like much in life, there's good news and bad news.

First, the good news: there are plenty of systems available (with new ones being introduced on a fairly regular basis). While this wasn't the case a few years ago, it is today. More and more vendors have come on the scene, many performance measurement software vendors who previously addressed other aspects of performance have added attribution, and even portfolio accounting vendors are now including attribution models in their systems.

Okay, so what's the bad news? Such searches are much more complex than what you would do for virtually any other kind of software.

THE TYPICAL SOFTWARE SEARCH

Looking for software systems is pretty much "old hat." Most people use fairly standard, boilerplate models to find systems. What's the process?

Step 1. Figure Out What You Need: Conduct a *Needs Analysis* or *Needs Assessment*

This means sitting down with the key people and asking what they need or want. One important question, of course, is "who are the key people?" Who's going to use the system? For attribution, we're probably talking about your performance measurement team, portfolio managers, and marketing. Also, your compliance department might have interest, too. Don't forget to ask the IT (Information Technology) group for input.

Your marketing (or client service) folks should be able to tell you what your clients expect. Will they be satisfied with the same reporting, or do any require additional information that you need to be able to satisfy?

If there's an existing system in place, your job is much easier: what do they like about this system; what's lacking; what don't they like? What do they like about the vendor, and what don't they like? You can come up with a "gap analysis," showing the differences between what you have and what you want or need.

And let's speak a moment about "needs" and "wants." There *is* a difference. I may *want* a 5000-square-foot home with six bedrooms, a billiard room, a sun room, an indoor pool, etc. What I *need is* a roof over my head, running water, air conditioning, and heat. Making the distinction can be very helpful with any search. Granted, what the boss says she "wants" may be interpreted as "needs" by others, but distinguishing between the two may prove helpful. Also, to assign priorities to these is helpful as well. Things you *must* have weigh a whole lot more than things you'd *like to* have.

If there is no attribution system in place, your job is a bit more challenging, since the people you're talking to might not have much of an idea of what they want. Imagine asking someone whose never driven, ridden in, or possibly even seen a car what they want. That's what we have here.

Whoever is asking the questions needs to know a fair amount about attribution. A key is to ask the right questions. Otherwise, you won't have the answers and information that's critically important.

Step 2. Identify Vendor Candidates

Who are you going to consider buying from? Assembling a list of vendor candidates can be a challenge. While there are no formal directories available, there are occasionally lists published and other resources you might turn to.[1]

---

[1]See, for example, *The Journal of Performance Measurement*, Technology Supplement, Volume 6.

You may want to have a consultant assist you, not only with this step, but with other aspects of the search. Someone who's familiar with the vendors will not only identify candidates but also will be able to help identify firms that you don't want to consider.

You shouldn't contact all the vendors simply to show that you did an exhaustive search. Why waste someone's time if you're not going to consider them anyway? Rule out vendors that you know or strongly believe won't have what you need, operate on the wrong system, have a bad reputation, or cost too much (or too little)?

Step 3. Create a Request for Proposal

We're big fans of RFPs. They're effective tools in a few respects:

1. They clearly identify what you're looking for.
2. They let the vendor know what you want and allow them to tell you what they can do.
3. They are effective in comparing the vendors who respond.
4. They serve as documented evidence of the vendors' claims. Whoever you pick has to live up to what they said they can do.

The information you obtained from the first step will serve as input to the RFP.

Ideally, you should ask *closed-ended questions.* These are questions that people can answer "yes" or "no" to, or provide a single response to. For example, "do you support the Brinson, Hood, Beebower model?" should have a "yes" or "no" response.

The alternative is *open-ended questions.* While you will no doubt have some of these, try to keep them to a minimum. A question like, "what attribution models do you support?" is an open-ended question and might get a response like "the Brinson, Hood, Beebower model."

Why do I prefer closed-ended questions? Because your analysis is easier, you have fewer words to read, and comparing vendors is much easier. Also, the vendors you respond to will have an easier time responding to closed-ended questions.

Much of your RFP will deal with the functional side of the system—meeting your particular needs. You should also ask questions about the technology. Perhaps you have certain technological constraints. For example, your IT department might mandate that all systems run on a particular type of computer, be of the client-server variety, or use a particular database. If these constraints are hard and fast, then it's critical that you know the technology of the vendor. In fact, you should probably assess some of this even before you bother to send the RFP out—why ask a vendor to fill out a lot of paper if, in the end, you'll reject them because their platform doesn't conform to your requirements?

Ask questions about the vendor themselves. For example:

- How long have you been in business?
- What's the ownership of your company (public, private, partnership)?
- What financial information can you provide us?
- How old is your system?
- How many full-time employees do you have?
- How many software developers do you have?
- How many client service people do you have?
- Where are your offices?
- Do you have a user group?
- How many new clients have you added in the past year?
- How many clients did you lose in the past year?
- How many clients are currently in production on your system?
- What's the process to get enhancements made to your system?
- How many new releases do you offer per year?

Make sure you ask for a list of representative clients. You'll want to contact some of these. But also do some homework and identify some clients that might not be on their list. Chances are that the vendor will give you names of clients that will say good things about them; getting other names might provide you with a more objective assessment of their client relationships.

When the RFP is completed, review it and validate that it meets your objectives. Then distribute it to the vendors you identified in step 2.

When you distribute the RFP, ask that it be returned by a set date. Ideally, ask that it be sent in an electronic format (perhaps e-mailed to you). This will allow you to pull the data together into a single report, for effective comparison or analysis in step 4.

Step 4. Review RFP Responses and Select Vendors for the Next Step

In step 2, you look at the universe of vendors and reduce the list, based upon what you and/or the consultant you brought in know about them. Now's your chance to further reduce the list. As you review the RFPs, identify the candidates that look like they best suit your needs.

You may want to bring the responses into a spreadsheet so you can easily compare one vendor with another.

Once you identify your vendors for the next round, proceed to step 5.

Step 5. Vendor Analysis

Now you'll want to see the system. Ideally, have the vendors come in and make presentations. You'll probably want to visit the vendor at their site, too, to get a good feel for the organization.

This is your chance to "kick the tires." To try the system out. To see how it operates. Essentially, to take it for a test drive.

If you can justify it, by your size and the eventual cost of the purchase, provide the vendor with some of your own data and see how the system behaves. Again, if you're a big enough firm, ask to have a copy installed that you can try out for a couple of months. You'll probably only want to do this with the final one to three vendors. Otherwise, it will take forever for you to find a system.

A couple of things that I like to look for:

- How easy is the system to operate? Has the system been designed so that it works in an intuitive manner (that is, you can pretty much figure out how to work it without a lot of training), or does it require extensive technical skills and/or training?

I've seen some systems that are *so* flexible that they're quite a challenge to use. There has to be a balance between flexibility and ease of use. Sometimes in gaining flexibility you pay for it in complexity![2]

■ Can I break the system?

I try to force bugs to occur, and often they do. You can do this by trying to do something that wouldn't be expected. See how the system behaves. See if the developer took into consideration all possibilities—even illogical ones.

As part of your vendor analysis, reach out to some of the vendor's clients. Ask them for report cards on the vendor. How has the system worked? Has the vendor kept their promises? How did the installation go? Any regrets? Any surprises? Would the client do the same thing knowing what they know today?

As noted earlier, don't limit this checking to the references the vendor gave you. Ask your consultant for names or do some research on your own. The client that your vendor forgot to list might have some interesting revelations for you.

If time and your budget permits, visit one or two of the vendor's clients. See how they use the system.

If you have any time constraints, you'll want to know if the vendor has room in their schedule to meet your needs. Ask what your responsibilities will be in the installation. If an interface is required (as it most likely will be) to your portfolio accounting or performance measurement system, find out if similar interfaces have been developed. If not, who will be responsible for developing it—what will your role be?

Obviously, you'll want to know what the system is going to cost. Vendors base cost on various criteria, for example:

■ assets under management
■ number of portfolios
■ number of users

If the system doesn't meet 100% of your needs, you need to decide if you want to pay for enhancements. For that matter, will

---

[2]While this statement may appear to be a contradiction, it isn't. Some vendors implement the flexibility by using rather low-level tools—perhaps close to a spreadsheet level of presentation. This requires the user to be pretty sophisticated in knowing how to use the tools. To carry our carpentry metaphor a bit further, what if, in buying a home, you were presented with a bunch of lumber, nails, etc. and told that you have the flexibility of building it how you choose? Probably not. Even though this, like many of my metaphors, is a stretch, it hopefully conveys what I mean by the above.

the vendor be willing to make the enhancements? These are important questions to pursue.

Often, vendors use a combination of these. Once your vendor has enough information about you, they should be able to tell you what the system will cost. What's the initial cost, will this be recurring, what costs will there be for implementation, and what are their consulting and custom developing costs?

Step 6. Picking the Vendor

By now you should have enough information to narrow the field down to one vendor. Once you do, the negotiations begin. Get a copy of their standard contract. Review it. Pass it by legal. See if it's acceptable to you.

What are your requirements? What do you want in writing? How will payment be made? Upon certain milestones being met? Will there be any penalty clauses added for vendor failure to make dates or deliver functionality?

SO, WHAT'S DIFFERENT FOR THE ATTRIBUTION SEARCH?

While there are many common aspects to a search for an attribution system and other software needs, there are some unique aspects to attribution that require additional work. Work that *you* need to do.

For example, you have to answer some questions:

1. What model do you want?

As we've shown, there are various ways to do attribution. If you agree to abide by the first law of attribution, then you need a model to meet your investment style. So what's that model? Does one exist, or do you need to develop one? Do you need more than one model? Do any of your clients require that you report in a particular model? These are key questions that you need to answer.

2. What linking methodology do you want?

As we discussed, there are various ways to link subperiods. Do you require or prefer one? If not, you'll at least want to know how the vendor does this to make sure that you're comfortable with it.

3. Daily or monthly?

While there may be appeal to doing daily attribution, there's a cost to pay in ensuring the accuracy of the underlying data. Can you afford it? Is it achievable?

4. Holdings- or transaction-based?

Do you have a preference? Is the perceived accuracy of a transaction-based approach justifiable or applicable to you?

5. What investment groups are you measuring?

If you're doing domestic equity, your requirements should be fairly easy to define. Global equity provides a bit more of a challenge. Domestic fixed income, as we showed, is complex and not well developed. Global fixed income will be even more complex. Figure this stuff out early on.

6. Geometric or arithmetic?

Have I convinced you that there are differences? Do the mathematical benefits of the geometric approach outweigh the lack of intuitive appeal of the arithmetic? Will your clients understand geometric? Do you need both?

In order to find an attribution system, you *must* get these (and probably more) questions addressed early on. If you're going to buy a car, you don't usually wait until you're inside the dealer's showroom to figure out if you want a van, a truck, or a two-seat sports car, right? You at least narrow the field down a bit, right? You need to do the same thing here.

WHAT ABOUT SPREADSHEETS?

Oh, the appeal of spreadsheets.

I look at spreadsheets as that little voice in your ear that's tempting you. "Come on, use me. I'm sitting right here on your computer. It won't cost you any more money. Use me. It's easy and fun. Use me."

Please, please, please. Do not give in to that voice. That voice is the voice of Satan, who is tempting you to make a huge mistake. Spreadsheets are not systems. They're for *ad hoc* use.

To build an attribution system on spreadsheets would violate what I would like to call attribution law #4—don't use spreadsheets for your attribution system![3]

Why not? Because spreadsheets are:

- time-consuming
- error prone
- manually intensive
- cumbersome
- not databases

If you want to do some *ad hoc* analysis, fine, use a spreadsheet. Construct a model and enjoy yourself. But if you plan to do sophisticated and continuous attribution analysis, please buy a system! Don't violate this law and commit this sin. You'll surely be sorry (and may be condemned to hell on earth!).

If your boss asks "can't we do attribution in a spreadsheet," answer "no!" While the appearance of an ability is surely there, it won't work. You would have to rekey all of the data or build some fairly sophisticated transfer programs that won't do the trick in the long run. Plus, there's no easy way to generate reports or to provide the data to others. So, the answer is "no." Buy a system!

I like spreadsheets for analysis to help you figure out what would work best for you—to try out various models—to test ideas. But don't build an attribution system with spreadsheets.

Here's a question for you: have I been too subtle, or do you get my point?

CONCLUDING REMARKS

Looking for an attribution system? Great! There are plenty to choose from, and you'll benefit from what they can offer.

But don't think you can go about it like you did for that trading or portfolio accounting system you bought last year. Your work will be harder. You have to do more thinking. You have to make some pretty serious decisions up front. But, if you do your homework and spend the time thinking as you should, you'll be successful! Good luck!

---

[3]Actually, it should be a global law: don't use spreadsheets for systems.

CHAPTER 13

The Future of Attribution

KF — Whol is the BM?

Linking

FI ettribution

"*Most of our future lies ahead.*"
Denny Crum

A book on such an important topic as performance attribution has to say something about its future. After all, attribution is dynamic, growing in importance, and will evolve considerably as we learn more about it and demand more from it.

ATTRIBUTION STANDARDS

Our industry might be tempted to create standards for attribution, just as we've done for performance measurement[1] and performance presentation.[2] But should we do such a thing?

I've had the opportunity to discuss this issue with many people and have found no one who supports the notion. When asked if he'd support such standards, Gary Brinson, who codeveloped two mathematical models for attribution[3] said, "I would be very opposed to that. I think when you talk about attribution you are talking about diagnosis."[4]

---

[1]See BAI [1968], ICAA [1971].
[2]See AIMR [1993, 1997, 2000, 2001].
[3]See Brinson [1985 and 1986]. Also, see chapter 3, Brinson, Hood, Beebower and Brinson-Fachler methods.
[4]Brinson [1999], page 32.

209

In early meetings with members of The Performance Measurement Forum,[5] we had occasions to discuss this idea. While there appeared to be some appeal to the idea, no one really seemed to feel that standards were needed. Rather, a series of "dos and don'ts" was preferred. But recently, we've seen changes in opinions begin to occur amongst this group's members.

I propose[6] and support the incorporation of a recommendation (and eventual requirement) to include attribution statistics as part of a manager's presentation in accordance with the Global Investment Performance Standards (GIPS®).[7] Just as these standards have evolved from providing rates of return to the requirement and/or recommendation for benchmarks, dispersion measures, and risk measures, attribution statistics seems to be the logical next step.

Such a requirement would mean that a manager must show to a prospect the *sources* of her returns. It's one thing to say that "I'm a great stock picker" or that "we pride ourselves in the analysis of economic data and industry analysis to develop optimum asset allocation strategies." But these statements are mere words without the numbers to back them up, and attribution analysis provides such numbers.

I highly encourage managers to include this analysis with their presentations. Hopefully, the IPC (Investment Performance Council) will see the wisdom of including this as a formal recommendation and eventual requirement of GIPS.

TRUE FIXED INCOME ATTRIBUTION

In chapter 4, we discuss the challenge of providing effective attribution tools for the fixed income manager. This will change. We will see the growth of various models that I refer to as "true" fixed income attribution models. These will not be equity models that have been recast as ones for fixed income, but models that adhere to our three laws and represent the investment approach of the fixed income manager.

[5]The Performance Measurement Forum is an international membership group of performance measurement professionals.
[6]I proposed this at the fall meeting of the Investment Performance Council in London on September 11, 2001.
[7]See AIMR [1999].

MORE LINKING RESEARCH

Chapters 6 and 7 addressed the linking of subperiod attribution effects to derive statistics for longer periods. We will surely see more such models developed. While the simpler "smoothing" method seems to offer a much easier approach to this difficult process, we showed how counterintuitive results can arise. We are also aware that some vendors who have methods similar to the logarithmic and optimized approaches have yet to present their logic to the public. Hopefully, these other vendors will make the details known.

But, given the need and desire for greater precision, we will see more models. Hopefully, some will be simpler, granted at the cost of mathematical elegance, and easier to comprehend.

ATTRIBUTION FOR PASSIVE MANAGERS

The models we discuss in this book, actually most of the book, deal with analysis of *active* portfolio managers: managers who are free to vary their portfolios' structures relative to the benchmarks in an attempt to gain superior performance results. The flip side of this is *passive* or *index* managers, who attempt to mirror or match the index. These managers want to achieve the identical performance results of the index.

Given that these managers make no real active decisions, is there a basis for attribution analysis? I believe that there is because it is rare that the manager can actually mirror the performance results of the index. First, in order to acquire the securities in the index, a cost must be paid: trade commission and transaction fees. This cost doesn't exist within an index. If an index provider decides to take two securities out and replace them with two new ones, it's a simple change, not unlike a magician pulling a hare from a hat. But the portfolio manager who is charged with matching the index must now sell two securities, often at the cost of commissions, plus a possible trade execution cost called market impact, and must simultaneously make purchases of the two new securities.

Likewise, the manager must periodically execute trades to keep the portfolio in balance, and he must make purchases when new cash comes in, or sales to generate cash when money is being withdrawn.

Given this, there will be an "excess return." Granted, it's probably not a positive number, but there will be a difference between the manager's return and the index. Wouldn't it be nice to provide some analysis to demonstrate the source(s) of the difference? Thus we'd have attribution analysis for the passive manager.

Nothing, to my knowledge, has yet been formally developed to provide for this, but I suspect that we'll see this in the future.

ATTRIBUTION FOR HEDGE FUND MANAGERS

The hedge fund industry has grown significantly. But with all its growth, we have very little to offer when it comes to performance measurement. There are no agreed-upon standards as to how to measure or report performance. But there seems to be a growing cry for such standardization.

And once we have it, we'll no doubt have the development of better attribution analysis, too.

A key part of attribution analysis is pairing up the active decisions of the manager with the appropriate component(s) of the benchmark, so that we can determine whether these decisions were correct. For example, in chapter 3 we compare our portfolio with the benchmark using industry. Our decisions are either to underweight or overweight the sectors, or to pick different securities. The analysis would not be possible unless we can match up our decisions with the part(s) of the benchmark we are varying against.

The same requirement has to exist with hedge fund attribution. The challenge is that pairing up such decisions vis-a-vis the benchmark may be difficult. If we short a security, then we should be able to match the security to either the same security in the benchmark, or at least to the industry. But what if we invest in futures or other derivatives that don't have a clearly defined match with the benchmark? Someone needs to tie these together. But once we do this, then the analysis should be relatively straightforward.

Again, this is a relatively new area within the hedge fund world, and more analysis and development is needed.

DOCUMENTED MODELS FOR TRANSACTION-BASED AND SECURITY-LEVEL ATTRIBUTION

In chapter 9, I present these two concepts. At the time, I mentioned that little has been written about these. And yet we're seeing increased attention, from both portfolio managers and software developers, to provide these levels of analysis.

Without documented research and mathematical models, it's difficult for much development to happen and needs to be satisfied. We can expect more work to come and much more discussion to occur.

MULTIFACTOR MODELS

In chapter 3, I touch very briefly on the idea of multifactor models. In these cases, the model looks at several factors simultaneously. In chapter 11, we show how this might be done when we look at country and industry together.

Granted, for many of us, we're just beginning to figure out the differences between the two-factor models. Many professionals don't fully appreciate how different models can generate vastly different results.

But if portfolio managers consider multiple criteria when they look to beat a benchmark, our analysis should present results that report on all of this criteria. And we can expect to see more work in this regard.

Most of the development work that has taken place to date deals with the two-factor approach. We should expect to see more interest in and work done on multifactor attribution in the future. For now, most people are satisfied with the single-factor approach.

TRANSACTION COST MEASUREMENT AND ATTRIBUTION

Damien Laker broached the subject of incorporating transaction costs into attribution analysis.[8] Transaction cost measurement (this goes by other terms, such as trade cost measurement) is a topic that the industry has been wrestling with for close to 20 years. Damien's perceptive analysis, which suggests a link between it and attribution, suggests that there's going to be a linking of various analytical tools, giving us the opportunity to leverage our analysis even further. I choose not to address this topic here, partly because of space and time. However, we can expect others to look to see how

[8]Laker [2001].

these two disciplines can be brought together to provide additional value to the portfolio management and trading processes.

CONCLUDING REMARKS

"Attribution, while not new, is an evolving process."[9]

I began this book with this quote from Gary Brinson. In the time I've been involved with performance measurement, I've seen some of this evolution. The saying, "the more we learn, the more we realize we don't know," is truly applicable to the subject of attribution.

As we move more deeply into it, the more new questions arise. And, with these questions, we need answers. And unfortunately, often these answers are slow to come. But trust me, the answers will come. And along with these answers, more questions.

I've seen a demand for attribution from people who had no idea what they were asking for. Just like the gadget-craving neighbor of yours who has to have the latest technological tool, even if he doesn't know what it's for, we have investment folks who want attribution because they heard about it and figure it's something they need. Well, the interest is much appreciated. And hopefully, it will generate the need for deeper awareness into what exactly attribution *is*, and what it can *do* for them.

Attribution provides us with tools. And just like the carpenter whose tool chests has items in it that didn't exist 20, 40, or 100 years ago, we'll see the performance measurement professional with new and evolving tools.

Knowing what they're intended for, what the resulting numbers mean, how to interpret them, and how to use these tools, is critical.

I hope that this book has provided you with some insights into the power of attribution analysis. This project has been a fun, although long, process. I hope it benefits you and your organization.

---

[9]Brinson [1986], page 40.

Exercise Solutions

CHAPTER 2—CONTRIBUTION

1. Table 2–S–1 shows the contributions of individual securities.

T A B L E   2–S–1

Contributions Using the Basic Formula

Security	ROR	Weight	Contribution
A	2.50%	13%	0.33%
B	−1.50%	9%	−0.14%
C	3.00%	12%	0.36%
D	0.44%	7%	0.03%
E	−2.00%	12%	−0.24%
F	1.63%	11%	0.18%
G	0.55%	8%	0.04%
H	0.90%	9%	0.08%
I	0.30%	8%	0.02%
J	−1.03%	11%	−0.11%

2. Table 2–S–2 includes the cash flows and their impact on all the individual security contributions. The overall return remains the same: 0.56%.

T A B L E   2–S–2

Contributions Using the Enhanced Formula

Security	ROR	BMV	CF Amt.	CF Day	CF Wt.	Wtd Flow	Contribution
A	2.50%	$13,000					0.32%
B	−1.50%	9,000	(5,000)	7	0.81	(4,032.26)	−0.07%
C	3.00%	12,000					0.36%
D	0.44%	7,000					0.03%
E	−2.00%	12,000					−0.24%
F	1.63%	11,000					0.18%
G	0.55%	8,000					0.04%
H	0.90%	9,000					0.08%
I	0.30%	8,000					0.02%
J	−1.03%	11,000	5,000	2	0.97	4,838.71	−0.16%
Portfolio		100,000				806.45	0.56%

CHAPTER 3—EQUITY ATTRIBUTION

Brinson, Hood, Beebower Model:

T A B L E   3–S-1

Quadrant Values

	Rate of Return		Weights		Quadrants			
	Portfolio	Index	Portfolio	Index	I	II	III	IV
Industrials	2.00%	3.00%	40.00%	25.00%	0.750%	1.200%	0.500%	0.800%
Transportation	3.00%	2.00%	20.00%	25.00%	0.500%	0.400%	0.750%	0.600%
Utilities	4.00%	5.00%	30.00%	25.00%	1.250%	1.500%	1.000%	1.200%
Financials	5.00%	4.00%	10.00%	25.00%	1.000%	0.400%	1.250%	0.500%
Total	3.10%	3.50%			3.500%	3.500%	3.500%	3.100%

T A B L E 3–S-2

Attribution Effects

	Quadrants				Effects			
	I	II	III	IV	Timing	Stk. Sel.	Other	Total
Industrials	0.750%	1.200%	0.500%	0.800%	0.450%	−0.250%	−0.150%	0.050%
Transportation	0.500%	0.400%	0.750%	0.600%	−0.100%	0.250%	−0.050%	0.100%
Utilities	1.250%	1.500%	1.000%	1.200%	0.250%	−0.250%	−0.050%	−0.050%
Financials	1.000%	0.400%	1.250%	0.500%	−0.600%	0.250%	−0.150%	−0.500%
Total	3.500%	3.500%	3.500%	3.100%	0.000%	0.000%	−0.400%	−0.400%

BHB Variation Model:

T A B L E 3–S-3

Attribution Effects Using the Variation of the BHB Model

	Rate of Return		Weights			
	Portfolio	Index	Portfolio	Index	Stk. Sel.	Ind. Sel.
Industrials	2.00%	3.00%	40.00%	25.00%	−0.400%	0.450%
Transportation	3.00%	2.00%	20.00%	25.00%	0.200%	−0.100%
Utilities	4.00%	5.00%	30.00%	25.00%	−0.300%	0.250%
Financials	5.00%	4.00%	10.00%	25.00%	0.100%	−0.600%
Total	3.10%	3.50%			−0.400%	0.000%

218

Exercise Solutions

Brinson-Fachler Model:

T A B L E   3–S–4

Attribution Effects Using the Brinson-Fachler Model

	Rate of Return		Weights		Effects	
	Portfolio	Index	Portfolio	Index	Stk. Sel.	Ind. Sel.
Industrials	2.00%	3.00%	40.00%	25.00%	−0.400%	−0.075%
Transportation	3.00%	2.00%	20.00%	25.00%	0.200%	0.075%
Utilities	4.00%	5.00%	30.00%	25.00%	−0.300%	0.075%
Financials	5.00%	4.00%	10.00%	25.00%	0.100%	−0.075%
Total	3.10%	3.50%			−0.400%	0.000%

CHAPTER 4—FIXED INCOME

Excess Return = Portfolio Return minus Benchmark Return
$$= 0.11 - 0.32 = -0.21.$$

T A B L E   4–S–1

Treasury Change Values for Benchmark and Portfolio

Sector	Portfolio Duration	Portfolio Treasury Change	Portfolio Treasury Effect	Benchmark Duration	Benchmark Treasury Change	Benchmark Treasury Effect
Treasuries	7.55	1.68	−12.85	7.55	1.68	−9.19
Mortgage-Backed	4.30	1.78	−7.52	4.30	1.78	−3.32
A-Rated Corp.	6.03	1.74	−10.31	6.03	1.74	−10.49
High-Yield	4.94	1.83	−9.54	4.94	1.83	−8.26
Emerging Markets	3.59	1.67	−11.59	3.59	1.67	−6.00

T A B L E   4–S–2

Formulas for Campisi's Returns

Return	Formula	Portfolio Effects
Income Effect	Coupon ÷ Price	$\dfrac{7.11}{\$98.11} = 7.21\%$
Treasury Effect	(−Duration) × Treasury Change	$(-5.55) \times (1.67) = -9.70$
Spread Effect	(−Duration) × Average Spread Change	$(-5.55) \times (-0.47) = 2.60$
Selection Effect	Total Return − Income Effect − Treasury Effect − Spread Effect	0.00

T A B L E   4–S–3

Attribution Effects for the Benchmark (Note: some rounding is taking place.)

	Returns	Income Effect	Treasury Effect	Spread Effect	Spread Change	Selection Effect
Portfolio	0.11	7.21	−9.70	2.60	−0.47	0.00
Benchmark	0.32	7.01	−8.64	1.27	−0.18	0.67
Difference	−0.21	0.19	−1.06	1.32	−0.29	−0.38

Note: The data I use for this example is totally fictitious. If it appears nonsensical, this is probably the reason. The exercise's purpose isn't to evaluate a real portfolio but rather to demonstrate how the math works. If you get these results, then you did the math correctly.

CHAPTER 5—GLOBAL ATTRIBUTION

$$Unhedged = R_i + E_{\$,i}$$

1.

T A B L E 5–S–1

Unhedged Returns

	Local Currency Return (R_i)	Exchange Rate Return ($E_{\$,i}$)	Unhedged Market Returns
Germany	5.00%	2.00%	7.00%
U.K.	11.00%	−2.50%	8.50%
Japan	9.00%	−1.50%	7.50%

$$Hedged = R_i + F_{\$,i} = R_i + (C_\$ - C_i)$$

T A B L E 5–S–2

Hedged Returns

	Local Currency Return (R_i)	3-Month Euro Currency Rate ($\$$)	3-Month Euro Currency Rate (C_i)	Hedged Market Returns
Germany	5.00%	8.00%	4.50%	8.50%
U.K.	11.00%	8.00%	9.00%	10.00%
Japan	9.00%	8.00%	7.50%	9.50%

$$Cross\text{-}Hedged = R_i + F_{j,i} + E_{\$,i} = R_i + (C_j - C_i) + E_{\$,i}$$

T A B L E   5–S–3

Cross-Hedged Returns (Hedging Using an Intermediate Country)

	Local Currency Return (R_i)	3-Month Euro Currency Rate (C_i) (into currency)	3-Month Euro Currency Rate (C_i) (from currency)	Exchange Rate Return ($E_{\$,i}$) (into currency)	Cross-Hedged Market Returns
		Cross-Hedging into Japan			
Germany	5.00%	7.50%	4.50%	−1.50%	10.00%
U.K.	11.00%	7.50%	9.00%	−1.50%	7.00%
		Cross-Hedging into Germany			
U.K.	11.00%	4.50%	9.00%	2.00%	4.00%
Japan	9.00%	4.50%	7.50%	2.00%	7.50%
		Cross-Hedging into the U.K.			
Germany	5.00%	9.00%	4.50%	−2.50%	11.50%
Japan	9.00%	9.00%	7.50%	−2.50%	12.50%

2.

T A B L E   5–S–4

Portfolio and Benchmark Returns

	Market-Weighted Risk Premium (Market Return)	Currency-Weighted Cash Return ($) (Currency Return)	U.S. Dollar Returns
Portfolio Return	1.22%	7.38%	8.60%
Benchmark Return	0.98%	7.25%	8.23%
Excess Return	0.24%	0.13%	0.37%

TABLE 5-S-5

Market Quadrant Values

	Quadrant (M)I		Quadrant (M)II		Quadrant (M)III		Quadrant (M)IV	
	Passive Weights	Passive Returns	Active Weights	Passive Returns	Passive Weights	Active Returns	Active Weights	Active Returns
Germany	35%	2.00%	50%	2.00%	35%	2.10%	50%	2.10%
U.K.	15%	−0.50%	20%	−0.50%	15%	−0.45%	20%	−0.45%
Japan	20%	1.00%	15%	1.00%	20%	1.10%	15%	1.10%
U.S.	30%	0.50%	15%	0.50%	30%	0.60%	15%	0.60%
Total		0.98%		1.13%		1.07%		1.22%

TABLE 5-S-6

Currency Quadrant Values

	Quadrant (C)I		Quadrant (C)II		Quadrant (C)III		Quadrant (C)IV	
	Passive Weights	Passive Returns	Active Weights	Passive Returns	Passive Weights	Active Returns	Active Weights	Active Returns
Germany	25%	6.00%	20%	6.00%	25%	5.90%	20%	5.90%
U.K.	25%	8.00%	35%	8.00%	25%	8.05%	35%	8.05%
Japan	25%	7.50%	15%	7.50%	25%	7.45%	15%	7.45%
U.S.	25%	7.50%	30%	7.50%	25%	7.55%	30%	7.55%
Total		7.25%		7.38%		7.24%		7.38%

TABLE 5-S-7

Market and Currency Attribution Effects

Market Selection	(M)II − (M)I	0.15%
Security Selection	(M)III − (M)I	0.09%
Other Market Effects	(M)IV − (M)III − (M)II + (M)I	0.00%
Total Market Effects	Sum [also, (M)IV − (M)I]	0.24%
Currency Selection	(C)II − (C)I	0.12%
Hedge Selection	(C)III − (C)I	−0.01%
Other Currency Effects	(C)IV − (C)III − (C)II + (C)I	0.02%
Total Currency Effects	Sum [also, (C)IV − (C)I]	0.13%
Total Effects		0.37%

CHAPTER 6—GEOMETRIC ATTRIBUTION

T A B L E   6–S-1

Calculating the Returns

	Rate of Return		Weights		Returns		
	Portfolio	Index	Portfolio	Index	R_p	R_b	R_s
Industrials	2.00%	3.00%	40.00%	25.00%	0.800%	0.750%	1.200%
Transportation	3.00%	2.00%	20.00%	25.00%	0.600%	0.500%	0.400%
Utilities	4.00%	5.00%	30.00%	25.00%	1.200%	1.250%	1.500%
Financials	5.00%	4.00%	10.00%	25.00%	0.500%	1.000%	0.400%
Total	3.10%	3.50%			3.100%	3.500%	3.500%

Portfolio excess return $= -0.386\%$

$$\frac{1 + .031}{1 + 0.35} - 1 = -0.386\%$$

T A B L E   6–S-1

Calculating the Effects

	R_p	R_b	R_s	Stk. Sel.	Asset Alloc.
Industrials	0.800%	0.750%	1.200%	−0.386%	−0.072%
Transportation	0.600%	0.500%	0.400%	0.193%	0.072%
Utilities	1.200%	1.250%	1.500%	−0.290%	0.072%
Financials	0.500%	1.000%	0.400%	0.097%	−0.072%
Total	3.100%	3.500%	3.500%	−0.386%	0.000%

As we can see, the total effects (−0.386%) equal the excess return.

CHAPTER 7—ARITHMETIC LINKING

1. The monthly excess return is 0.24%. When we sum the month's attribution effects (0.34% and −0.09%), we obtain our excess return.[1] Since our three months have the same data, we can geometrically link the returns to determine our quarterly portfolio and benchmark results, which are found to be 16.92% and 16.13%, respectively. Our quarterly excess return is 0.80%. This is what we will attempt to link our attribution effects to arrive at.

Arithmetic Linking

Arithmetically linking our effects yields the results in Table 7–S–1.

T A B L E   7–S-1

Applying Arithmetic Linking to Our First Exercise

	Month 1		Month 2		Month 3		Quarter	
	Stk. Sel.	Ind. Sel.	Stk. Sel.	Ind. Sel.	Stk. Sel.	Ind. Sel.	Stk. Sel.	Ind. Sel.
Equities	0.38%	0.28%	0.38%	0.28%	0.38%	0.28%	1.13%	0.83%
Bonds	−0.04%	−0.42%	−0.04%	−0.42%	−0.04%	−0.42%	−0.12%	−1.26%
Cash	0.0%	0.05%	0.0%	0.05%	0.0%	0.05%	0.00%	0.15%
Portfolio	0.34%	−0.09%	0.34%	−0.09%	0.34%	−0.09%	1.01%	−0.28%
Net Effects		0.24%		0.24%		0.24%		0.72%

The sum of our arithmetic linked attribution effects is 0.72%, falling 8 basis points short of our goal of 0.80% (to match our linked excess return).

---

[1] Unfortunately, we're experiencing some rounding, which belies the reality of our addition. Our stock selection is actually 0.335%; our industry selection is −0.95%; adding these gives us the 0.240% we need to satisfy our first law of attribution.

Geometric Linking

The geometric linking results are in Table 7–S–2 which follows.

T A B L E   7–S-2

Applying Geometric Linking to Our First Exercise

	Month 1		Month 2		Month 3		Quarter	
	Stk. Sel.	Ind. Sel.	Stk. Sel.	Ind. Sel.	Stk. Sel.	Ind. Sel.	Stk. Sel.	Ind. Sel.
Equities	0.38%	0.28%	0.38%	0.28%	0.38%	0.28%	1.13%	0.83%
Bonds	−0.04%	−0.42%	−0.04%	−0.42%	−0.04%	−0.42%	−0.12%	−1.25%
Cash	0.0%	0.05%	0.0%	0.05%	0.0%	0.05%	0.00%	0.15%
Portfolio	0.34%	−0.09%	0.34%	−0.09%	0.34%	−0.09%	1.01%	−0.28%
Net Effects		0.24%		0.24%		0.24%		0.72%

Again, the sum of our linked effects (as a result of geometric linking) yields 0.72%, which falls short of our goal of 0.80%.

Logarithmic Linking

The next two tables show the results of applying Cariño's logarithmic linking methodology.

T A B L E 7-S-3

Applying the Cariño Linking Methodology to Our
First Exercise

		Portfolio	Index	Excess Return
Month 1		5.35%	5.11%	
Month 2		5.35%	5.11%	
Month 3		5.35%	5.11%	
		16.92%	16.13%	0.80%

$$k_t = \frac{\ln\left(1 + R_{P_t}\right) - \ln\left(1 + R_{B_T}\right)}{R_{P_t} - R_{B_t}}$$

$$k = \frac{\ln\left(1 + R_p\right) - \ln\left(1 + R_B\right)}{R_p - R_B}$$

k_1	0.9503
k_2	0.9503
k_3	0.9503
K	0.8582

$$\beta_t^{Log} = \frac{k_t}{k}$$

$$\sum_t \beta_t^{Log}\left(Rp_t - Rb_t\right)$$

		Test
beta1	1.11	0.0027
beta2	1.11	0.0027
beta3	1.11	0.0027
		0.80%

T A B L E   7-S-4

Calculating the Logarithmic Attribution Effects to Our
First Exercise

		Mkt. Effect		
		Stk. Sel.	Ind. Sel.	Total
	Month 1	0.34%	−0.09%	0.24%
$k_t \times A_{i,t}$	Month 2	0.34%	−0.09%	0.24%
	Month 3	0.34%	−0.09%	0.24%
	$k_1{}^*AE$	0.32%	−0.09%	
	$k_2{}^*AE$	0.32%	−0.09%	
	$k_3{}^*AE$	0.32%	−0.09%	
$AE_i = \sum_t \dfrac{k_t \times A_{i,t}}{k}$	Linked AE	1.11%	−0.32%	0.80%

We see that our linked stock selection for the period is 1.11%, and
our linked industry selection is −0.32%; summing these yields the
0.80% we had hoped for.

Optimized Approach

Applying the Menchero optimized approach yields the results that we show in the next two tables.

TABLE 7-S-5

Creating the Beta Factor—Optimized Approach—for Our First Exercise

			Portfolio	Index	Excess Return
$$A = \frac{1}{T} \times \left[\frac{\left(R_P - R_B\right)}{\left(1 + R_P\right)^{1/T} - \left(1 + R_B\right)^{1/T}} \right]$$		Month 1	5.35%	5.11%	
		Month 2	5.35%	5.11%	
		Month 3	5.35%	5.11%	
			16.92%	16.13%	0.80%
		A term	1.1073		
$$\alpha_t = \left[\frac{R_P - R_B - A \sum_{j=1}^{T}\left(R_{P_J} - R_{B_J}\right)}{\sum_{j=1}^{T}\left(R_{P_J} - R_{B_J}\right)^2} \right] \times \left(R_{P_t} - R_{B_t}\right)$$		alpha1 (α_1)	0.0000		
		alpha2 (α_2)	0.0000		
		alpha3 (α_3)	0.0000		
		Test	0.0027		
			0.0027		
			0.0027		
$$R_P - R_B = \sum_{j=1}^{T}\left(A + \alpha_t\right) \times \left(R_{P_t} - R_{B_T}\right)$$		Constraint	0.80%		
$$\beta_t^{Opt} = A + \alpha_t$$		betaOpt1	1.1073		
		betaOpt2	1.1073		
		betaOpt3	1.1073		

T A B L E   7-S-6

Calculating the Optimized Attribution Effects for Our
First Exercise

| | | Mkt. Effect | | |
		Stk. Sel.	Ind. Sel.	Total
	Month 1	0.34%	−0.09%	0.24%
	Month 2	0.34%	−0.09%	0.24%
	Month 3	0.34%	−0.09%	0.24%
$Adj'\ dAE_t = \beta_t^{Opt} \times AE_t \longrightarrow$	betaOpt*AE1	0.37%	−0.11%	
	betaOpt*AE2	0.37%	−0.11%	
	betaOpt*AE3	0.37%	−0.11%	
$AE_t = \sum \beta_t^{Opt} \times AE_t \longrightarrow$	Sum'd AE	1.11%	−0.32%	0.80%

We obtain results identical to Cariño: linked stock selection effect of 1.11%, industry selection effect of −0.32%, and the desired summed attribution effect of 0.80%

Smoothing Techniques

We have two methods for smoothing. But first, let's look at the basic geometrically linked results we obtained earlier.

T A B L E   7-S-7

Geometrically Linked Results for Exercise #1

Industry Selection Effect	−0.28%
Stock Selection Effect	1.01%
Total Attribution Effect	0.72%
Linked Excess Return	0.80%
Difference	−0.08%

T A B L E   7-S-8

Applying Smoothing Method 1 to Exercise #1

Ratio of Actual to Calculated	0.80 / 0.72	1.11
Adjusted Industry Selection Effect	1.11 × (−0.28)	−0.32%
Adjusted Stock Selection Effect	1.11 × 1.01	1.12%
Adjusted Total	−0.32 + 1.12	0.80%

T A B L E   7-S-9

Applying Smoothing Method 2 to Exercise #1

Proportion from Ind. Selection	(−0.28) / (0.72)	−0.40%
Proportion from Stk. Selection	1.01 / 0.72	1.40%
Adjusted Ind. Selection	−0.40 × 0.80	−0.32%
Adjusted Selection	1.40 × 0.80	1.12%
Adjusted Total		0.80%

We obtain identical results, which are comparable to what we saw with the logarithmic and optimized methods, with industry selection of −0.32% and industry selection of 1.12%, yielding a combined effect of 0.80% which matches our excess return. The very slight difference is attributable to rounding.

2. We begin by deriving the quarterly portfolio and index return, as well as the quarter's excess return.

T A B L E   7-S-10

Calculating the Quarterly Returns and Excess Return

Month 1		Month 2		Month 3		Quarter (linked)	
Portfolio	Index	Portfolio	Index	Portfolio	Index	Portfolio	Index
2.12%	0.86%	0.66%	0.62%	0.72%	0.55%	3.53%	2.04%
				Quarterly Excess Return			1.49%

Method #1—Arithmetic Linking

We'll add the individual effects of the three months for these sectors, which is shown in Table 7–S–11.

T A B L E   7-S-11

Applying Arithmetic Linking to Our Portfolio

Month 1		Month 2		Month 3		Quarter	
Stk. Sel.	Ind. Sel.	Stk. Sel.	Ind. Sel.	Stk. Sel.	Ind. Sel.	Stk. Sel.	Ind. Sel.
0.20%	0.04%	0.02%	0.00%	0.02%	0.00%	0.23%	0.04%
0.24%	−0.06%	0.01%	−0.06%	−0.02%	0.03%	0.22%	−0.10%
0.04%	−0.02%	0.02%	0.00%	0.04%	0.00%	0.09%	−0.02%
0.22%	0.00%	−0.01%	0.00%	−0.01%	0.00%	0.21%	0.00%
0.00%	0.00%	−0.01%	0.00%	−0.01%	0.00%	−0.02%	0.00%
0.22%	0.02%	0.04%	−0.01%	0.02%	0.02%	0.29%	0.03%
0.01%	−0.01%	0.02%	0.00%	0.01%	0.00%	0.04%	−0.01%
0.08%	0.01%	−0.01%	0.02%	0.01%	0.01%	0.08%	0.05%
0.10%	0.01%	−0.03%	−0.01%	0.02%	0.02%	0.09%	0.03%
0.16%	0.01%	0.02%	0.02%	−0.02%	0.02%	0.16%	0.05%
1.26%	−0.01%	0.07%	−0.03%	0.07%	0.10%	1.40%	0.07%
Total	1.25%		0.04%		0.17%		1.47%

Method #2—Geometric Linking

TABLE 7-S-12

Applying Geometric Linking to Our Portfolio

Month 1		Month 2		Month 3		Quarter	
Stk. Sel.	Ind. Sel.	Stk. Sel.	Ind. Sel.	Stk. Sel.	Ind. Sel.	Stk. Sel.	Ind. Sel.
0.20%	0.04%	0.02%	0.00%	0.02%	0.00%	0.23%	0.04%
0.24%	−0.06%	0.01%	−0.06%	−0.02%	0.03%	0.22%	−0.10%
0.04%	−0.02%	0.02%	0.00%	0.04%	0.00%	0.09%	−0.02%
0.22%	0.00%	−0.01%	0.00%	−0.01%	0.00%	0.21%	0.00%
0.00%	0.00%	−0.01%	0.00%	−0.01%	0.00%	−0.02%	0.00%
0.22%	0.02%	0.04%	−0.01%	0.02%	0.02%	0.29%	0.03%
0.01%	−0.01%	0.02%	0.00%	0.01%	0.00%	0.04%	−0.01%
0.08%	0.01%	−0.01%	0.02%	0.01%	0.01%	0.08%	0.05%
0.10%	0.01%	−0.03%	−0.01%	0.02%	0.02%	0.09%	0.03%
0.16%	0.01%	0.02%	0.02%	−0.02%	0.02%	0.16%	0.05%
1.26%	−0.01%	0.07%	−0.03%	0.07%	0.10%	1.40%	0.07%
Total	1.25%		0.04%		0.17%		1.47%

Method #3—Logarithmic Linking

TABLE 7-S-13

Applying the Cariño Linking Methodology to Our Portfolio

		Portfolio	Benchmk.	Excess Return
	Month 1	2.12%	0.86%	
	Month 2	0.66%	0.62%	
$k_t = \dfrac{\ln\left(1 + R_{P_t}\right) - \ln\left(1 + R_{B_T}\right)}{R_{P_t} - R_{B_t}}$	Month 3	0.72%	0.55%	
		3.53%	2.04%	1.49%
	k_1	0.9853		
$k = \dfrac{\ln\left(1 + R_P\right) - \ln\left(1 + R_B\right)}{R_P - R_B}$	k_2	0.9936		
	k_3	0.9937		
	k	0.9729		
$\beta_t^{Log} = \dfrac{k_t}{k}$				Test
	beta1	1.01		0.0127
	beta2	1.02		0.0004
$\sum_t \beta_t^{Log}\left(Rp_t - Rb_t\right) = R_p - R$	beta3	1.02		0.0018
				1.49%

T A B L E   7-S-14

Calculating the Attribution Effects Using the
Logarithmic Method

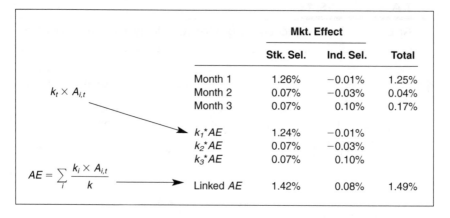

		Mkt. Effect		
		Stk. Sel.	Ind. Sel.	Total
$k_t \times A_{i,t}$	Month 1	1.26%	−0.01%	1.25%
	Month 2	0.07%	−0.03%	0.04%
	Month 3	0.07%	0.10%	0.17%
	$k_1{}^*AE$	1.24%	−0.01%	
	$k_2{}^*AE$	0.07%	−0.03%	
	$k_3{}^*AE$	0.07%	0.10%	
$AE = \sum_i \dfrac{k_i \times A_{i,t}}{k}$	Linked AE	1.42%	0.08%	1.49%

Method #4—Optimized Approach

TABLE 7-S-15

Creating the Beta Factor—Optimized Approach—for Our Second Exercise

	Portfolio	Index	Excess Return
Month 1	2.12%	0.86%	
Month 2	0.66%	0.62%	
Month 3	0.72%	0.55%	
	3.53%	2.04%	1.49%

$$A = \frac{1}{T} \times \left[\frac{\left(R_P - R_B\right)}{\left(1 + R_P\right)^{1/T} - \left(1 + R_B\right)^{1/T}} \right]$$

A term   1.0185

$$\alpha_t = \left[\frac{R_P - R_B - A \sum_{j=1}^{T}\left(R_{P_J} - R_{B_J}\right)}{\sum_{j=1}^{T}\left(R_{P_J} - R_{B_J}\right)^2} \right] \times \left(R_{P_t} - R_{B_t}\right)$$

alpha1 (α_1)	−0.0038
alpha2 (α_2)	−0.0001
alpha3 (α_3)	−0.0005
Test	0.0127
	0.0004
	0.0018

$$R_P - R_B = \sum_{t=1}^{T}\left(A + \alpha_t\right) \times \left(R_{P_t} - R_{B_T}\right)$$

Constraint   1.49%

$$\beta_t^{Opt} = A + \alpha_t$$

betaOpt1	1.0147
betaOpt2	1.0184
betaOpt3	1.0180

TABLE 7-S-16

Calculating the Attribution Effects Using the
Optimized Approach for Our Second Exercise

		Stk. Sel.	Ind. Sel.	Total
		Mkt. Effect		
	Month 1	1.26%	−0.01%	1.25%
	Month 2	0.07%	−0.03%	0.04%
	Month 3	0.07%	0.10%	0.17%
$Adj'\ dAE_t = \beta_t^{Opt} \times AE_t \longrightarrow$	betaOpt*AE1	1.28%	−0.01%	
	betaOpt*AE2	0.07%	−0.03%	
	betaOpt*AE3	0.07%	0.11%	
$AE_t = \sum \beta_t^{Opt} \times AE_t \longrightarrow$	Sum'd AE	1.42%	0.07%	1.49%

Method #5—Smoothing

From the geometric linking, we obtain the following:

TABLE 7-S-17

Geometrically Linked Results

Industry Selection Effect	0.07%
Stock Selection Effect	1.40%
Total Attribution Effect	1.47%
Linked Excess Return	1.49%
Difference	−0.02%

T A B L E   7-S-18

Applying Smoothing Method 1 to Second Exercise

Ratio of Actual to Calculated	1.49 / 1.47	1.01
Adjusted Sector Allocation Effect	1.01 × 0.07	0.07%
Adjusted Stock Selection Effect	1.01 × 1.40	1.42%
Adjusted Total	0.07 + 1.42	1.49%

T A B L E   7-S-19

Smoothing Method 2

Proportion from Allocation	0.07 / 1.47	0.05%
Proportion from Selection	1.40 / 1.47	0.95%
Adjusted Allocation	0.05 × 1.49	0.07%
Adjusted Selection	0.95 × 1.49	1.42%
Adjusted Total	0.07 + 1.42	1.49%

CHAPTER 8—GEOMETRIC LINKING

1. We've summarized the results of the math in the following tables.

As you'll see, the excess return for the quarter is 0.69%, the same as our linked effect, thus satisfying our third law.

T A B L E   8-S-1

The Index Returns, Weights, and Returns to Derive the Geometric Attribution Effects

	ROR		Weight		Returns		
	Portfolio	Index	Portfolio	Index	R_p	R_b	R_s
Equities	6.00%	5.50%	75.00%	70.00%	4.50%	3.85%	4.13%
Bonds	4.00%	4.20%	20.00%	30.00%	0.80%	1.26%	0.84%
Cash	1.00%	1.00%	5.00%	0.00%	0.05%	0.00%	0.05%
Portfolio	5.35%	5.11%	100.00%	100.00%	5.35%	5.11%	5.02%

T A B L E   8–S–2

The Geometric Attribution Effects

	Returns			Effects		
	R_p	R_b	R_s	Stk. Sel.	Ind. Sel.	Combined
Equities	4.50%	3.85%	4.13%	0.36%	0.02%	0.38%
Bonds	0.80%	1.26%	0.84%	−0.04%	0.09%	0.05%
Cash	0.05%	0.00%	0.05%	0.00%	−0.20%	−0.20%
Portfolio	5.35%	5.11%	5.02%	0.32%	−0.09%	0.23%

T A B L E   8–S–3

Monthly and Quarterly Returns; Geometric Excess Return for Quarter

Month 1		Month 2		Month 3		Quarter (linked)	
Portfolio	Index	Portfolio	Index	Portfolio	Index	Portfolio	Index
5.35%	5.11%	5.35%	5.11%	5.35%	5.11%	16.92%	16.13%
						Quarterly Geometric Excess Return	0.69%

T A B L E   8–S–4

Monthly and Quarterly Attribution Effects

	Stock Selection	Industry Selection	Combined Effect
Month 1	0.32%	−0.09%	0.23%
Month 2	0.32%	−0.09%	0.23%
Month 3	0.32%	−0.09%	0.23%
Quarter	0.96%	−0.27%	0.69%

2. Again, we've summarized the results in the following tables.

T A B L E   8–S-5

Calculation of Returns for Month 1

	ROR		Weight		Returns		
	Portfolio	Index	Portfolio	Index	R_p	R_b	R_s
Basic Materials	3.66%	2.01%	12%	10%	0.439%	0.201%	0.241%
Industrials	4.52%	2.15%	10%	13%	0.452%	0.280%	0.215%
Consumer Cyclicals	2.45%	2.12%	11%	12%	0.270%	0.254%	0.233%
Utilities	1.73%	−0.31%	11%	10%	0.190%	−0.031%	−0.034%
Energy	−0.85%	−0.83%	10%	10%	−0.085%	−0.083%	−0.083%
Financial	2.88%	1.04%	12%	10%	0.346%	0.104%	0.125%
Healthcare	0.45%	0.37%	8%	10%	0.036%	0.037%	0.030%
Technology	2.02%	1.09%	9%	8%	0.182%	0.087%	0.098%
Telecom	2.17%	1.10%	9%	8%	0.195%	0.088%	0.099%
Consumer Non-Cyc.	1.15%	−0.82%	8%	9%	0.092%	−0.074%	−0.066%
Portfolio	2.12%	0.86%	100%	100%	2.117%	0.863%	0.858%
Excess ROR		1.24%					

T A B L E   8–S-6

Calculation of Returns for Month 2

	ROR		Weight		Returns		
	Portfolio	Index	Portfolio	Index	R_p	R_b	R_s
Basic Materials	1.50%	1.35%	10%	10%	0.150%	0.135%	0.135%
Industrials	1.30%	1.20%	8%	13%	0.104%	0.156%	0.096%
Consumer Cyclicals	−0.80%	−0.95%	12%	12%	−0.096%	−0.114%	−0.114%
Utilities	0.04%	0.12%	10%	10%	0.004%	0.012%	0.012%
Energy	0.08%	0.15%	10%	10%	0.008%	0.015%	0.015%
Financial	0.07%	−0.30%	12%	10%	0.008%	−0.030%	−0.036%
Healthcare	1.20%	1.00%	10%	10%	0.120%	0.100%	0.100%
Technology	2.30%	2.45%	9%	8%	0.207%	0.196%	0.221%
Telecom	−0.80%	−0.50%	9%	8%	−0.072%	−0.040%	−0.045%
Consumer Non-Cyc.	2.30%	2.10%	10%	9%	0.230%	0.189%	0.210%
Portfolio	0.66%	0.62%	100%	100%	0.663%	0.619%	0.594%
Excess ROR		0.04%					

T A B L E   8–S-7

Calculation of Returns for Month 3

	ROR		Weight		Returns		
	Portfolio	Index	Portfolio	Index	R_p	R_b	R_s
Basic Materials	−0.80%	−0.95%	10%	10%	0.150%	0.135%	0.135%
Industrials	−0.80%	−0.50%	8%	13%	0.104%	0.156%	0.096%
Consumer Cyclicals	0.04%	−0.30%	12%	12%	−0.096%	−0.114%	−0.114%
Utilities	0.07%	0.12%	10%	10%	0.004%	0.012%	0.012%
Energy	0.08%	0.15%	10%	10%	0.008%	0.015%	0.015%
Financial	1.20%	1.00%	12%	10%	0.008%	−0.030%	−0.036%
Healthcare	1.30%	1.20%	10%	10%	0.120%	0.100%	0.100%
Technology	1.50%	1.35%	9%	8%	0.207%	0.196%	0.221%
Telecom	2.30%	2.10%	9%	8%	−0.072%	−0.040%	−0.045%
Consumer Non-Cyc.	2.30%	2.45%	10%	9%	0.230%	0.189%	0.210%
Portfolio	0.72%	0.55%	100%	100%	0.663%	0.619%	0.594%
Excess ROR		0.17%					

T A B L E   8–S-8

Calculation of Attribution Effects for Month 1

	R_p	R_b	R_s	Stk. Sel.	Ind. Sel.
Basic Materials	0.439%	0.201%	0.241%	0.20%	0.02%
Industrials	0.452%	0.280%	0.215%	0.23%	−0.04%
Consumer Cyclicals	0.270%	0.254%	0.233%	0.04%	−0.01%
Utilities	0.190%	−0.031%	−0.034%	0.22%	−0.01%
Energy	−0.085%	−0.083%	0.083%	0.00%	0.00%
Financial	0.346%	0.104%	0.125%	0.22%	0.00%
Healthcare	0.036%	0.037%	0.030%	0.01%	0.01%
Technology	0.182%	0.087%	0.098%	0.08%	0.00%
Telecom	0.195%	0.088%	0.099%	0.10%	0.00%
Consumer Non-Cyc.	0.092%	−0.074%	−0.066%	0.16%	0.02%
Portfolio	2.117%	0.863%	0.858%	1.25%	−0.01%

T A B L E 8–S–9

Calculation of Attribution Effects for Month 2

	R_p	R_b	R_s	Stk. Sel.	Ind. Sel.
Basic Materials	0.150%	0.135%	0.135%	0.01%	0.00%
Industrials	0.104%	0.156%	0.096%	0.01%	−0.03%
Consumer Cyclicals	−0.096%	−0.114%	−0.114%	0.02%	0.00%
Utilities	0.004%	0.012%	0.012%	−0.01%	0.00%
Energy	0.008%	0.015%	0.015%	−0.01%	0.00%
Financial	0.008%	−0.030%	−0.036%	0.04%	−0.02%
Healthcare	0.120%	0.100%	0.100%	0.02%	0.00%
Technology	0.207%	0.196%	0.221%	−0.01%	0.02%
Telecom	−0.072%	−0.040%	−0.045%	−0.03%	−0.01%
Consumer Non-Cyc.	0.230%	0.189%	0.210%	0.02%	0.01%
Portfolio	0.663%	0.619%	0.594%	0.07%	−0.03%

T A B L E 8–S–10

Calculation of Attribution Effects for Month 3

	R_p	R_b	R_s	Stk. Sel.	Ind. Sel.	Excess ROR
Basic Materials	−0.080%	−0.095%	−0.095%	0.015%	0.01%	0.00%
Industrials	−0.064%	−0.065%	−0.040%	−0.024%	−0.02%	0.05%
Consumer Cyclicals	−0.004%	−0.036%	−0.036%	0.040%	0.04%	0.00%
Utilities	0.007%	0.012%	0.012%	−0.005%	0.00%	0.00%
Energy	0.008%	0.015%	0.015%	−0.007%	−0.01%	0.00%
Financial	0.144%	0.100%	0.120%	0.024%	0.02%	0.01%
Healthcare	0.130%	0.120%	0.120%	0.010%	0.01%	0.00%
Technology	0.135%	0.108%	0.122%	0.013%	0.01%	0.01%
Telecom	0.207%	0.168%	0.189%	0.018%	0.02%	0.02%
Consumer Non-Cyc.	0.230%	0.221%	0.245%	−0.015%	−0.01%	0.02%
Portfolio	0.721%	0.548%	0.652%	0.069%	0.07%	0.10%

242

Exercise Solutions

TABLE 8-S-11

Monthly and Quarterly Returns; Geometric Excess Return
for Quarter

Month 1		Month 2		Month 3		Quarter (linked)	
Portfolio	Index	Portfolio	Index	Portfolio	Index	Portfolio	Index
2.12%	0.86%	0.66%	0.62%	0.72%	0.55%	3.53%	2.04%
						Quarterly Geometric Excess Return	1.46%

TABLE 8-S-12

Monthly and Quarterly Attribution Effects

	Stock Selection	Ind. Selection	Combined Effect
Month 1	1.25%	−0.01%	1.24%
Month 2	0.07%	−0.03%	0.04%
Month 3	0.07%	0.10%	0.17%
Quarter	1.39%	0.07%	1.46%

Our quarterly excess return (1.46%) matches the quarterly combined effect, thus satisfying our third law of attribution.

References

AIMR. *Performance Presentation Standards.* Charlottesville, Va: Association for Investment Management and Research, 1993.

AIMR. *Performance Presentation Standards Handbook.* Charlottesville, VA: Association for Investment Management and Research, 1997.

AIMR. *Global Investment Performance Standards.* Charlottesville, VA: Association for Investment Management and Research, 1999.

AIMR. *AIMR Performance Presentation Standards.* Charlottesville, VA: Association for Investment Management and Research, 2001.

Bacon, Carl. Various e-mail messages with the author. 2002.

BAI. *Measuring The Investment Performance of Pension Funds.* Park Ridge, IL: Bank Administration Institute, 1968.

Brinson, Gary P., and Nimrod Fachler. "Measuring non-U.S. equity portfolio performance," *Journal of Portfolio Management* (Spring 1985: 73–76).

Brinson, Gary P., L. Randolph Hood, and Gilbert L. Beebower. "Determinants of Portfolio Performance," *Financial Analysts Journal* (July–August 1986: 39–44).

Brinson, Gary P., Brian D. Singer, and Gilbert L. Beebower. "Determinants of Portfolio Performance II: An Update," *Financial Analysts Journal* (May–June 1991: 40–48).

Brinson, Gary. "The Journal Interview," *Journal of Performance Measurement* (Fall 1999: 29–34).

Buzan, Tony. *Use Both Sides of Your Brain.* New York, NY.: Plume, 1991.

Campisi, Stephen. "Primer on Fixed Income Performance Attribution," *Journal of Performance Measurement* (Summer 2000: 14–25).

Campisi, Stephen. Various e-mails shared with the author. 2002.

Cariño, David. "Combining Attribution Effects Over Time," *Journal of Performance Measurement* (Summer 1999: 5–14).

Contingency Analysis. On-line glossary (www.contingencyanalysis.com/glossary.htm) 1996–2000.

Davies, Owen, and Damien Laker. "Multiple-Period Performance Attribution Using the Brinson Model," *Journal of Performance Measurement* (Fall 2001: 12–22).

EIPC. "EIPC Guidance for users of Attribution Analysis." Published by the European Investment Performance Committee. This document is in development. A draft copy was graciously provided to the author to use as a reference in this text. 2001.

Frongello, Andrew. "Linking Attribution Effects Over Time," *Journal of Performance Measurement*. (Spring 2002, pp 10–22).

Gazalé, Midhat. *Gnomon: From Pharaohs to Fractals*. Princeton, N.J.: Princeton University Press, 1999.

Gazalé, Midhat. *Number: From Ahmes to Cantor*. Princeton, N.J.: Princeton University Press, 2000.

Higgs, Peter J., and Stephen Goode. "Target Active Returns and Attribution Analysis," *Financial Analysts Journal* (May–June 1993: 77–80).

ICAA. *The Standards of Measurement and Use For Investment Performance Data*. New York, NY: Investment Council Association of America, 1971.

Karnosky, Denis, and Brian Singer. *Global Asset Management and Performance Attribution*. Charlottesville, VA: The Research Foundation of The Institute of Chartered Financial Analysts, 1994.

Laker, Damien. "What is this Thing Called 'Interaction'?," *Journal of Performance Measurement* (Fall 2000: 43–58).

Laker, Damien. "Incorporating Transaction Cost Measurement Into Performance Attribution," *Journal of Performance Measurement* (Summer 2001: 13–24).

Laker, Damien. E-mail messages with the author. 2002.

Laker, Damien. "Karnosky Singer Attribution: a Worked Example," Unpublished paper (available at http://www.ipoglobal.biz/fund3.htm) 2002.

Lord, Timothy J. "The Attribution of Portfolio and Index Returns in Fixed Income," *Journal of Performance Measurement*. Fall 1997.

Menchero, Jose. "An Optimized Approach to Linking Attribution Effects Over Time," *Journal of Performance Measurement*. (Fall 2000: 36–42).

Menchero, Jose. Materials provided to the author to clarify linking issues, as well as commentary on the draft manuscript. 2002.

Ramaswamy, Srichander. "Fixed Income Portfolio Management: Risk Modeling, Portfolio Construction and Performance Attribution," *Journal of Performance Measurement* (Summer '01: 58–70).

Spaulding, David. *Measuring Investment Performance*. New York, NY.: McGraw-Hill, 1997.

Terhaar, Kevin. "Currency Management," Presentation at the Thomson Financial Software Solutions Global Client Conference. 2002.

Terhaar, Kevin. Various e-mail messages with author. 2002.

The Working Group of the Society of Investment Analysts. "The Measurement of Portfolio Performance for Pension Funds." 1972.

The Spaulding Group. "Performance Measurement Attribution Survey." Partial results cited. 2002.

Appendix—Additional Resources

Here are additional resources that you may want to consider to assist you with performance attribution or other aspects of performance measurement.

The Journal of Performance Measurement®. This quarterly publication was launched in 1996 and has become "the bible" of investment performance measurement. Articles on various aspects of attribution regularly appear in the journal, and several are referenced within this book.

Performance, Attribution, and Risk Measurement Reference Guide. This handy, pocket-sized guide is a glossary of investment performance formulas, terms, and concepts.

The Performance Measurement Forum. This membership-only group meets twice a year in Europe and twice a year in North America. Unlike a conference, the meetings are highly interactive, with a lot of sharing and discussion. Members tend to be senior representatives from money management firms, software providers, and other institutions involved with the investment industry.

Performance Measurement Training. David Spaulding conducts various training classes, including a two-day Introduction to Performance Measurement, a one-and-a-half-day class on Performance Measurement, and a one-day class on Performance Measurement for Plan Sponsors and Investment Consultants.

Research. The Spaulding Group regularly conducts research for the industry on various aspects of performance measurement. Such projects have included surveys on attribution, the presentation standards, and performance measurement technology. All participants receive complimentary copies of the results.

For further information about these and other services and products relating to performance measurement, contact The Spaulding Group at 001-732-873-5700, or info@SpauldingGrp.com.

Index